Wonders of the Ancient World

National Geographic Atlas of Archaeology

Prepared by the Book Division, National Geographic Society, Washington, D.C.

WONDERS OF THE ANCIENT WORLD:
National Geographic Atlas of Archaeology

Norman Hammond, *Professor of Archaeology,*
    Boston University, Consultant

Published by
    The National Geographic Society
Gilbert M. Grosvenor,
    President and Chairman of the Board
Michela A. English, *Senior Vice President*

Prepared by the Book Division
William R. Gray, *Vice President and Director*
Margery G. Dunn, Charles Kogod,
    Assistant Directors

Staff for this book
Mary B. Dickinson, *Editor*
Carolinda E. Hill, Bonnie S. Lawrence,
    Assistant Editors
David Ross, *Illustrations Editor*
Jody Bolt, *Art Director*
Alexandra Littlehales, *Assistant Art Director*
Ron Fisher, *Contributing Editor*
Elisabeth B. Booz, Elizabeth W. Fisher,
Judson T. Heartsill, Ann Nottingham Kelsall,
Kimberly A. Kostyal, Anne E. Withers,
    Researchers
Carl Mehler, *Map Editor*
Sven M. Dolling, *Map Research*
Sandra F. Lotterman, *Editorial Assistant*
Artemis S. Lampathakis,
    Illustrations Assistant
Lewis R. Bassford,
    Production Project Manager
Richard S. Wain, Timothy H. Ewing,
    Production
Karen F. Edwards, Elizabeth G. Jevons,
Peggy J. Oxford, Teresita Cóquia Sison,
Robin S. H. Tunnicliff, *Staff Assistants*

Manufacturing and Quality Management
George V. White, *Director*
John T. Dunn, *Associate Director*
Vincent P. Ryan, *Manager*
R. Gary Colbert

Diane L. Coleman, *Indexer*

Page 1: Ceramic figure, Veracruz, ca A.D. 600-900
Pages 2-3: Pueblo Bonito, Chaco Canyon, ca A.D. 900-1200
Pages 4-5: Detail from gold and silver greave, Thrace, ca 375 B.C.
Page 6: Rock-cut dwellings, Cappadocia, Turkey,
since the 4th century A.D.

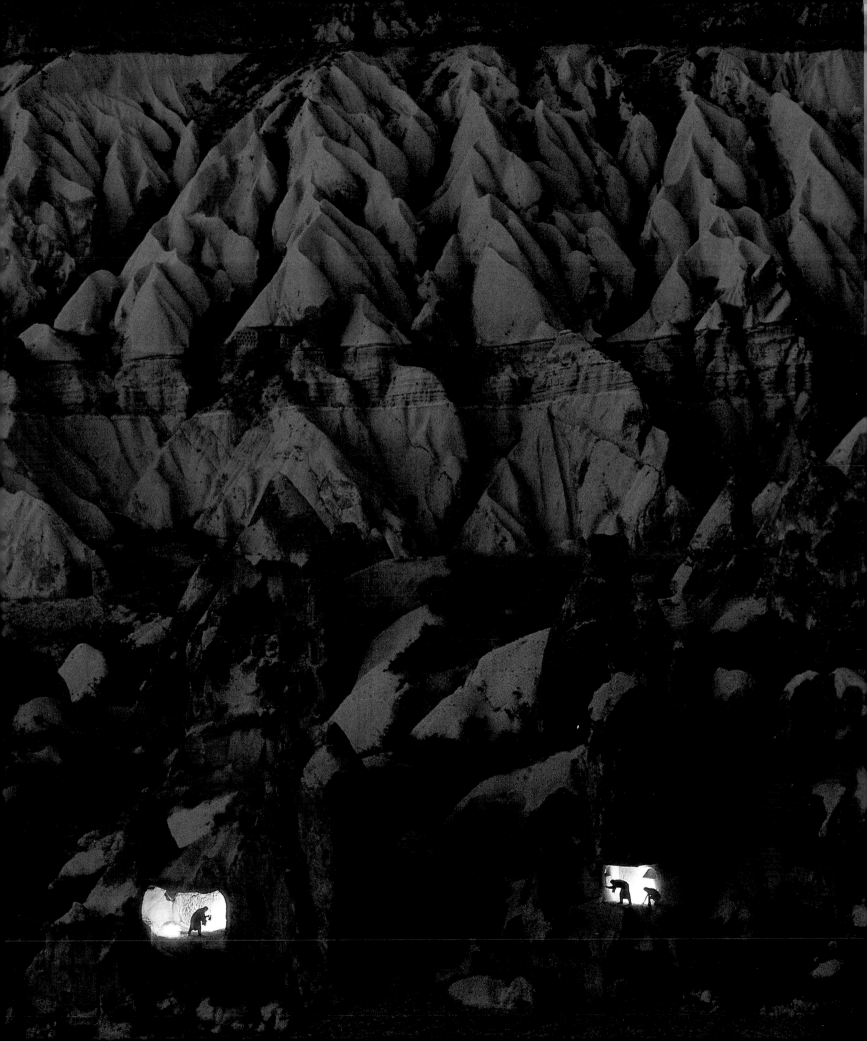

Contents

Introduction 8
  by George E. Stuart
  National Geographic
  Staff Archaeologist

Portfolio:
Tools of Archaeology 10
  by Tom Melham

Human Origins 18

In the Beginning 20
  by Leslie Allen

Peopling the Earth 26
  by Leslie Allen

**The Middle East
and Europe** 32

Early Settlements 34
  by Toni Eugene

Portfolio:
First Farmers 40
  by Catherine Herbert Howell

Cities and Civilizations 46
  by Cynthia Russ Ramsay

Portfolio:
Origins of Writing 68
  by John F. Ross

The Classical World 76
  by Catherine Herbert Howell

Crossroads of Faith 98
  by Catherine Herbert Howell

Europe: Into the North 110
  by Toni Eugene

Sub-Saharan Africa 126

Ancient Kingdoms 128
  by John F. Ross

Portfolio:
Metal Ages 144
  by K. M. Kostyal

Asia and Oceania 152

The Indian Subcontinent 154
  by Cynthia Russ Ramsay

Southeast Asia 164
  by Cynthia Russ Ramsay

East Asia 176
  by Ann Nottingham Kelsall

Portfolio:
Textile Treasures 192
  by Margaret Sedeen

Central and North Asia 200
  by Jennifer C. Urquhart

Pacific Islands 210
  by Ron Fisher

The Americas 224

North America 226
  by Tom Melham
  John F. Ross

Portfolio:
The Potter's Art 246
  by Jennifer C. Urquhart

Mesoamerica 254
  by Mary Ann Harrell

South America 276
  by Toni Eugene

Illustrations Credits and
  Acknowledgments 298

Index 300

Introduction

In 1836, the American travel writer John Lloyd Stephens went to what he called the "ancient and extraordinary" city of Petra (opposite), now one of the great archaeological treasures of Jordan. There, he contemplated an astonishing and imposing temple intricately carved into the rose-red cliff. "I can well imagine," he later wrote in New York, "that the first view of that superb facade must produce an effect which could never pass away." By virtue of his observations on ancient ruins, whether Petra, the Pyramids of Egypt, or the magnificent Maya palaces of Uxmal, Stephens was but one of many whose devotion to ancient things helped to create modern archaeology—the science of the study of the past.

Clues to the lives of vanished peoples can take any number of forms: the ruins of a deserted city; a single tooth, worn by diet and polished by time; a faded king list rendered in an extinct script; or a charred cereal grain from an ancient hearth. Such pieces of evidence, and the context in which they are discovered, form the raw material for the reconstruction of human history and for the re-creation of ancient lifeways. Probably most important of all, archaeologists seek to provide some understanding of *why* human culture has changed through time.

Archaeologists sometimes isolate the occurrences of changes in the past—shifts in the way food is procured, the appearance of a nobility in the social hierarchy, or variations in the way art looks—then seek the reasons for them. Perhaps the cause was population movements, warfare, fluctuations in climate, the spread of disease, or the introduction of key inventions. Archaeology may be seen as the seeking of a relationship between known events or objects made by people on the one hand and human behavior on the other. Armed with computers, laboratory analysis, and hypotheses about society and culture, archaeologists even attempt to reach into the minds of those who made the artifacts.

Wonders of the Ancient World concisely summarizes the findings of archaeologists and their colleagues in other disciplines about the human past. It embraces a span of time from the earliest known hominids in what is now East Africa to around, or shortly after, A.D. 1600.

Following the introductory chapter on human origins, sections of the book deal in turn with geographical regions of the world, beginning with the Middle East and ending with the Americas. Each of these sections contains essays on the cultures and main archaeological sites of the area, along with maps showing those sites and the natural features of their settings. Illustrations of artifacts are accompanied by discussions of what they reveal about the lives of the people who made them. At intervals throughout the volume, special portfolios examine broad topics that reach across the global landscape—agriculture, writing, and various technologies that created the giant steps of human development.

As you peruse *Wonders of the Ancient World,* the search for the past goes forward in every corner of the world. Archaeologists continue to locate and evaluate the evidence that lies all about us—and to reassess old discoveries as well, finding new insights into their meaning.

—George E. Stuart
*National Geographic
Staff Archaeologist*

Nabataean tomb, Petra, Jordan, ca 1st-2nd century A.D.

Mammoth-bone shelters at Kostenki on the Don River, Russia

Tools of Archaeology

Over many centuries, archaeology—the science that seeks to interpret the material evidence of vanished cultures—has made excavation its primary tool. How else do you locate the remains of civilizations buried under tons of accumulated debris, both natural and man-made?

In Russian steppes north of the Caucasus, partly unearthed bones give the jumbled impression of a mammoths' graveyard (left). Careful excavation, however, reveals that human hunters arranged the bones into enduring shelters some 23,000 years ago. As archaeologists painstakingly peel back layer after layer, they record exact positions of every bone, tool, ornament, and other artifact. Photographs and sketches augment written observations. Such diligence helps reconstruct how the huts were built and what they looked like. It also turns up evidence that this hunting society was more complex and sedentary than was first supposed.

Excavators have not always been so conscientious. As recently as the 19th century, "archaeologists" often were glorified treasure hunters more interested in a pharaonic tomb's golden artifacts than in its dusty mummies or hieroglyphic records; they cared even less about the civilization that spawned such trappings. Napoleon and Lord Elgin, among others, blithely carted off remnants of ancient Egypt and Greece—showing more concern for grandeur than for archaeological context.

Today's archaeologists are infinitely more aware of their own impact, as well as the need to extract

E
24

E
24
floor
3

E
24
floor
4

E
24
floor
5

E
24
floor
6

E
24
floor
7

E
24
floor
8

E
24
floor
9

E
24
floor
10

E
24
floor
11

Before and after: Aztec bat god

Techniques of Restoration

Part gravedigger, part architect, part trash picker, part forensic scientist: Today's archaeologist uses many skills to find and interpret clues from the refuse and ruins of the past. Stratigraphy—that is, defining and dating different layers at a site—relies on the fundamental principle that lower means older. At the Sumerian site of Nippur, tags identify the remains of 12 different floors (opposite). Artifacts often emerge from a dig in need of conservation and repair, as well as analysis. Using diverse techniques, restorers and conservators work wonders. In their hands, a scattering of clay bits from Mexico City gradually coalesces into an image of a Mesoamerican bat god. Reconstruction of a different sort— computer modeling—creates three-dimensional views of buildings and cities now vanished or in ruins. Primed with archaeological field data, computers breathe new reality into Africa's ancient Kingdom of Kush.

the information a site possesses.

They know that even the most careful and correct excavation is destructive, for it is an archaeological given that a site can be dug only once. The very act of bringing it to light paradoxically destroys it. While individual objects may endure, the site's archaeological value to succeeding generations is lost. All that survives, apart from such artifacts, are the excavator's data.

Today, archaeologists are far less likely to dig than they once were— and more likely to unearth only part of a site when they do excavate. There are two reasons: excavation's intrusiveness and the continuing evolution of technology. Increasingly sophisticated methods— including such remote-sensing techniques as infrared photography and

Computer-generated three-dimensional digital image of Royal Cemetery of Kush, Nuri, Sudan

ground-penetrating radar—complement and at times even supplant traditional brush-and-trowel work. Tomorrow's generations will possess more and more advanced tool kits, yielding more information than we can extract now, and will do so less invasively. Thus it makes sense to save some sites for the future.

Excavation still goes on, of course. A worker at a Sumerian site occupied in the third millennium B.C. trowels through a dozen successive floors, each built atop an older one (page 12). This stack of strata enables her to date recovered objects relatively, if not absolutely.

When archaeologists want to know the absolute date of a site, they can often go beyond simple stratigraphy. Historical records, coins, and other date-bearing objects can help—if they exist. But even prehistoric sites contain records—written in nature's hand. For example, tree rings. Scientists can link generations of trees by the thickness of their rings. Dendrochronology (literally, "tree time") dates wooden artifacts by matching their ring patterns to known records, which, in some areas of the world, span several thousand years.

Carbon dating, another tech-

nique, stems from the principle that carbon 14, a naturally occurring radioactive isotope, decays at a known rate. All living things contain C^{14} in the same relative proportion until their deaths,

Moche gilded copper man-crab, 24 in

Treasures of a Moche Tomb

Thriving black markets, regional poverty, and soaring worldwide demand for Native American relics fuel illicit pothunting and despoliation of archaeological sites. At Sipán, Peru, armed guards (opposite) patrol the tomb of a Moche warrior-priest after police were alerted to looting there. Plundered sites never tell their tales. Looters make the job of archaeologists difficult—and in places even hazardous. Their spoils fetch high prices from collectors, but take a devastating toll on a more valuable commodity—knowledge of past cultures. To extract as much information as possible at digs, excavators make detailed sketches; this one comes from the Moche site, which yielded, among other artifacts, an anthropomorphic crab of gilded copper necklaced with owl-head beads.

Site drawing of Moche Tomb 3, Sipán

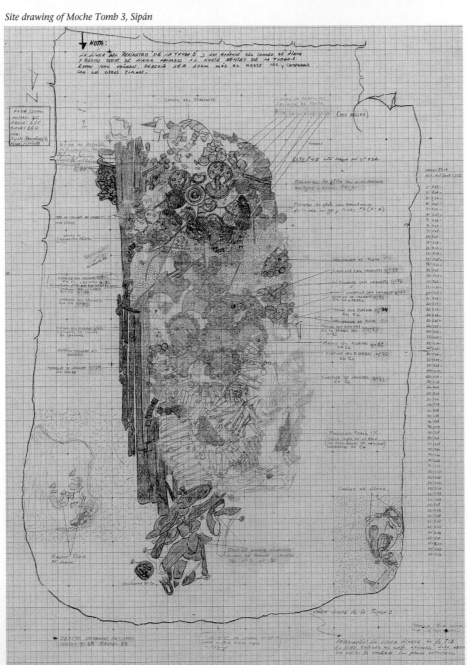

when C^{14} atoms begin to decay. Organic objects up to 50,000 years old—bone, leather, wood, charcoal, or food—can thus be dated.

For even older dates, archaeologists sometimes use methods such as potassium-argon, which can determine when a rock or mineral was formed. It extends measurable time farther, up to millions of years. It is considered the best method for dating early hominid fossils, by gauging the date of the rock in which the fossilized bones are embedded.

There are other methods for revealing when a rock was used by humans. For example, obsidian, the dark volcanic glass often prized by Stone Age peoples, absorbs water when it is chipped or broken. Measuring the absorption can yield dates for worked pieces of obsidian. Similarly, dating pottery sherds by thermoluminescence can tell when clay was fired by humans.

Modern archaeologists study chemistry as well as physics, because blood chemistry and the tracking of DNA, both of which can be done

from skeletons, provide information on the diet of early peoples and on their relationships and migrations.

The same technology used by engineers, architects, and scientists can help archaeologists in new ways. Satellites such as LANDSAT reveal ancient trails and structures; sophisticated computer technology such as CAD (Computer Aided Design) can reconstruct monuments or whole cities; and GIS (Geographic Information Systems) helps archaeologists see the broad patterns of human behavior over time.

Nor is this technological revolution restricted to land: Nautical archaeologists increasingly delve into the ocean's hoard of human history, from ancient Mediterranean ships to the storied *Titanic*. Current tools include new developments in scuba gear and metal detectors, photogrammetry, hand-held sonar plotters, and submersibles both human-piloted and robotic. Giant "airlifts" vacuum away overburden, while air-filled balloons raise heavy artifacts sunk in the distant past.

Diving into the Past

At sea as well as on land, technological innovation yields archaeological success. Flanked by amphorae and other cargo from one of the world's oldest known shipwrecks, a scuba-equipped archaeologist at Ulu Burun off the Turkish coast hefts a copper ingot (opposite) that dates to the late Bronze Age, about 3,400 years ago. Nearby, a Canaanite amphora still holds chunks of yellow terebinth resin—an aromatic substance used as incense in Egyptian rites. One of the ship's several storage jars, known as pithoi, *yields Cypriot crockery, including a small juglet. Also aboard: an array of pottery from Mycenaean Greece, Cyprus, and Palestine; bronze swords of Mycenaean and Canaanite design; small bronze Canaanite cymbals; and ingots of cobalt-rich blue glass used by both Egyptians and Greeks. Numerous bronze*

Terebinth resin from a Canaanite amphora

Cypriot crockery includes a juglet

Pottery, swords, and cymbals

Blue glass ingots

spearheads, ebony-like exotic wood, and ingots of tin as well as copper round out the cargo. The goods indicate this ship was a valued merchantman. Diverse origins offer clues about trade routes and everyday commerce in the Bronze Age.

Human Origins

In the Beginning

4,000,000 to 1,800,000 B.C.

As perplexing as any other questions we humans ponder are the ones that concern our own origins: How did humanity itself begin? And when? The "where" of the human dawn—Africa—was first suggested by Charles Darwin in the mid-19th century. But proof awaited the 20th, when a series of fossil discoveries kept turning up ever older ancestors. Scientists named these creatures australopithecines, or southern apes. But unlike real apes—and like modern humans—the australopithecines were hominids, creatures who stood upright and negotiated their world on two legs.

One of the earliest hallmarks of the ancestors who would evolve into modern humans was this habitual upright locomotion, or bipedalism. Most scientists believe that it began to occur after apes and humans split from a common lineage and went separate evolutionary ways between two and a half and eight million years ago. Environmental change may have triggered the divergence, as millions of years of warmth gave way to falling temperatures and the moist forests that blanketed Africa to areas of grassland. The apes' knuckle-walking posture and long, grasping limbs—vital for life in the trees— were ill suited to the open savanna, where the need for long-distance foraging favored bipedalism.

Starting in 1924, fossil-rich sites along the Great Rift Valley in eastern Africa and caves in southern Africa yielded evidence that australopithecines were thriving from one to two million years ago. Then, in 1974, a team led by paleoanthropologist Donald C. Johanson began to find fossils of even older, more primitive-looking hominids in the dusty

Australopithecus afarensis   *A. africanus*   *A. robustus*   *A. boisei*   *Homo habilis*

gullies of Ethiopia's Afar Desert. One of these was "Lucy," the remarkably complete skeleton of a small adult female who walked upright more than three million years ago; nearby were found the remains of at least 13 other individuals, including young and elderly adults and children who lived about the same time as Lucy.

Later, in 1978, archaeologist Mary Leakey's team at Laetoli, Tanzania, identified long, parallel trails of footprints made by hominids 3.6 million years ago in damp volcanic ash that later dried and hardened. Now known collectively as *Australopithecus afarensis,* these very early bipeds from Laetoli, Afar, and other East African sites date back three to four million years. The strikingly modern-looking Laetoli footprints appear to be those of an adult couple walking together.

In 1992, the discovery in the Afar region of the first nearly complete *A. afarensis* skull—at some three million years old the youngest one found—added to the information about this species. When pieced together, the skull, that of a male larger than Lucy, showed very little change from the earliest *A. afarensis* finds of nearly a million years before. The species appears to have long remained stable, then suddenly diversified.

With their low foreheads, jutting jaws with massive back teeth, and flat noses, the earliest known

Australopithecus to Homo

Long evolutionary strides over four million years culminate in modern Homo sapiens, *a newcomer perhaps 100,000 years old. By contrast,* H. erectus, *who evolved into* H. sapiens, *survived some 1.5 million years. Evolution was not really as linear as the illustration below suggests:* Australopithecus robustus *and* A. boisei *died out;* H. sapiens *(Neandertal) may have, too. But* A. afarensis *is generally agreed to be all hominids' common ancestor.*

PRECEDING PAGES: Workers sift soil for fossils in South Africa's Border Cave, a cradle of modern H. sapiens.

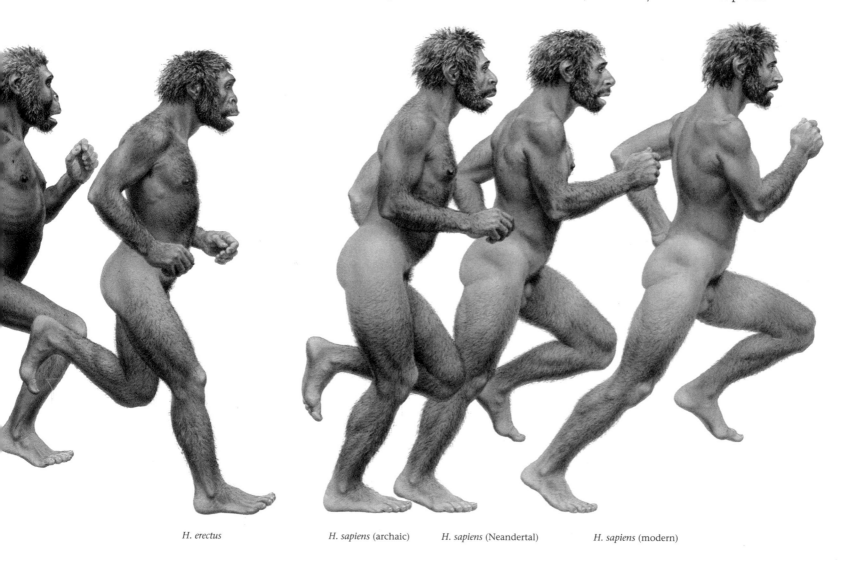

H. erectus   H. sapiens (archaic)   H. sapiens (Neandertal)   H. sapiens (modern)

australopithecines bore little resemblance to modern humans. Their brains were only about a third the size of ours. Hands, with slightly curving fingers, were relatively humanlike. But there is no sign that *A. afarensis* made tools, even though bipedalism had freed its hands.

The earliest known tools, sharpened rocks, were made about 2.5 million years ago in northern Ethiopia, not far from where Lucy and her kind lived. By then, though, *A. afarensis* had disappeared from the fossil record, and its descendants were proliferating. They probably included two, and possibly three, kinds of massive-jawed, dish-faced "robust" australopithecines, as well as the more lightly built "gracile" australopithecines, *A. africanus*.

Though little is known about how early hominids lived, some of what we do know comes from the tools found in Tanzania's Olduvai Gorge, a chasm that slices through two million years' worth of overlying sediments to the site of an ancient lake bed 300 feet below the rim. There, over several decades, Mary Leakey recorded the location and details of more than 37,000 flakes, cobbles, and other stone tools. Along with its trove, Olduvai Gorge yielded a name, Oldowan, for the world's first toolmaking industry.

Early hominids used hammerstones to knock flakes from pieces of rock and shape them into tools. Sometimes, they transported unworked stones several miles, sharpening them when they encountered the carcass of an elephant or another large animal they could butcher for food. After examining sites where tools and bones lie together, some archaeologists believe that the early hominids may also have scavenged meat and bones from carnivore kills and taken them back to places where they cached their tools. Whether they actually hunted animals is uncertain.

Clearly, the early Oldowan toolmakers moved heavy raw materials over large distances, suggesting that they could cooperate and perhaps lived in groups. But who were they?

When Mary Leakey and her husband, anthropologist Louis Leakey, found the 1.8-million-year-old skull of a robust australopithecine in Olduvai Gorge in 1959, they believed that its kind had been the early toolmakers. But soon afterward they began finding hominid remains at Olduvai that were strikingly different from the australopithecine's—though about the same age. The most important difference was in the skull,

which had clearly encased a larger, more complex brain, possibly even capable of speech. Louis Leakey named the newfound hominid *Homo habilis,* or "handy man," and declared that its kind were the real originators of Oldowan toolmaking.

Standing side by side with *Australopithecus*, *H. habilis* would have looked slightly less apelike—its head higher and rounder, its face less protruding, its molars less massive. In evolutionary terms, *H. habilis*, modern humans' direct ancestor, began to branch away from the more primitive australopithecines possibly 2.5 million years ago. Many scientists

Australopithecus afarensis

Re-created in dental plaster, the skeleton of "Lucy," a three-million-year-old member of Australopithecus afarensis, *reveals a hominid at ease in bipedal movement. Lucy's pelvis—unlike an ape's—flares outward to help bear the upper body's weight, while femurs, or thighbones, angle under her body. Whereas an ape's thumblike big toe serves to grasp, Lucy's toes all align to propel her forward. The arch, the biped's shock absorber, is evidenced here in a 3.6-million-year-old footprint at Laetoli, Tanzania. At Kenya's Koobi Fora, yet another fossil trove along the crack in Africa's crust known as the Rift Valley, Richard Leakey and Meave Epps—later Leakey's wife—ponder an australopithecine skull (opposite); beyond, visiting professor Paul Abell and Kamoya Kimeu, the team's deputy leader, catalog finds.*

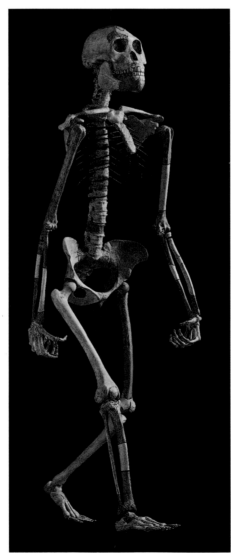

Plaster model of Lucy, 3 ft 8 in tall

Fossilized footprint, Laetoli, about 7.5 in long

believe that gracile *A. africanus* evolved into *H. habilis,* while the robust australopithecines died out about 1.5 million years ago.

H. habilis and at least one australopithecine, together with a huge variety of now-extinct animals, shared Rift Valley watering holes such as Kenya's Lake Turkana for more than half a million years. And for some of that time there was a newcomer, *Homo erectus,* on this crowded stage.

In 1984, members of a team headed by paleoanthropologists Richard Leakey and Alan Walker found and assembled, in jigsaw-puzzle style, hundreds of bits of bone from someone who had lived by Lake Turkana about 1.6 million years ago. One of the most complete fossil skeletons yet found, it is also the oldest known skeleton of *H. erectus,* the descendant of *H. habilis.*

The bones belonged to a youth, nicknamed "Turkana Boy," who was not more than 12 years old when he died. His brain was only slightly larger than that of *H. habilis.* But at five feet four inches, he was taller than most modern boys his age. His limbs were more humanlike than those of *H. habilis;* in fact, from the neck down, he was quite modern-looking. Turkana Boy disproved the theory that humans have grown larger through time. He also proved to some scientists that different parts of the body evolved at varying rates.

Tools began to change markedly about the time Turkana Boy lived. Called Acheulian, one new industry that arose with *H. erectus* produced hand axes and cleavers that were worked on both sides—sophisticated new tools that both reflected and enhanced the early humans' newfound skills. Besides being used for cutting, scraping, and even throwing, hand axes served as reservoirs of raw material for other new tools.

Another possible tool was the firebrand. *H. erectus* may have learned to tame and conserve brush-fire from lightning for warmth, cooking, and protection from predators. Armed with firebrands, the hominids could venture into unfamiliar territory and extend their home range, which would have helped them to find the greater amounts of food that their large bodies required.

In East Africa, *H. erectus* was the first hominid to move from the lower lying savannas into higher elevations and more open, sparsely vegetated lands. Increasing brainpower would poise *H. erectus* to spread beyond the continent of Africa into other parts of the Old World.

A: ca 2.3 million years old

B: ca 1.8 million years old

C: ca 1.6 million years old

D: ca 150,000 years old

E: 35,000 B.C.

Newfound Skills

Their early makers' sense of stone's potential survives in an Oldowan lava chopper (A), a developed Oldowan protohand ax (B), and an Acheulian hand ax (C). A Homo sapiens tool kit from about 1.5 million years later (D, from left) contains a prepared flake, an oval hand ax, an upended point, and a disk core used for making tools. Upper Paleolithic industry (E, from left) invented more refined stone scrapers, burins, and points, along with needles of bone.

Quest for fire brings an incredulous Homo erectus *band to a savanna wildfire, perhaps sparked by lightning. Ignited branches may serve as firebrands to ward off large predators* or perhaps light a cooking fire. Traces of domesticated fire may date back to 1.6 million years ago in Kenya and South Africa. But thoroughly documented proof that humans mastered fire only occurs when Homo erectus *settled at a much later time in temperate China. Warmth became a key to survival during frigid winters in that vast country's northern reaches.*

Peopling the Earth

1,800,000 to 4500 B.C.

Shortly after members of our own genus, *Homo,* showed up in tropical Africa, humans began a northward trek that would lead them into vastly different environments in Asia and Europe. Venturesome *Homo erectus* proved highly successful in new homelands, judging by his long history. Starting about 460,000 years ago, his kind inhabited a certain locality in China's Zhoukoudian Caves for about 150,000 years. The Zhoukoudian people were hunter-gatherers and roasted meat and fruits over open hearths. They left behind choppers, scrapers, awls, and other tools, mostly made from quartz flakes or river pebbles.

Life was often short and brutal for the Zhoukoudian people—thick-skulled individuals who stood more than five-and-a-half-feet tall. According to scientists who studied the remains of more than 40 individuals found in the caves, they had died of injuries before the age of 14.

Archaeologists trace a rising arc of cooperative behavior as the millennia passed. In western Europe, groups of hominids began to band together to butcher and perhaps hunt large game animals as much as

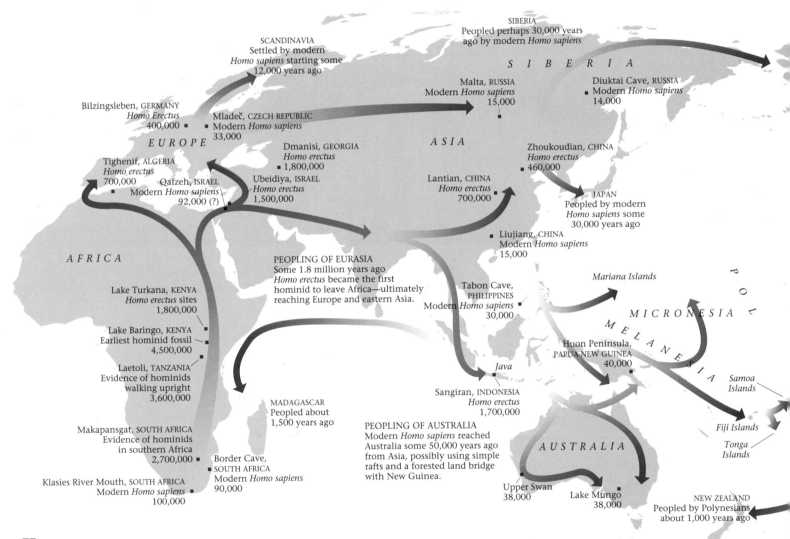

SIBERIA
Peopled perhaps 30,000 years ago by modern *Homo sapiens*

SIBERIA

SCANDINAVIA
Settled by modern *Homo sapiens* starting some 12,000 years ago

Malta, RUSSIA
Modern *Homo sapiens*
15,000

Diuktai Cave, RUSSIA
Modern *Homo sapiens*
14,000

Bilzingsleben, GERMANY
Homo Erectus
400,000

Mladeč, CZECH REPUBLIC
Modern *Homo sapiens*
33,000

EUROPE

Dmanisi, GEORGIA
Homo erectus
1,800,000

ASIA

Zhoukoudian, CHINA
Homo erectus
460,000

Tighenif, ALGERIA
Homo erectus
700,000

Qafzeh, ISRAEL
Modern *Homo sapiens*
92,000 (?)

Ubeidiya, ISRAEL
Homo erectus
1,500,000

Lantian, CHINA
Homo erectus
700,000

JAPAN
Peopled by modern *Homo sapiens* some 30,000 years ago

Liujiang, CHINA
Modern *Homo sapiens*
15,000

AFRICA

PEOPLING OF EURASIA
Some 1.8 million years ago *Homo erectus* became the first hominid to leave Africa—ultimately reaching Europe and eastern Asia.

Mariana Islands

POL

Lake Turkana, KENYA
Homo erectus sites
1,800,000

Tabon Cave, PHILIPPINES
Modern *Homo sapiens*
30,000

MICRONESIA

Lake Baringo, KENYA
Earliest hominid fossil
4,500,000

MELANESIA

Huon Peninsula, PAPUA NEW GUINEA
40,000

Laetoli, TANZANIA
Evidence of hominids walking upright
3,600,000

Java

Samoa Islands

Makapansgat, SOUTH AFRICA
Evidence of hominids in southern Africa
2,700,000

MADAGASCAR
Peopled about 1,500 years ago

Sangiran, INDONESIA
Homo erectus
1,700,000

Fiji Islands

Tonga Islands

PEOPLING OF AUSTRALIA
Modern *Homo sapiens* reached Australia some 50,000 years ago from Asia, possibly using simple rafts and a forested land bridge with New Guinea.

AUSTRALIA

Border Cave, SOUTH AFRICA
Modern *Homo sapiens*
90,000

Klasies River Mouth, SOUTH AFRICA
Modern *Homo sapiens*
100,000

Upper Swan
38,000

Lake Mungo
38,000

NEW ZEALAND
Peopled by Polynesians about 1,000 years ago

Human Migration

Humans first appeared outside Africa some 1.8 million years ago, as Homo *erectus began to reach Asia and then Europe. Another major dispersal occurred as modern* Homo sapiens *migrated beyond the Old World and into the New, reaching Australia some* 50,000 years ago and the Americas later. But theorists clash over what occurred between these two dispersals. Did modern humans arise in Africa before 100,000 years ago

400,000 years ago. Sites at Torralba and Ambrona in Spain indicate that they may have used fires to drive migrating elephant herds into swamps and trap them there.

One theory holds that, as brain capacity increased, *H. erectus* was evolving into another species, *Homo sapiens*. At all events, between about 300,000 and 200,000 years ago, *H. erectus* disappeared altogether.

Though *sapiens* means "wise," the best known of early *H. sapiens*—the Neandertals who lived in Europe from about 180,000 to about 35,000 years ago—were long unjustly ridiculed as dim-witted, cartoonish cavemen. Named for Germany's Neander Valley, where miners found the first skeleton in 1856, the Neandertals had strong bodies, large heads, jutting brow ridges, and big, broad noses.

Their brains were, in fact, at least as large and as developed as ours, giving them an evolutionary edge that allowed them to survive in extremely cold climates and to become expert hunters. Creating the technology called Mousterian, they crafted sophisticated new tools for specific purposes—to chop branches, to whittle, to work animal hides, to strip meat, or to prepare vegetables.

Neandertals were the first humans known to bury their dead, and the care they lavished on burials hints at a belief in an afterlife. In Iraq, archaeologists concluded that flowers had been buried with a corpse when they found traces of pollen in the grave. Nearby lay the remains of an old man who had lost an eye and an arm and was so hobbled by leg injuries that he must have depended on the compassion of his companions for food and care.

About 35,000 years ago, the last Neandertal mysteriously disappeared. Was the Neandertal subspecies of *Homo sapiens* killed off or displaced by newcomers of our own subspecies, *H. sapiens sapiens?* Did the Neandertals interbreed with these modern *H. sapiens,* who succeed them in the fossil record? Or did Neandertals simply evolve, over time, into modern humans?

As troubling as these unanswered questions are, they form only part of a larger debate, which flares again with each new find. On one side are scientists who believe that *H. erectus* populations in many different places evolved separately into archaic *H. sapiens*—which includes Neandertals—and then into modern *H. sapiens.* On the other side are those who believe that modern *H. sapiens* arose in one place, Africa, and then spread throughout the Old World, somehow replacing archaic *H. sapiens.*

Some recent studies in the field of molecular biology, though controversial, support the theory of an African cradle for modern humankind. Scientists have also found in African sites by far the earliest known remains of modern *H. sapiens,* dating back more than 100,000 years.

Modern humans began to spread

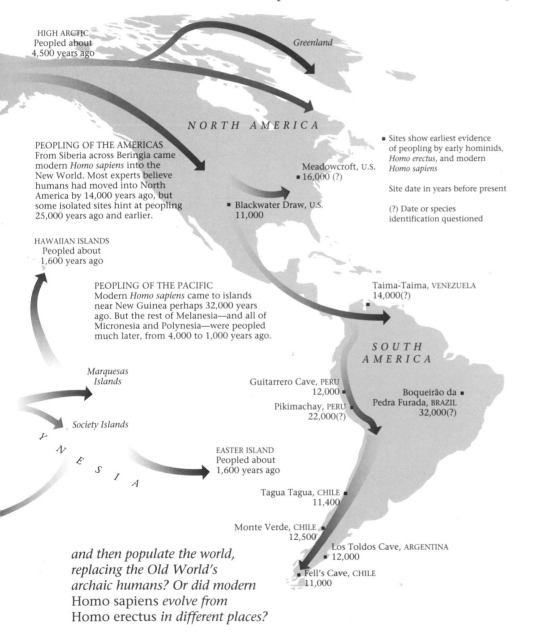

HIGH ARCTIC
Peopled about
4,500 years ago

Greenland

NORTH AMERICA

PEOPLING OF THE AMERICAS
From Siberia across Beringia came modern *Homo sapiens* into the New World. Most experts believe humans had moved into North America by 14,000 years ago, but some isolated sites hint at peopling 25,000 years ago and earlier.

■ Sites show earliest evidence of peopling by early hominids, *Homo erectus,* and modern *Homo sapiens*

Site date in years before present

(?) Date or species identification questioned

Meadowcroft, U.S.
■ 16,000 (?)

■ Blackwater Draw, U.S.
11,000

HAWAIIAN ISLANDS
Peopled about
1,600 years ago

PEOPLING OF THE PACIFIC
Modern *Homo sapiens* came to islands near New Guinea perhaps 32,000 years ago. But the rest of Melanesia—and all of Micronesia and Polynesia—were peopled much later, from 4,000 to 1,000 years ago.

Taima-Taima, VENEZUELA
14,000(?)
■

SOUTH AMERICA

Marquesas Islands

Guitarrero Cave, PERU
12,000 ■

Boqueirão da ■
Pedra Furada, BRAZIL
32,000(?)

Pikimachay, PERU
22,000(?)

Society Islands

P O L Y N E S I A

EASTER ISLAND
Peopled about
1,600 years ago

Tagua Tagua, CHILE ■
11,400

Monte Verde, CHILE
12,500

and then populate the world, replacing the Old World's archaic humans? Or did modern Homo sapiens *evolve from* Homo erectus *in different places?*

Los Toldos Cave, ARGENTINA
■ 12,000

■ Fell's Cave, CHILE
11,000

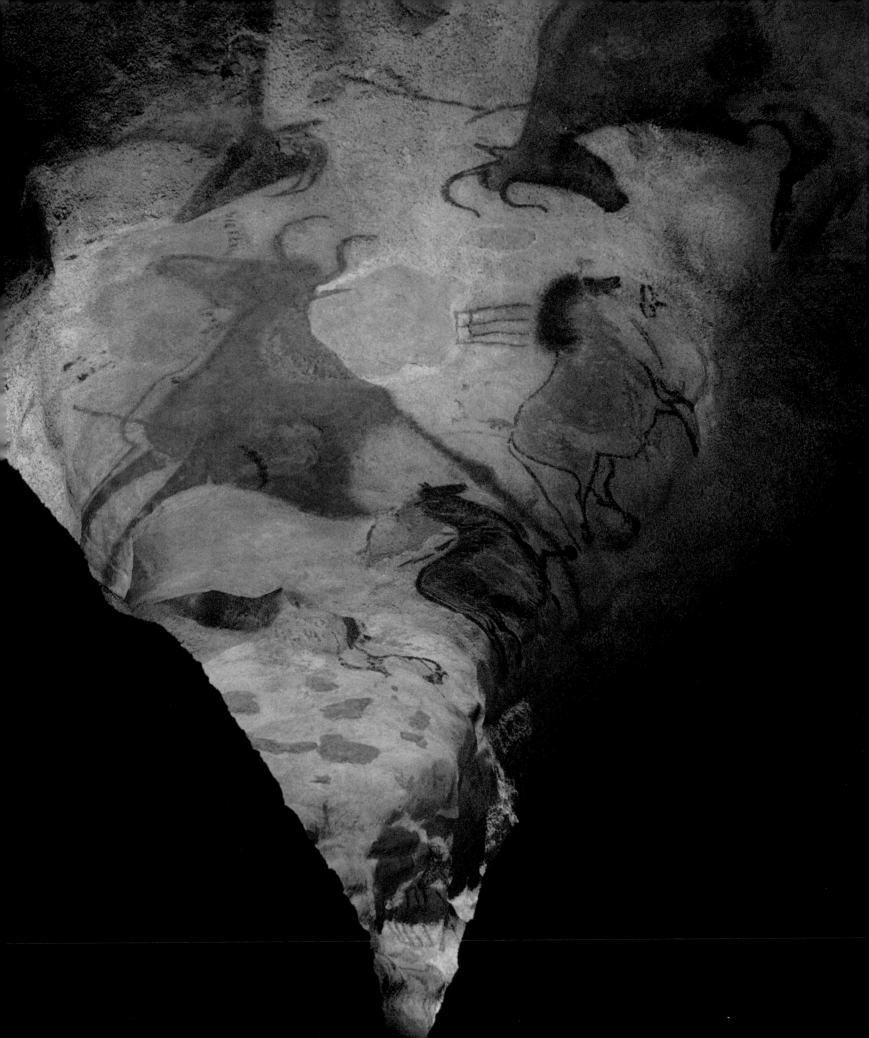

rapidly through Europe, Asia, and Australia about 50,000 years ago. Despite the harsh cold of glacial periods, modern *H. sapiens* was thriving. In fact, climate itself was an important factor that affected settlement of the habitable world. While ice sometimes impeded settlement, glaciation lowered sea levels, joining islands and forging migration routes.

Exposed seafloor linked Australia and New Guinea, forming a landmass called Sahul, while much of another called Sunda—consisting of Indonesia, the Philippines, and Borneo—was connected to mainland Southeast Asia. Still, no matter what route Australia's first colonists took, they would have had to cross large stretches of open sea. Though archaeologists have found no proof that they could build rafts, these migrants may have been the first humans to venture out of sight of land.

As populations grew, so did the size and complexity of the sites they occupied—whether caves, tents, or huts made of mammoth bones. Some sites were used seasonally or even longer, perhaps as gathering places for several bands who joined forces in the quest for food.

Such gatherings were probably times of ritual and ceremony among the Cro-Magnons of western Europe.

Groups of people exchanged lore and gifts—ornaments of seashells or amber. Increasingly, their elegant tools and weapons—fishhooks of bone, antler harpoons, slender spear throwers—and personal ornaments took on varying styles that came to identify different groups of people.

Brilliant sculptors, these Ice Age Europeans are even better known for the paintings and engravings they made deep inside the caves of northern Spain and southern France. Bulls, wild horses, reindeer, and other animals thunder across walls at Lascaux, Altamira, and other sites where artists swept on pigments made from ochers and manganese oxides.

The first Americans crossed from Siberia into Alaska over a land bridge called Beringia that spanned the Bering Strait between 25,000 and 14,000 years ago. The earliest known settlement near Beringia, at Bluefish Caves in Canada's Yukon, dates back to about 12,000 years ago. There, humans left behind spear-tipping stone microblades of a style first made in Siberia. But older settlements in South America suggest much earlier migration across Beringia. By 12,500 years ago, the

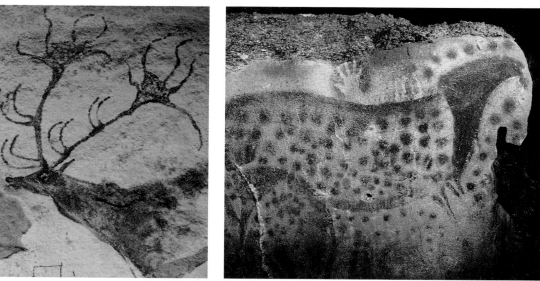

Cave paintings: roaring stag, Lascaux (above left); dappled horse, Pech-Merle (above right)

Ice Age Artistry

A hunter's spear pierces the chest of a bovine painted perhaps 17,000 years ago in the Axial Gallery of France's Lascaux Cave (opposite). Nearby, magnificent antlers curl like tentacles from a roaring stag. Spots such as those dappling a steed and the surrounding wall at Pech-Merle, France, elude interpretation. These and handprints—common cave art motifs—may have held magical meaning. Below, an ivory portrait, or Venus figurine, a whinnying horse, and a bison licking an insect bite exemplify the delicacy of sculptures created by European Ice Age artists.

Ivory head, Brassempouy, France, 1.4 in

Bison, La Madeleine, France, 4.1 in

Horse's head, Mas d'Azil, France, 2.2 in

In the Americas

Ice sheets beat a northward retreat beyond hunters butchering an elk north of the Meadowcroft site in

Ice sheets beat a northward retreat beyond hunters butchering an elk north of the Meadowcroft site in Pennsylvania. One man wields a knife resembling an artifact shown below him—14,000 to 16,000 years old. Giant spearpoints of chalcedony, from Washington State, bear distinctive fluted bases carved by Clovis knappers. In Patagonia, hands haloed in ocher and other pigments wave from a wall decorated by Toldense people at least 7,000 years ago.

Hunters north of Meadowcroft site, Pennsylvania

Clovis points, Washington State, ca 9000 B.C., 9 in

people of Monte Verde, in southern Chile, were using hide-covered timber dwellings that contained clay hearths. The vast number of medicinal and food plants they used showed a profound knowledge of their environment.

The first well-documented inhabitants of the Americas were the Clovis people, hunters of large game who flourished on the Great Plains and spread across North America and even into South America. Known primarily by the distinctive stone spearpoints that littered their kill sites, the Clovis people lasted only about 500 years, and then, around 11,000 years ago, disappeared—roughly at the same time that many of their quarry became extinct.

Their successors lived in a warmer, more diverse, and bountiful world. Over time, humans became skilled exploiters of their local environments. This may have led hunter-gatherers in both the New World and the Old to start giving up their far-ranging ways. Deliberate cultivation of crops—agriculture—favored a sedentary existence and in turn set the stage for changes that gave rise to the world's great civilizations.

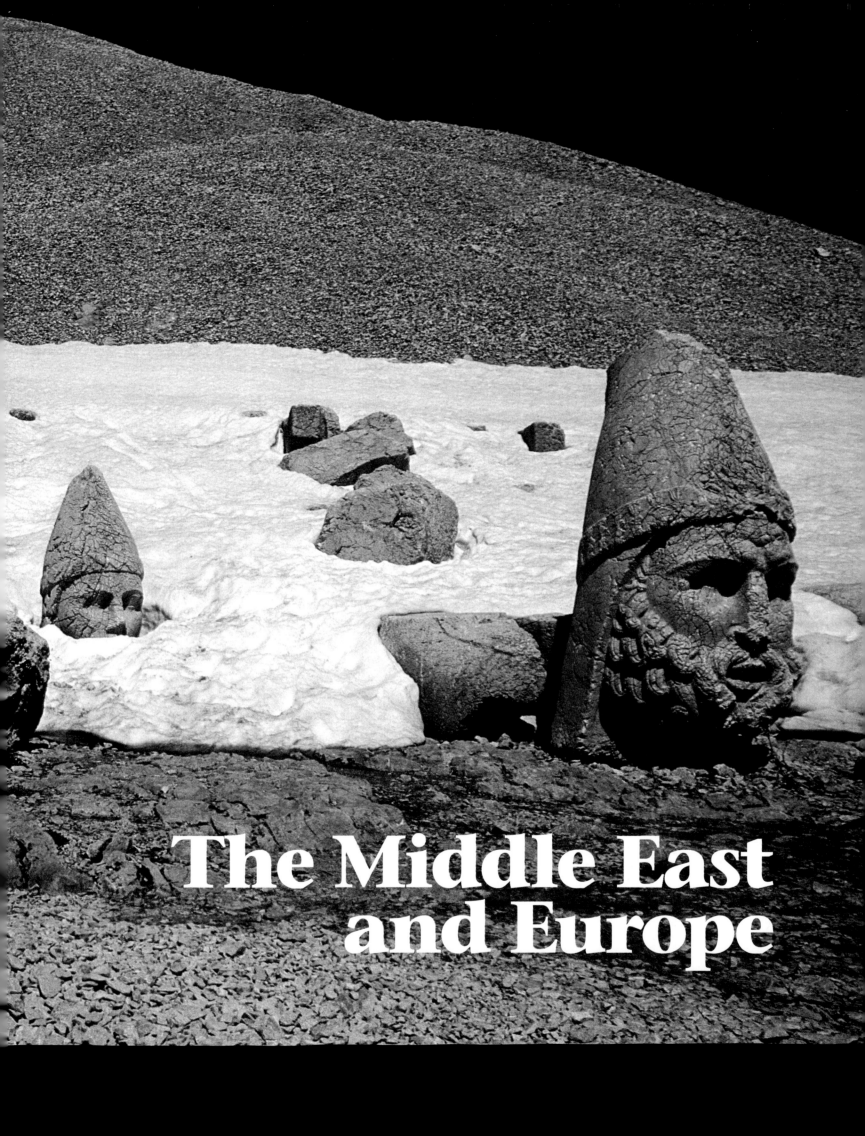

The Middle East
and Europe

Early Settlements

9000 to 4000 B.C.

In the hills and grasslands of the Middle East, some of the world's first farmers domesticated wild cereals and animals that were the ancestors of agricultural staples still in use today. Southwest Asia afforded flat, arable land, and the climate there grew warmer and wetter as the last ice age receded.

To begin with, hunter-gatherers harvested wild grains. At two of the earliest known agricultural villages in the area—Abu Hureyra and Mureybit in northern Syria—archaeologists have recovered wild cereals from pit dwellings that date back to between 9000 and 7500 B.C. More and more people turned from the nomadic lifestyle of hunter-gatherers to settle in permanent communities.

By 8000 B.C. settlers at Ali Kosh, in lowlands near the Zagros Moun-tains, were herding domesticated sheep and goats. At the walled village of Jericho in the Jordan Valley, farmers harvested domesticated barley and wheat. Harvesting and storing grain assured farmers a year-round food supply, so the trend toward settlement continued.

The 25 mud houses at Jarmo, in the Zagros foothills, had clay ovens for baking the stored grain. Columns and terrazzo floors at Çayönü, in southeastern Turkey, denote a skill in advanced building techniques, as do the plastered walls of Hacilar, a farming village founded in southwestern Turkey about 6700 B.C.

By 6000 B.C. agriculture had spread throughout southwest Asia, and prosperous farming villages had become widespread. Farmers grew peas, lentils, bitter vetch, barley, and wheat; they raised pigs and cattle as well as tending sheep and goats.

Trade in a variety of commodities developed between villages. A prehistoric settlement at Tell Brak in eastern Syria evolved over time into a hundred-acre trading center. Bartering native obsidian helped Çatal Hüyük in Anatolia to grow and flourish. Archaeologists have unearthed evidence of trade in the volcanic glass as far south as Beidha.

Agriculture—together with trade—fostered the establishment of permanent communities and thus paved the way for the rise of urban civilizations in the Middle East.

PRECEDING PAGES: Toppled Greco-Persian gods gaze across the Euphrates River from the site of Nemrud Dagh in Turkey. Antiochus I of Commagene erected them in the first century B.C., placing his own image among them.

BLACK SEA

CASPIAN SEA

ANATOLIA

Hacilar
Çatal Hüyük
Nemrud Dagh
Çayönü
Tell Brak
ZAGROS MOUNTAINS

TAURUS MTS.

Mureybit

Abu Hureyra

Jarmo

Tigris

Euphrates

Ali Kosh

SEA

Jordan River

Jericho

Dead Sea

Beidha

PERSIAN GULF

RED SEA

● Ancient and modern town site

◆ Archaeological site only

0   400 mi

0   600 km

Jericho

9000 to 4000 B.C.

Much more than the well-known biblical story of walls tumbling at the sound of Joshua's trumpets assures Jericho's fame. Jericho is one of the world's earliest communities and the oldest known walled town. It lies six miles west of the Jordan River, north of the Dead Sea.

As early as 9000 B.C., hunter-gatherers camped on the east side of Jericho near a perennial spring that still spouts more than a thousand gallons of water every minute.

Later, beside the spring, settlers built beehive-shaped huts of mud brick, the first known use of the building material that is standard throughout the rural Middle East today. By 8000 B.C.—in the Late Neolithic, or Late Stone Age—farmers in Jericho were herding flocks of domesticated sheep and goats; they cultivated and stored barley and wheat that show the characteristics of domesticated grains.

By 6000 B.C., as many as 3,000 people lived in Jericho. Archaeological evidence suggests that the village was part of an extensive trading network, bartering Dead Sea salt for obsidian from Anatolia.

From time to time, Jericho lay abandoned, but other settlers arrived. As mud-brick dwellings collapsed, new ones were built on top of the rubble, creating a mound. Such a mound of settlement debris, called a *tell* or a *hüyük,* is typical of archaeological sites in this region.

Excavations at 70-foot-high Tell es-Sultan—ancient Jericho—by two British archaeologists have yielded exciting finds but left many questions unanswered. In the 1930s, John Garstang found evidence documenting Jericho's existence in 6000 B.C. But more dramatic discoveries occurred in the 1950s, when Kathleen Kenyon pushed the history of Jericho back to the ninth millennium B.C., prompting scholars to reevaluate when agriculture and the domestication of animals began.

Kenyon's discoveries raised questions, too, about the accuracy of the biblical narrative. Partly because of the absence of imported Bronze Age pottery, she concluded that Jericho was destroyed in the 16th century B.C., long before the time of Joshua.

Archaeologist Bryant Wood disagrees. He notes, among other things, that Kenyon's dig was limited and that Garstang found local pottery dating from about 1400 B.C.

Puzzles still remain. Jericho lies in a region of frequent earthquakes; could one have toppled its walls? And why were they built—to defend Jericho or to prevent flooding? Further study is hampered by the site's location in an area of civil unrest.

Tower steps, looking up from base

Plastered, painted skulls, ca 7000 B.C.

Mysteries Amid the Ruins

Rising amid ruins inside the outer wall of Jericho, a stone tower (opposite) excavated in the 1950s by Kathleen Kenyon still baffles archaeologists. Did it serve as a watchtower? Water and food storage bins found nearby suggested to Kenyon that Jericho's leader used the 30-foot-high tower as a stronghold; 22 narrow steps rise from base to top. Plastered, painted skulls with eyes of seashell found at the site may hold spiritual meaning. A plaster bust of a later date also has shell eyes.

Plaster bust, ca 6000 B.C.

Çatal Hüyük

7000 to 5600 B.C.

Farmers settled at Çatal Hüyük, in the fertile grasslands of Anatolia, about 7000 B.C. They herded cattle and cultivated wheat, barley, and peas, along with numerous other crops. Çatal Hüyük forms one of the earliest links between the rise of farming and the development of urban life.

Bartering obsidian from quarries in the Taurus Mountains, Çatal Hüyük flourished as the center of an extensive trading complex. Local craftsmen grew skilled in weaving, in smelting lead and copper, and in the necessary technology for shaping the metals.

By 6000 B.C., Çatal Hüyük had mushroomed into a town of some 5,000 people that covered 32 acres. Archaeologists have discovered no other Neolithic settlement in the Middle East nearly as large. Not only did its size render Çatal Hüyük unique. It was a much more sophisticated community than Jericho and other farming villages. Yet, unlike those settlements, which were inhabited for many thousands of years, excavations in the west mound revealed that Çatal Hüyük was occupied only in the Neolithic and was abandoned by 5600 B.C.

Its remains lay undisturbed until British archaeologist James Mellaart discovered the 55-foot-high mound in 1958. During four seasons in the 1960s, Mellaart and his team unearthed walls, shrines, statues, tools, and paintings whose variety and complexity were startling for such an ancient site. By the third day of digging, Mellaart said, "we knew we were in clover."

He excavated small, rectangular houses of mud brick coated with plaster. Although they shared no common walls, the houses were so tightly clustered they looked like an Indian pueblo; access was by ladder from a hole in the roof. Mellaart also unearthed storerooms and shrines.

Perhaps the biggest surprises were the wall paintings, such as a hunting scene the team found on the third day. Bold in style and color, the paintings are the earliest known to have been done on man-made walls. They were found mostly in shrines.

The paintings, along with sculptures of female deities and images of bulls discovered in the shrines, suggest that Çatal Hüyük may have been a ceremonial center. Like the excavations at Jericho, however, those at Çatal Hüyük were limited. Mellaart's dig covered only about an acre—less than one-thirtieth of the total area. Perhaps it centered on the sacred quarter of town and was not representative of the whole settlement.

After a gap of nearly 30 years, work began again at Çatal Hüyük in 1993, but speculation continues.

Mother goddess, 6.5 in

Images of Settled Life

Horned effigies—four bulls and a ram—jut from the walls of a reconstructed shrine (opposite) from Çatal Hüyük in south-central Turkey. More than 40 shrines adorned with fertility symbols such as these have been found at Çatal Hüyük, the largest Neolithic site in the Middle East. A restored baked-clay figure, depicting a mother goddess giving birth, was found in a grain bin. Similar figures unearthed at the dig led archaeologists to suggest the existence of an agricultural fertility cult. Polished obsidian mirrors from burial sites near shrines may have been associated with priestesses. Bone forks and spatulas recovered from the ruins most likely served as food utensils. Spatulas, spoons, and ladles were often present in burials of a mother and child.

Fork and spatulas

Obsidian mirror

Chinese painting of rice workers, ca 13th century A.D.

First Farmers

On the threshing floor at left, four Chinese men use a hand bar to operate the crank that turns a grain-hulling mill. Others winnow, vigorously tossing rice in flat baskets to separate the grain from the chaff.

Rice cultivation, like all traditional forms of agriculture, required an organized, settled population and demanded intensive labor. Good years produced surpluses, but annual harvests were always subject to floods, droughts, and other vagaries of nature. Success was never guaranteed.

Archaeologists have tried to learn where, when, how, and why people made the sometimes perilous shift from the flexible and often less demanding lifestyle of the hunter-gatherer to the deliberate manipulation of plant and animal species that is the basis of agriculture.

Locating the threshold of agriculture in any part of the world is a difficult task. In their search, archaeologists often must rely on small amounts of plant or animal material: charred remains of meals, stored grain adhering to pottery fragments, discarded bones, or microscopic bits of pollen. They look for other indications of organized food production: permanent settlements, pottery vessels for food storage or preparation, and tools or tool-making equipment. But because the difference between some wild and domesticated species of both plants and animals may be minimal, it is often impossible to determine the presence of cultivation or animal husbandry with certainty.

In the 19th century, theorists sought a single source for world agriculture. Some experts thought it might be the brainchild of a lone prehistoric planter. Others suggested the possibility of a post-Pleistocene drought, which essentially corralled all plant and animal species into well-watered oases where domestication eventually occurred. But archaeological evidence did not support a single-source scenario, and such theories were abandoned.

Most scholars now believe that hunter-gatherer societies in widely separated parts of the world turned gradually to cultivating the soil, growing crops, and domesticating animals, thus effecting the worldwide shift to agriculture that took place between 10,000 and 4000 B.C. —a very short time in the context of all human history.

In several areas of Mesopotamia, northern China, Southeast Asia, and Mesoamerica, the bones of animals and the preserved remains of wheat, rice, maize, and other cereal plants provide evidence of organized agricultural activity. In South America and parts of Africa, where far fewer animals were domesticated and farmers relied on root crops and tuberous vegetables that usually decay without a trace, documentation of early agricultural activity is much more difficult to obtain.

In the Fertile Crescent, the uplands that arc from the southeastern Mediterranean to the broad plains between the Tigris and the Euphrates Rivers, wild wheat and barley grew in abundance, and ancestors of the sheep and goat roamed the nearby Zagros Mountains. Local hunters harvested grain with flint knives and gradually developed greater dependence upon this readily available food source. They also began to herd the wild sheep and goats, which provided them with food and clothing. Simple attempts to improve on what nature provided—scattering seeds to enlarge production or controlling the feeding and breeding of herd animals— slowly laid the foundations of an agricultural society and a more settled way of life.

Tomb of Sennedjem, Thebes, ca 1200 B.C.

Beasts, Butter, and Beer

Figures in clay and stone record aspects of animal husbandry and food production in western Asia. This pottery pig from Anatolia represents an

Pottery pig, Anatolia, ca 5600 B.C., 10.2 in

Pottery toys, Indus Valley, ca 2500 B.C., about 1.5 to 2.8 in

Detail of the Standard of Ur, Sumer, ca 2600-2400 B.C., width 19 in

Limestone figurine,
Saqqara, Egypt,
ca 2450 B.C.,
10.6 in

animal first domesticated about 7000 B.C. Clay toys portray animals raised thousands of years ago in the Indus Valley: a dog, a chicken, a duck, and oxen hitched to a cart. A Sumerian mosaic panel unearthed in the royal cemetery at Ur depicts a procession of people, sheep, cattle, and goats. Butter making occupies Sumerian priests shown on a limestone frieze from Ubaid. In Egypt, a tomb painting reveals planting and harvesting techniques. A tomb figurine shows a woman making beer. She works barley mash through a sieve in an earthen jar.

Frieze, Ubaid, 3rd millennium B.C.

To the west, in the Levant and Anatolia, archaeological remains of numerous settlements—among them Abu Hureyra, Jericho, and Hacilar—bear witness to flourishing agriculture during the tenth and ninth millennia B.C. Over the next few thousand years, agricultural skills also developed in other parts of the Asian continent, in Egypt, and on the Balkan Peninsula, which is the site of Europe's earliest known farming communities.

By 6000 B.C., many of the plants and animals that sustain modern agriculture had been domesticated, and numerous agricultural villages were thriving in the Middle East.

The central role of agriculture and the details of its undertaking are frequently preserved not only in archaeological remains but also in the historical and artistic records of all great civilizations. A 14th-century B.C. tomb painting from Thebes (pages 42-3) depicts the harvesting of wheat and

Antler sickle, Bulgaria, 8.2 in

Pottery figure, Hungary, ca 4500 B.C., 10 in

flax, the bounty of well-tended orchards, the use of oxen, and the irrigation of fields—an improvement that followed the unification of Egypt in 3100 B.C.

On the Indian subcontinent, the northwestern highlands have provided substantial evidence of the earliest agricultural development in southern Asia. During the seventh millennium B.C., farmers at Mehrgarh, in what is now Pakistan, grew barley and wheat and also kept cattle, sheep, and goats.

Southeast Asian sites have yielded animal and plant remains from as early as 9000 B.C., but proof of organized agriculture at that date remains to be found. Firm evidence of domesticated rice has been dated to about 5000 B.C.

In East Asia, Chinese farmers living on the delta of the Yangtze River were cultivating rice in irrigated fields well before 5000 B.C. Such labor-intensive work demanded organization and cooperation in the construction of dams, dikes, and canals. In northern China, millet cultivation, sericulture, and the domestication of both pigs and dogs characterized village life from about the seventh millennium B.C.

In the New World, Mesoamerican farmers developed seed crops such as maize, beans, and squash during the sixth millennium B.C., while in South America root crops that included manioc and potatoes

are thought to have predominated.

Compared to modern corn, the prehistoric maize plant bears only a tiny nub of kernels; early farmers experimented with hybrids of many varieties to improve their yields. Eventually, maize production would fuel the economies of the great empires of Mesoamerica.

Early farmers of both the Old and the New Worlds used simple tools—digging sticks, hoes, and knives—all of which retained their importance in the Americas and in parts of Africa until relatively modern times. In Asia and in Europe, however, the invention of the plow made possible the use of draft animals, the development of larger fields, and the cultivation of heavier soils.

The techniques of agriculture and its attendant way of life spread steadily from its original centers, in many cases coexisting with hunter-gatherer societies and eventually displacing them in all but inhospitably arid parts of the earth.

When nature cooperated, organized agriculture enabled greater production and larger settlements. Farmers could invest more time and energy in the construction of dwellings and the development of material goods. The change in both occupation and lifestyle brought about by agriculture was a necessary precursor to most subsequent developments in the ever changing nature of human civilization.

Detail of steatite vessel, Hagia Triada, Crete, ca 1500 B.C.

Ceramic figure,
Ecuador,
ca A.D. 200-400,
12 in

Old World and New

Early communities in the Old and the New Worlds fashioned agricultural artifacts both artistic and utilitarian. A deer-antler sickle, with flint blades embedded in it, harvested grain growing near the Danube some 8,000 years ago. Jubilant Minoan farmers celebrate their harvest on this 16th-century B.C. vessel from Crete. The dignified figure found at a 5th-millennium B.C. site in Hungary carries what may be a sickle over his right shoulder. A detailed ceramic figure from Ecuador, wearing a garment with a seed motif and carrying a seed bag and digging stick, suggests ritual preparations for planting. The Maya attributed human origin to corn plants, as illustrated in this 8th-century A.D. mural from Mexico. In coastal Peru, Moche potters elaborated brilliantly on plant and animal forms. Dating from the 4th century A.D., this vessel depicts a flute player in the shape of a peanut.

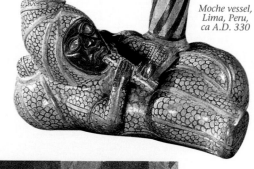

Moche vessel,
Lima, Peru,
ca A.D. 330

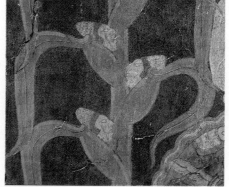

Section of mural, Cacaxtla, 8th century A.D.

ETRURIA

Rome

Ibiza

Mycenae • • Salamis

Carthage •

MEDITERRANEAN

Cities and Civilizations

4000 to 30 B.C.

Some time after 4000 B.C., Sumerians living along the Tigris and Euphrates Rivers in what is today Iraq succeeded in producing the first food surplus in human history. This achievement set in motion a process that was to lead to the rise of Western civilization.

With irrigation, the rich alluvial soil of southern Mesopotamia—"land between the rivers"—yielded harvests large enough to support a relatively dense population. But no longer did everyone need to labor in the fields. Farming occupied only one segment of the workforce.

This far-reaching change gave other individuals the freedom to develop specialized skills and new ideas. Villages were transformed into urban centers, and writing evolved as

a way of keeping records. A society of specialists emerged—scribes, teachers, carpenters, masons, potters, and other artisans—ruled by a religious and political elite. Technology, art, and religious ritual became hallmarks of these urban communities by 3500 B.C. Sustained by intensive agriculture and by trade, they developed into prosperous city-states.

As wealth accumulated, the cities became tempting targets for invaders from neighboring regions. An epic succession of alien peoples—the Gutians, Amorites, Elamites, Hittites, Hurrians, Kassites, Assyrians, Chaldeans, Medes, and Persians—advanced into the fertile plains and bordering areas of Mesopotamia.

These newcomers adopted the cultures of the cities they conquered. By the third millennium B.C.,

civilization had spread out from the Mesopotamian floodplain in a great arc—reaching north from the Persian Gulf into Anatolia and Syria and south to Egypt—an area that became known as the Fertile Crescent.

The first empire in history was forged in Mesopotamia around 2300 B.C. by Sargon, ruler of Akkad, a kingdom to the north of Sumer. His conquests extended from the Persian Gulf to the Mediterranean Sea. Other empires followed, succeeding one another over the centuries.

Egypt embarked on its interrelated journey to civilization after 3050 B.C. when, following unification of the kingdom, rulers mobilized the population in large-scale irrigation projects. Again, a rich agricultural base underlay this ancient empire's long-lived civilization.

BLACK SEA

CASPIAN SEA

Bosporus

◆ Alaca Hüyük

◆ Hattusha

MILID

HITTITES

ANATOLIA

LYDIA

Carchemish ◆ ◆ Til Barsip

◆ Khorsabad ● Gaugamela
Nineveh ◆

◆ Ebla

ASSYRIA

Nimrud ◆

Arwad ◆

◆ Ashur

MESOPOTAMIA

ZAGROS

◆ Ecbatana

SEA

◆ Byblos

● Sidon

Euphrates

Tigris

MOUNTAINS

PERSIA

Tyre ◆

CANAAN

PALESTINE

● Jerusalem

Babylon ● ◆ AKKAD

Nippur ◆ ◆ Girsu

● Susa

E L A M

LOWER
EGYPT

BABYLONIA

SUMER ◆ Lagash

Giza ◆

Eridu ◆ ◆ Ur

◆ Pasargadae

Memphis ●

◆ Persepolis

Nile

PERSIAN GULF

◆ Tell el-Amarna

UPPER
EGYPT

Valley of the Kings ◆ ◆ Karnak

THEBES ● Luxor

Nile

◆ Abu Simbel

RED SEA

NUBIA

● Ancient and modern town site

◆ Archaeological site only

0   400 mi

0   600 km

Sumerians

3500 to 1950 B.C.

The world's first civilization emerged about 3500 B.C. in the lower reaches of Iraq's Tigris and Euphrates Rivers. There, in ancient Sumer in southern Mesopotamia, urban living and literacy flourished in cities with names such as Ur, Lagash, Eridu, and Nippur. Sumerians were early users of wheeled vehicles and were among the first metallurgists, blending metals into alloys, extracting silver from ore, and casting bronze in complex molds. Sumerians were also the first to invent writing, a skill called for by the need to keep track of the accounts of the temple treasuries. Archaeologists have uncovered thousands of clay tablets incised with a reed stylus in a wedge-shaped script called cuneiform. New discoveries of tablets in adjacent Syria and Turkey indicate that writing skills spread earlier and farther than formerly thought. While scholars were deciphering texts—commercial records, laws, and royal proclamations—archaeologists were unearthing cities of mud brick, each with its own god, king, and powerful priesthood.

At Ur, where according to legend Abraham was born, British archaeologist Sir Leonard Woolley excavated

Bottom section, one side of Standard of Ur, width 19 in

Bull's head, 11.6 in, mounted on harp

Ziggurat of Ur, 20th-century restoration

the treasure-filled tombs of royalty in the 1920s and '30s. Sumerians produced fine wares and works of art from metals and materials not available on the alluvial plain. The demand for luxuries and for timber and stone for construction led to a far-flung trade that contributed to the flowering of Sumerian civilization around 3000 B.C. It may also account for the rapid rise of other cities beyond Sumer's borders in the following centuries.

Trappings of Civilization

Steep main stairway ascends Ur's ziggurat, or temple platform, restored with ancient brick. Atop this "hill of heaven," which rose in three tiers to about 70 feet, priests washed, fed, and clothed a statue of the moon god, Nanna. A gilded head of a bull adorns a harp found in one of the royal tombs at Ur, where exquisite furnishings and an entourage accompanied monarchs

to the grave. A mosaic of shell and lapis lazuli depicts a battle scene on an object of unknown function dubbed the Standard of Ur. A limestone head illustrates the refinement of sculpture during the third dynasty of Ur, about 2050 to 1950 B.C., the last period of Sumerian independence.

Limestone head, 4.5 in

Hittites

2000 to 700 B.C.

Hittites entered the civilized world about 2000 B.C. when they migrated to Turkey's mountainous Anatolian Plateau from the steppelands north of the Black Sea. After some 400 years the Hittites began making a bid for empire, setting out from their hilltop capital of Hattusha. The heavily fortified city was dominated by a citadel-palace and surrounded by massive double stone walls, reinforced with stone sentry towers.

Warriors were led into battle by a sovereign who was also the high priest responsible for propitiating the storm god Teshub, the sun goddess Hebat, and a large pantheon of lesser nature deities. On military campaigns, the Hittites used battering rams and a fighting force of war chariots and infantrymen in bronze armor, equipped with bronze-tipped arrows and bronze daggers, swords, and battle-axes. The warlike Hittites were also master diplomats, negotiating alliances, often based on royal marriages, to extend their domain.

By the 14th century B.C., at the zenith of their power, this warrior elite had gained hegemony over the cities and petty states in southern Anatolia and Syria, forging an empire on the borders of Mesopotamia bound together by treaties and laws. The Hittites had also sacked storied Babylon and had repeatedly challenged the mighty kingdom of Egypt.

Yet the once powerful Hittites all but disappeared from the annals of history until 1906, when the archives of the empire were retrieved from the ruins of Hattusha. Thousands of clay tablets inscribed in wedge-shaped Mesopotamian cuneiform recorded treaties, royal decrees, laws, prayers, and rituals, as well as such mundane details as price lists and inventories.

Some of the texts were in Akkadian, which was the diplomatic language of the ancient Middle East and was readily translated by scholars. But the bulk of the cuneiform writings were in an unknown language that was not deciphered until 1915. Hittite was not one of the Semitic languages of the region but a branch of the Indo-European family, which includes Latin, English, and Slavic. More baffling to scholars were the Hittite hieroglyphs (opposite). This script inscribed on stone monuments was not deciphered until the 1960s.

The written record reveals that the Hittites

Warrior-god, Hattusha, 6.5 ft

were reasonable men, tolerant of local customs. They had a high regard for the rule of law, which provided protection even to slaves.

About 1200 B.C. the empire abruptly collapsed, and Hattusha was razed by invaders whose identity remains a mystery. But a surge of migrations and invasions had put the whole region in turmoil. Vestiges of the culture lingered, but by 700 B.C. these Neo-Hittites also had vanished, and Assyrians controlled the region.

Bronze stag, 20 in

Neo-Hittite king, 10.3 ft

Lion gate, Hattusha

Hieroglyphs, 9th century B.C.

Kings and Gods

Stone lions stand sentinel at a gateway to Hattusha, the heart of the Hittite Empire. Prisoners of war, refugees, and conscripted villagers built the double walls that form a four-mile perimeter around the city. Gripping a battle-ax, a warrior-god bas-relief guards another entrance. He wears a Hittite warrior's conical helmet with flaps to cover the cheeks. A bronze stag figurine, inlaid with an alloy of silver and gold, was recovered from the royal tombs of Alaca Hüyük, a city that flourished some 300 years before the Hittites arrived. Found in Milid, one of the petty states where a diluted form of Hittite culture survived, a 10.3-foot stone statue portrays a king with curly beard and hair in the Assyrian style. A gold figurine from the late Neo-Hittite period at the city of Carchemish depicts a Hittite god.

Neo-Hittite figurine of god, 0.6 in

51

Babylonians

1792 to 539 B.C.

A minor village when Sumerians made their breakthrough to civilization, Babylon rose from obscurity under the monarch Hammurapi, who began his reign in 1792 B.C. He took advantage of the chaotic situation in Mesopotamia that had existed since Sumer fell to invaders around 2000 B.C. and consolidated the warring states into what is now known as the Old Babylonian Empire.

A direct heir to the culture of ancient Sumer, Babylon remained the great metropolis and cultural hub of western Asia, unrivaled in prestige for two thousand years. Biblical tradition associated Babylon with decadence and vice, but the city was, in fact, a center of learning and religion.

Little is known of Hammurapi's Babylon because the 18th-century B.C. layer of ruins lies below the water table, inaccessible to archaeologists. But clay tablets from the period attest to achievements in mathematics, astronomy, and literature, which would bequeath to the world the 60-minute hour, the 360-degree circle, the 12-month year, and literature such as the *Epic of Gilgamesh*—the tale of a legendary Sumerian king's futile quest for immortality.

Under Hammurapi, Babylon developed a centralized administration, a bureaucracy, and a professional merchant class. Hammurapi promulgated the famous legal code based on the principle of an "eye for eye, tooth for tooth" that is also set forth in the Old Testament.

After the sack of Babylon by the Hittites in 1595 B.C., barbarians from the north called Kassites imposed their rule on the city and all Babylonia. But the long-established civilization of Babylonia, with its esteemed expertise in science and divination and its venerable scribal schools, prevailed. The Kassite conquerors adopted local customs and reinstalled Marduk, the chief god of Babylon, in his shrine.

The end of four centuries of Kassite rule ushered in another period of instability, followed by Assyrian conquests in the ninth century B.C. Babylon was absorbed into an empire that embraced most of the Fertile Crescent. But even at the peak of Assyrian power, the tradition-bound city retained its cultural importance.

By this time the Chaldeans, a tribe from southern Mesopotamia, had established a dynasty in Babylon. In 612 B.C., Chaldeans and their allies struck the mighty Assyrian Empire a deadly blow, and Nebuchadrezzar II, the monarch of Babylon, brought new grandeur to his ancient capital. Lavish royal palaces and the famed Hanging Gardens, with their multiple terraces, date from this Neo-Babylonian period.

Persians subdued Babylon in 539 B.C., and two centuries later Alexander the Great inaugurated a period of

Alabaster figurine of Ishtar, 9 in

Detail of basalt stela, 7.3 ft, inscribed with Law Code of Hammurapi

Kassite boundary stone

Restored facade of throne room, Babylon

By the Walls of Babylon

Decorated with lions, columns, and conventional designs, the restored, glazed-brick facade of King Nebuchadrezzar II's throne room typifies the architecture of the Neo-Babylonian period of the seventh century B.C., when Babylon became an imperial capital for the second time. The city had been a center of learning for more than a thousand years, but it achieved its greatest fame under the Neo-Babylonian kings, when Nebuchadrezzar II lavishly rebuilt it. Babylon continued to dominate the cultural life of the region, even after the Persian conquest in 539 B.C. An alabaster figurine from the fourth century B.C. portrays Ishtar, the Babylonian goddess of love and war and the preeminent goddess of western Asia. Babylon first gained ascendancy under Hammurapi, the monarch who created the Old Babylonian Empire in the 18th century B.C. The most important relic from this era, a black stela inscribed in cuneiform with the Law Code of Hammurapi, shows the law-giver before the seated sun god, Shamash, patron of justice. Little survives from the succeeding Kassite period, beginning in 1595 B.C., except for boundary stones such as this oval-shaped basalt monument. Embellished with divine symbols, it records a gift of land. A tablet from the sixth century B.C. bears a map of the world encircled by the sea. Names inscribed on it include "Babylon" and "Assyria."

Tablet inscribed with world map

Hellenistic rule. He died in Babylon.

In A.D. 116, Roman emperor Trajan wintered in Babylon and found the city in ruins. For centuries its magnificent structures lay buried in sandy mounds. Then, in excavations between 1899 and 1917, German archaeologist Robert Koldewey revealed something of Babylon's ancient glory. Today, the Iraqi government is restoring parts of the city to their former grandeur.

Assyrians

1500 to 612 B.C.

Headdress, Nimrud

From their homeland on the fertile plains in northern Mesopotamia, a succession of Assyrian monarchs waged bloodthirsty campaigns that terrorized the Middle East and raised their state to the rank of a great empire. Assyria first rose to prominence around the 14th century B.C. Periods of glory alternated with intervals of internal weakness and chaos as the Assyrians resisted nomadic raids

the number of people they butchered like sheep, impaled on stakes, burned in fires, blinded, and mutilated. These atrocities were part of a strategy of terror to discourage resistance. Entire conquered populations were uprooted and forced into slave labor. These prisoners of war created the ornate palaces and temples, the marvels of sculpture, and the mighty walls with their great gateways flanked by winged bulls or lions that made the capitals of Nimrud and Nineveh cities of splendor. Under Ashurbanipal, the last great Assyrian king, Nineveh also assembled a huge library of all the literary masterpieces of Sumer, Babylon, and Assyria.

In 612 B.C., Nineveh fell to a coalition of subject states led by Babylon, and Assyrian domains were absorbed into the Neo-Babylonian Empire. Assyria was obliterated. Nothing remained but its reputation for cruelty until the 1840s, when French consul Paul Botta and, subsequently, Englishman Austen Henry Layard, discovered Assyria's ancient glories buried in mounds of dirt.

Crown (above), plaque (below), Nimrud

and other foreign incursions. Two kings of the ninth century B.C. laid the foundations of the empire, but Assyria was at the height of its power from 745 to 612 B.C., ruling the lands from the Zagros Mountains to the Mediterranean, and for a short time it even held Egypt in thrall. Under Tiglath-pileser III, who ruled from 745 to 727 B.C., Assyria streamlined the administration of its conquered territories. Military reforms created a powerful war machine consisting of a light infantry of archers, a sword-and-spear-wielding heavy infantry, and a mobile archer-cavalry that gradually replaced old-fashioned charioteers. Assyrian monarchs boasted of

Alabaster bas-relief of King Ashurbanipal hunting lions, Nineveh

Royal Art and Treasure

In a hunting scene carved with dramatic realism in the seventh century B.C. for a palace at Nineveh, King Ashurbanipal spears a lion from horseback. Assyrian monarchs decorated their palace walls with graphic bas-reliefs and compositions in colored tile extolling their courage and skill as hunters and as warriors. Remembered mostly for their ruthless military exploits, Assyrian monarchs also patronized the arts, fostering sculpture of great vitality and power. This statue of a colossal winged bull with a bearded human head once guarded the entrance to the throne room in Khorsabad, a city founded by Sargon II in 717 B.C. and abandoned at his death around 705. Artistic convention gave these mythical sentinel figures a fifth leg, so that they appeared natural when viewed from the front or in profile. Golden treasure from eighth-century B.C. royal tombs in Nimrud, one of Assyria's capitals, reveals an elegant taste in finery. Three rows of rosettes decorate a crown, one of hundreds of pieces of jewelry found by Iraqi archaeologists in 1989. A headdress and palm-crested plaque feature ornate gold tassels. Assyrian art often reflects the affluence of luxury-loving royalty, portraying rulers wearing embroidered robes and living in opulent palaces.

Winged bull, palace of Sargon II, Khorsabad

Phoenicians

1200 to 146 B.C.

Beginning about 1200 B.C., Phoenician galleys laden with cargo dominated shipping in the Mediterranean for more than a thousand years. Phoenician traders were also braving the perilous reaches of the Atlantic by 600 B.C., sailing down the coast of Africa and up into northern waters, perhaps venturing as far as England. An account set down by the Greek historian Herodotus suggests that skilled Phoenician mariners may even have circumnavigated Africa.

At first the mariners ruled the seas from the ports of Byblos, Tyre, Sidon, and Arwad located in modern Lebanon. The cities were part of Canaan, a region settled earlier by a Semitic tribe of herders and farmers. Those Canaanites who lived along the coast turned to maritime trade and in time came to be known as Phoenicians. By 2600 B.C. their ships were transporting logs to Egypt, including the coveted cedars of Lebanon. By 1500 B.C. returning ships carried grain, linen, gold, and papyrus to homeland ports, which had become distribution centers for products transported to or from the hinterland by caravan.

For several hundred years Egypt held sway over these seafaring Canaanites. But as the pharaoh's power crumbled in 1200 B.C. under invasions by the mysterious "sea peoples," and as the Mycenaean Greeks lost control over local sea lanes, the Phoenicians seized the opportunity to seek new markets in order to expand their trade.

During the Phoenician golden age that followed, these traders plied the seas unchallenged, establishing trading posts and colonies on many islands and along the North African coast. Carthage, in modern Tunisia,

Glass pendant, 1.5 in

Wall relief of Phoenician ships, 8th century B.C.

eventually became the most important outpost, eclipsing even the homeland cities.

Phoenicians also were known for their skill as craftsmen; they manufactured wares that have been found from one end of the Mediterranean to the other. Artisans excelled in making glass, in working bronze, gold, and ivory, and in fashioning wood furniture. Purple textiles, dyed with an extract from sea snails, were prized by kings. The Israelite king Solomon relied heavily on Phoenician carpenters and stonemasons to build his temple in Jerusalem.

To keep track of their far-flung business activities, Phoenicians developed a writing system far simpler than the cuneiform script, which had hundreds of characters. Their alphabet, which used a letter to represent a consonant sound, was a forerunner of the modern Western alphabet.

From around 750 B.C., the wealthy but vulnerable home cities began to suffer repeated invasions—first by Assyrians and then by Babylonians and Persians. Carthage became a haven for Phoenicians fleeing conquerors who exacted heavy tribute. By 650 B.C. this African metropolis ruled the seas, edging out Greek and Etruscan rivals. Under King Hannibal, Carthage also posed a threat to Rome until defeated in the Second Punic War in 202 B.C. The city was utterly destroyed by Romans in 146 B.C.

Phoenicians left few written records, and until archaeologists began digging into their past, information came mostly from the sometimes hostile accounts of others. In Carthage, excavations have confirmed eyewitness reports of child sacrifices made to appease the gods. Thousands of urns containing the ashes and bones of children were unearthed in a temple precinct. No such grim evidence has been found in Phoenician sites in their original homeland in Lebanon.

Bronze votive figures, Byblos, 9 in

Ivory carving, 4 in

Sea Traders of Antiquity

Phoenician ships with horse-headed prows transport logs in a scene on an Assyrian wall relief. Most logs are being towed behind, but one of the ships carries timber on board as well. Merchant vessels had deep, rounded hulls designed for cargo space, while Phoenician warships, built for speed, had a streamlined shape. Both fleets relied on oars and used a single sail. Skilled Phoenician artisans also produced glass beads and vessels for their export trade. This pop-eyed miniature pendant in colored glass, found on the Balearic island of Ibiza, hangs from a necklace of beads and amulets. Traces of gold leaf still remain on bronze figures that once stood in a temple at Byblos as offerings to the gods. In a masterpiece of Phoenician ivory carving found in Assyria, a lioness attacks a Nubian boy in a papyrus grove. Such panels, embellished with gold and precious stones, decorated Phoenician wood furniture. Bronze deities in a chariot show Egyptian influence on Phoenician artists, who often adapted the artistic styles of others.

Bronze deities in chariot, 6.3 in

Medes and Persians

702 to 330 B.C.

Under the Achaemenid dynasty, the Persians ruled an empire that extended 2,600 miles from present-day eastern Libya to western India. Heirs to the empires of Babylon and Assyria, the Persians were the descendants of one of the Indo-European nomadic tribes that had entered the Iranian plateau from the northeast a little before 1000 B.C. Eventually they migrated to the backcountry of the ancient kingdom of Elam, situ-

ated on the border of Mesopotamia.
Another tribe, the Medes, was part of this wave of Indo-European invaders. They had challenged the Assyrians as early as 702 B.C. and became a major power with an empire of their own that lasted until

Persepolis

Stone procession of envoys mounts a stairway at Persepolis, the ceremonial capital of the Achaemenids. Subject nations bearing tribute to the king ascended these steps to enter the great

audience hall. Only a few of the 65-foot columns that supported the chamber's roof remain. Alexander the Great sacked Persepolis in 330 B.C. and carried off its treasure. Rubble helped preserve this stairway until excavation in the 1930s.

550 B.C., when they were absorbed into the rapidly expanding realm of their Persian cousins.

Cyrus the Great, who ascended the throne in 559 B.C., was a military genius, personifying the Achaemenid virtues of "riding well, shooting straight, and speaking the truth." The empire's great organizer and administrator was Darius I (the Great). During his reign—from 522 to 486 B.C.—he welded the multitude of city-states and tribal nations into a single cosmopolitan state. Persian rule

Gold rhyton

was tolerant toward subject peoples, allowing, for example, the Jews to return to Jerusalem from their Babylonian exile. The Achaemenids relied on special inspectors, referred to as the "king's eyes," to keep tabs on the provinces, or satrapies. A courier system with relays of horseback riders enhanced communications within the empire. Old caravan trails were graded and improved to form such major routes as the famed 1,600-mile Royal Road. Darius I also helped unify the economy by adopting a monetary system based on coinage invented by King Croesus of Lydia.

For a long time the Achaemenids were known mainly through Greek historians. The latter chronicled the Greco-Persian wars, which began in 513 B.C., when Darius I crossed the Bosporus into Europe on a floating

bridge of several hundred boats. The wars ended with the defeat of the Persian navy at Salamis in 480 B.C.

Excavations in the 1930s at Persepolis, one of the empire's four capitals, revealed the great wealth, grand architecture, and fine metalwork of this Persian civilization. They also revealed the glories of Pasargadae, site of coronations, of Susa, the administrative center, and of Ecbatana, the summer capital.

Although corruption and poor administration weakened the empire during its last hundred years, the lavish lifestyle of the Persian court continued until Alexander the Great defeated Darius III at the battle of Gaugamela in 331 B.C. Persepolis was demolished, Greek troops looted the treasuries, and Persia of antiquity became part of the Hellenistic world.

Cities and Tombs

Rock-hewn tomb of Xerxes (opposite), near Persepolis, reproduces the grandeur of Achaemenid architecture. Above the facade, the king, standing on a dais supported by his subjects, worships before the Zoroastrian god Ahura Mazda, a supreme being who opposes the forces of evil. In a glazed brick relief from Susa, Ahura Mazda appears as a winged sun disk above two winged lions with human heads. A bas-relief from Persepolis portrays Darius I accompanied by attendants. This gold, animal-shaped cup, called a rhyton, reflects the artistry of Achaemenid metalwork.

Glazed brick relief, palace of Darius I, Susa (above); Darius I and attendants, Susa (right)

Egyptians

3050 to 30 B.C.

The great span of ancient civilization along the Nile began around 3050 B.C. with the unification of the provinces—or nomes—of Lower Egypt in the north with the nomes of Upper Egypt in the south under a single ruler. This shadowy figure, traditionally known as Narmer or Menes, founded Egypt's first dynasty. His authority relied largely on his role as intermediary with the gods. As succeeding pharaohs assumed this mantle of god-king, a powerful priestly class arose to minister to their needs.

Egypt's physical geography, which created barriers to foreign contact, also helped shape a stable, monolithic society. Desert hemmed in the Nile Valley, keeping invaders and alien ideas at bay. The easily navigable Nile had a centralizing effect, linking each village to the pharaoh and the royal household, which controlled trade and much of the economy. For centuries, Egypt was spared the frequent warfare that disrupted the Mesopotamian states.

The river's annual flood, besides bringing waters for irrigation, renewed the soil by depositing a fresh layer of rich, dark silt through fields far beyond its banks. Ancient Egyptians called their country *kemet,* the black land, after this crop-sustaining alluvial soil. Rulers were responsible for maintaining the agricultural cycle by interceding with the gods. In times of low floodwaters and famine, dynasties toppled.

The flowering of Egyptian civilization is divided into three periods known as "kingdoms." The first, called the Old Kingdom, lasted from about 2686 to 2160 B.C. Old Kingdom rulers built huge pyramids, culminating in the Great Pyramid of Khufu and its companions at Giza. To construct the Great Pyramid, some 100,000 men labored several months each year for about 20 years, quarrying and moving 2.3 million blocks of stone that averaged 2.5 tons apiece. Egyptian farmers were conscripted after the harvest to work on such construction projects and on the huge temples, splendid tombs, and gigantic statues that came to characterize later stages of the civilization.

Many tomb and temple walls were covered with royal and religious texts, written in a hieroglyphic script made up of pictographic symbols. Recent evidence suggests that the earliest hieroglyphs served administrative purposes—an idea perhaps imported from Sumer.

Royal barge made of cedar, Giza, 142 ft

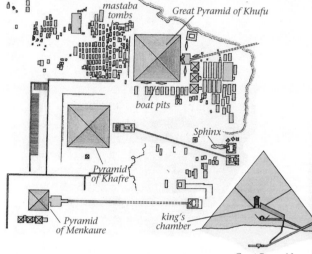

mastaba tombs

Great Pyramid of Khufu

boat pits

Sphinx

Pyramid of Khafre

Pyramid of Menkaure

king's chamber

Great Pyramid

Sunbursts in Stone

Famous pyramids at Giza have towered over the desert near Cairo for 4,500 years. Built as tombs for rulers—from the front, Menkaure, Khafre, and Khufu, or Cheops—they may have been designed as stairways in the form of stone sunbursts, by which the dead kings could ascend to the sky. Sloping corridors that pierce the Great Pyramid of Khufu, largest of these three monuments, were filled with stone blocks in a vain effort to thwart robbers. Flat-roofed mastaba tombs for the nobility were placed near Khufu's pyramid. A royal barge, one of two found dismantled in boat pits nearby, was likely meant to serve the king in his afterlife. Skilled workmen reassembled its 1,224 cedar pieces.

Famine or other unrest brought down the Old Kingdom. A period of anarchy followed, and then Middle Kingdom dynasties achieved prosperity, beginning around 2040 B.C. A second period of chaos in the 1700s culminated in 1674 B.C. in the fall of the capital, Memphis, to the Hyksos. These aliens from western Asia introduced the horse and chariot to Egypt and ruled in the north for about a century, finally being expelled by Theban princes.

The victors established the New Kingdom about 1558 B.C. and ruled a reunited Egypt from Thebes in the south. Amun, patron god of Thebes, had been linked with the sun god Re to become the national deity, Amun-Re, during the Middle Kingdom. Now, magnificent temples, obelisks, and inscriptions honored him at Karnak and Luxor in ancient Thebes.

Pharaohs were buried in the Valley of the Kings, a royal necropolis west of the Nile. Egyptians believed in a full life after death. Cut into the limestone cliffs, the tombs included jewelry, furniture, weapons, chariots, and wall paintings, as well as the mummy in a sarcophagus.

The Hyksos invasions had put an end to Egypt's virtual isolation. Pharaohs now embarked on military campaigns north into Syria and Palestine and south into Nubia. Relying on professional soldiers, they expanded their empire until, at its height in the 1400s, it stretched a thousand miles. Tribute and trade poured riches into Egypt.

During this long period of prosperity, Egyptian culture remained remarkably constant. But, during a 17-year reign that began around 1350 B.C., King Akhenaten made revolutionary changes in religion and art. In a foretaste of monotheism, he banished traditional gods and extolled the Aten, the sun disk, as the universal deity. After his death, the powerful priests in Thebes destroyed his temples, razed his

palace at Tell el-Amarna with its charming, naturalistic decorations, and restored the old order under a boy-king known to us chiefly through the treasures found in his tomb—Tutankhamun.

Warrior-pharaohs of the Ramesside era fought valiantly to maintain their empire. But decline set in by the death of Ramses III around 1166

B.C. The kingdom split in two and foreign dynasties ruled. Following conquest by Alexander the Great in 332 B.C., the Greek Ptolemies adapted to Egypt's unique culture until their kingdom fell to Rome in 30 B.C.

Ankh-shaped mirror case, 10.6 in

Gold-sheathed throne, 45 in

Case for
mummified liver,
15.4 in

Tutankhamun's Treasure

In 1922, British archaeologist Howard Carter saw "wonderful things" as he gazed into the virtually intact tomb of 18-year-old King Tutankhamun. It contained nearly 5,000 items from the 14th century B.C. They included a miniature mummy case for the king's

Pectoral
with winged scarab
and eye of Horus,
5.9 in

Gold
dagger and sheath,
12.75 in

liver, a gold-sheathed wooden throne, and objects to delight King Tut in his afterlife: a pectoral bearing a falcon-winged scarab, which symbolized resurrection; a mirror case in the shape of an ankh, the emblem of life; and a finely wrought gold dagger and sheath.

Imperial Splendor

Massive pillars, covered with reliefs and hieroglyphic inscriptions, form a central nave (opposite) in the Temple of Amun-Re at Karnak, part of ancient Thebes. A total of 134 pillars fills the vast hypostyle hall and once supported a painted slab ceiling. The 12 columns forming the main aisle are 12 feet in diameter and almost 80 feet tall; the other pillars are smaller. Beyond the colonnaded chamber stood the sanctuary of Amun, patron god of Thebes, who joined with the sun god Re to become mightiest of the Egyptian pantheon. Hewn out of rock, an immense statue of Ramses II sits on his throne at the doorway to the Temple of Abu Simbel. Three others help flank the entrance. Beside the legs of each colossus stand smaller figures representing members of the king's family. Religious texts and paintings of the gods cover the ceiling and walls of a tomb in the Valley of the Nobles, on the western bank of the Nile. Above the head of the dead man, the magical eye of Horus, holding aloft a bowl of incense, prepares to usher the deceased into the presence of Osiris, god of the underworld and stern judge of souls.

Seated Ramses II, Abu Simbel (above); tomb of Peshedu, Valley of the Nobles (right)

Cuneiform tablets from Ebla, ca 2500 B.C.

Origins of Writing

In 1975, while excavating a 50-foot-tall mound in northwestern Syria, Paolo Matthiae of the University of Rome discovered treasure far more valuable than gold. Lying broken in heaps were some 15,000 clay tablet fragments, each covered with ancient writing. Once translated, these 4,500-year-old tablets provided glimpses of the great power and majesty of Ebla, a city that archaeologists now believe rivaled those of Mesopotamia and Egypt. Until this find, the region containing present-day Syria was considered little more than a way station between great civilizations. These tablets and surrounding ruins are now forcing scholars to rethink theories about the emergence of civilization in this area.

Thanks to the work of English officer Henry C. Rawlinson and others who painstakingly decoded the ancient script in the 19th century, some of the writing was recognizable, but even today the tablets are far from fully translated. During the past two centuries, great progress has been made in deciphering ancient writing systems. Linguistic codebreakers have solved the mysteries of Sumerian cuneiform, Egyptian hieroglyphics, and early Greek Linear B. Such breakthroughs have enabled archaeologists to peer back into hitherto unknown corners of human history. Other scripts remain unbroken.

Writing first emerged in the Middle East, probably spawned by the need to record vital business transactions. One theory claims that the development of the earliest writing system began about 8000 B.C. in Sumer, in Mesopotamia, when

Clay tokens,
8000-3500 B.C.

Tokens and clay ball "envelope,"
3500 B.C.

Impressed tablet,
3100 B.C.

Wall painting of Assyrian scribes, Til Barsip, ca 730 B.C.

Tokens to Tablets

According to one theory, ancient clay tokens, whose shapes or markings recorded such items as animals, units of land, or jars of oil, may have led to writing. By 3500 B.C., they were being enclosed inside "envelopes"—hollow clay balls. Before tokens were sealed inside, their form was pressed onto the ball's surface, enabling others to "read" the contents. Often the ball was stamped, too, with a mark of ownership

Sumerian pictographs,
ca 3000 B.C.

rolled on with a cylinder seal. Since the surface could now be read, tokens were no longer needed, and impressions on clay tablets alone were used. At first, writing consisted of literal-minded pictographs—such as a hand or a tree. Combinations of symbols in boxes might express abstract concepts, as in the chart opposite, where a mouth plus a bowl of food means "eat." In time, symbols were turned on their sides—perhaps for greater ease in writing—and evolved into cuneiform script, incised with a wedge-tipped stylus. Examples here include an IOU for

ten shekels of silver, a list of livestock sacrificed during the journey of a ruler's wife, and a record of Gudea of Lagash's accomplishments. Scribes, such as the two above, became important functionaries. Refined into a linear script, cuneiform was used for everything from memorials on cylinders buried in temple foundations to attributes of magical guard dogs.

Sumerian IOU and clay
envelope, 2030 B.C.

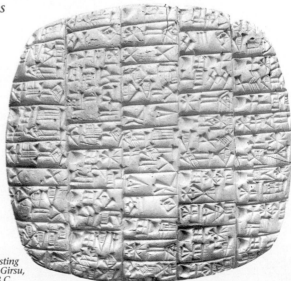

Tablet listing
sacrifices, Girsu,
2350 B.C.

merchants made marks on clay tokens as bills of lading. By 3100 B.C., according to this theory, these markings had evolved into cuneiform script. About the same time, the Egyptians developed a hieroglyphic writing system. A thousand years later, the Chinese created their own written language. And by the seventh century B.C., Mesoamericans in the New World had begun to develop writing. These systems evolved gradually, independent of one another.

Each system depended on one or a combination of the following methods: pictograph, word-sign, syllabary, or alphabet. Sumerians and Egyptians used picture symbols to denote particular meanings. It was only when the Sumerians started to develop a uniform script based on their picture symbols that a true written language emerged.

Whereas symbols previously were interpreted literally—the drawing of a mouth, for instance, meant "mouth"—Sumerian scribes invested written figures with more abstract and complex meanings. As a word-sign, the mouth could now signify the concepts of eating or talking. Scribes began using a blunt reed stylus with a triangular tip to make wedgelike shapes in the clay, creating more uniform, stylized symbols. The term "cuneiform" comes from the Latin word *cuneus,* meaning "wedge." Early in the development of cuneiform, certain symbols began to represent the sounds found in spoken language, rather than just denoting objects or concepts.

After the Sumerians developed cuneiform, the Akkadians, Babylonians, and Assyrians adapted it to write their own Semitic languages. It was also adapted by the Hittites to write their Indo-European language, and by other peoples, such as the Elamites, who lived in what is now Iran.

At about the same time that the earliest pictograms were being drawn on clay in Mesopotamia, the Egyptians almost one thousand miles away were developing their own writing system. Known as hieroglyphics, this system also was based on pictographs, word-signs, and syllabary meanings. Hieroglyphs were the symbols carved on stone in temples or tombs. Subsequently, the Egyptians developed cursive hieratic and demotic scripts for recording more routine religious and secular matters, usually on sheets made from the papyrus reed.

The Egyptians swelled their written vocabulary by use of the "rebus principle"— combining word sounds to write other words. In a classic English example, the pictures of "bee" and "leaf" form "belief." Hieroglyphics are full of such puns and word games, which complicated attempts to decode the language. The discovery of the Rosetta Stone, which carried the same message in hieroglyphs, demotic script, and Greek, enabled French scholar Jean François Champollion to decipher hieroglyphics in 1822.

Between 1800 and 1300 B.C., Semitic peoples living near the eastern Mediterranean developed an alphabet that borrowed elements from Egyptian

Akkadian cylinder seal, 2300 B.C., and modern impression

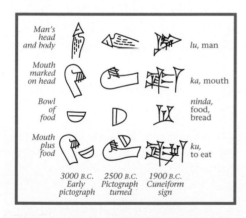

Man's head and body			lu, man
Mouth marked on head			ka, mouth
Bowl of food			ninda, food, bread
Mouth plus food			ku, to eat

3000 B.C. Early pictograph — 2500 B.C. Pictograph turned — 1900 B.C. Cuneiform sign

Gudea, ruler of Lagash, ca 2130 B.C.

Babylonian clay cylinder, 604-562 B.C.

Assyrian guard dogs, buried beside doorway for protection, ca 645 B.C.

Spoken Sounds

Around 1450 B.C., the Mycenaeans in the Aegean wrote an early form of Greek in a script now known as Linear B. A tablet from Pylos lists an inventory of pots, wine jars, cauldrons, and goblets—a typical record of administrative details. An alphabetic script based on consonants, invented by Semitic people around the same time, was adapted by the Phoenicians and refined by Greeks and Etruscans. These gold votive tablets,

Mycenaean Linear B clay tablet, Pylos, Greece, ca 1100 B.C.

with similar texts in Phoenician and Etruscan, offer clues to the enigmatic Etruscan language, which introduced the letter "c." By Roman times, the modern alphabet was in use.

hieroglyphs. The invention of this alphabet created a revolution in written communication: Instead of requiring hundreds, if not thousands, of different signs, all the consonants in a spoken language were represented by single symbols. Because there are usually no more than 40 separate sounds in a spoken language, written communication was dramatically simplified.

The principle of alphabetic writing was adopted by speakers of other Semitic languages, and the seafaring Phoenicians carried it far afield. Vowel symbols were not included. This proved a problem in other languages, especially Greek. Consequently, the Greeks adopted five unused Semitic consonants as vowels. This is why only five letters are used for vowels in modern English, even though there are fourteen spoken vowel sounds.

The Etruscans in western Europe adapted the early Greek alphabet, changing some letters and discarding others. The Roman alphabet descended from the Etruscan and was used to write Latin, which became the language of scholarship in Europe. Romance languages evolved from it. In a separate evolution, early Greek developed into the Cyrillic alphabet in eastern Europe.

Some four thousand years ago, an entirely different writing system arose in China. It was based on

Gold tablets from Pyrgi, Italy: Phoenician (left) and Etruscan (two at right), ca 500 B.C.

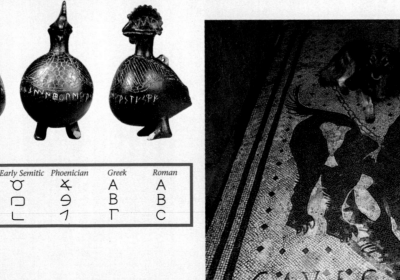

Etruscan alphabetic rooster inkwell, three views

Early Semitic	Phoenician	Greek	Roman
∀	✕	A	A
◖	ዓ	B	B
∟	૧	Γ	C

Roman "Beware of the dog" mosaic, Pompeii, Italy

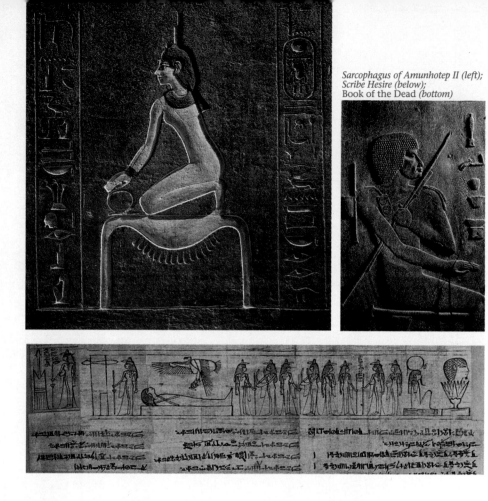

Sacred Carvings

Egyptian hieroglyphs—"sacred carvings" in Greek—were the earliest Egyptian written script. Hieroglyphs identify the kneeling woman on the sarcophagus of King Amunhotep II as the goddess Isis; the dead ruler's name is enclosed in an oval cartouche. From hieroglyphs emerged a cursive script called hieratic, which was usually written on papyrus. This Book of the Dead, a series of magic spells written in hieratic, helped speed an Egyptian princess into the afterworld. Scribes became important members of the Egyptian bureaucracy. Hesire, the chief royal scribe of his day, is immortalized on a 4,700-year-old wood carving. Proudly slung over his shoulder are the tools of his trade: a slate palette for holding ink cakes, a wood case for a rush brush, and a jug of water to moisten the brush.

pictographs supplemented by ideograms that convey meaning. The system changed little after it was codified in the third century B.C. Characters have changed their form since then, but Chinese remains the oldest continuously used writing system in the world. The survival of the character system in China reflects a regional situation unsuited to employment of the sound-based alphabet. The vast array of spoken

Bones and Bronzes

The earliest confirmed record of Chinese writing dates back to the Shang dynasty between 1700 and 1000 B.C. Angular marks inscribed on animal bones or turtle shells were accounts of communications by oracles with the spirits of their ancestors. The bones were heated and the resulting pattern of cracks interpreted as divine messages. Recent generations thought the oracle bones were "dragon bones" and ground them up for medicine. During the Zhou dynasty, records were inscribed inside ritual bronze vessels such as this food container called a dou. The original character for this

vessel resembled it in shape. Later characters became more stylized. In Chinese writing, emphasis is placed on the form as well as the function of the characters. Although these three columns all read "house full of precious things," the examples contrast different styles of archaic, everyday, and flowing, artistic calligraphy.

Turtle shell, 7.3 in

Chinese calligraphy

Archaeological Puzzle

Script on one-to-two-inch steatite seals continues to tantalize students of the 4,500-year-old Harappan culture of the Indus River Valley in Pakistan and India. Its approximately 400 distinct symbols remain undeciphered.

Steatite seal, 1 in

Bronze dou, Zhou dynasty, 17.8 in

73

dialects in China creates numerous disparities in pronunciation and word use among the different regions. An ideographic system can best serve the needs of this diverse population of about one billion people. The greatest limitation is the necessity of memorizing large numbers of characters. Some 60,000 exist today, but only 3,500 to 4,000 are in common use.

In the New World, written language originated in Mesoamerica. The first evidence of glyphs emerges as early as 700 B.C. on a stone carving in the modern state of Oaxaca in Mexico. But the earliest deciphered text comes from Veracruz. Here, descendants of the

Painting on Maya pot

Cacao pot, Río Azul, 5th century A.D.

Olmec or a related people created in the mid-second century A.D. an eight-foot stela carved with a lengthy and complicated hieroglyphic text.

It was the Maya who developed the New World's most complex writing system and carried the calendar to its most elaborate expression. Using any one of some 800 signs, the scribe could show whole words or "spell" them out with syllables. Today, much of the script has been deciphered, despite the fact that many Maya books were destroyed by the Spanish in the 16th century.

By A.D. 900, the Mixtec had developed a script based on pictographs, using sounds for proper names only. By 1400, the Aztecs had adapted this script to their own use.

The development of writing counts as one of humankind's most profound inventions. It enabled early societies to accumulate the knowledge that led to major developments in mathematics, science, and the arts and left later generations an eyewitness record of past cultures.

Glyphs and Codices

Mesoamerica was the first location in the New World to develop a true written language. The drawing of a stela from La Mojarra reveals the earliest deciphered writing from the New World. Among its 465 glyphs, dates corresponding to May 21, A.D. 143, and July 13, 156, may mark the reign of post-Olmec warrior-king Harvest Mountain Lord. Later, Maya glyphs relied on the same interplay of

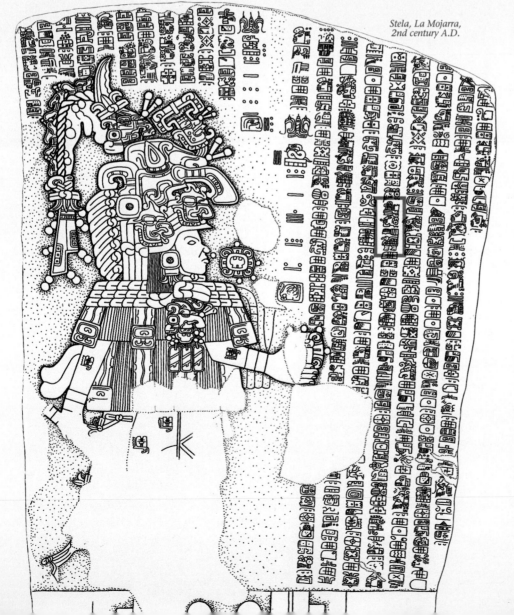

Stela, La Mojarra, 2nd century A.D.

Limestone lintel, Yaxchilan, A.D. 526

Mixtec marriage: Codex Nuttall, ca A.D.1330

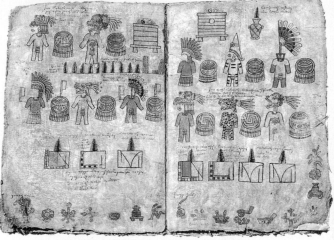

Aztec: Matrícula de Tributos, ca A.D.1519, with later annotations

Pre-Columbian Inca quipu, Peru

symbols. In a painting on a pot, a scribe with brushes tucked into his hat recites bar-and-dot numbers in a cartoonlike "balloon." On a limestone lintel from Yaxchilan, heads of gods designate numbers, while full figures represent blocks of time. The monkey at center right represents one day, and the two heads 6 and 10, so the glyph means "16 days." The whole panel spells out the equivalent of February 11, A.D. 526. In a breakthrough in 1986, archaeologist David Stuart deciphered the Maya glyph on a pot from Río Azul as "cacao," a finding borne out by chocolate residue inside. A pot of chocolate cements the marriage of a Mixtec ruler and his bride, an event depicted in a codex, or book. And a 16th-century pictographic Aztec record catalogs tribute paid to the rulers of Tenochtitlan. Peoples of South America had no written language, but the Inca of Peru kept records on a quipu, an intricate system of knotted cords of different colors.

BRITAIN

Hadrian's Wall

GAUL

SPAIN

Segovia

ETRURIA

Arezzo

Tiber

Tarquinia

ITALY

Rome

Satricum

Herculaneum

Pompeii

MEDITERRANEAN

Sicily

Carthage

MACEDON

Samothrace

Byzantium
(Constantinople)

BLA

Verghina

Mt. Olympus

AEGEAN

Troy

ANA

GREECE

Chaeronea

Thebes

LYDIA

Corinth

ATTICA

Mycenae

Athens

SEA

Salamis

Peloponnese

Argos

Pylos

Sparta

Delos

CYCLADES

Thera

Crete

Knossos

Arkalochori

Zakros

SEA

Leptis Magna

Alexandria

LIBYA

EGYPT

● Ancient and modern town site

◆ Archaeological site only

0   400 mi

0   600 km

The Classical World

2000 B.C. to A.D. 476

A second generation of civilizations in the ancient world rose on the islands and shores of the Mediterranean. The sea had aided the movement of peoples and ideas for thousands of years before settlers from the east came to the island of Crete. About 2000 B.C., a civilization formed there that bore traces of the established cultures in Egypt and the Middle East. In turn, this Minoan civilization of Crete sent not only valued shipments of timber, olive oil, pottery, and wool cloth, but also elements of *its* culture to the older civilizations. Spiral patterns, for instance, a fashion in Egypt around 2000 B.C., may have originated in fabric imported from Crete.

Minoan Crete traded heavily with mainland Greece. When the palace culture of Crete faltered in the 15th century B.C., mainlander Mycenaeans took over. The Mycenaeans' fortress-kingdoms in southern Greece accumulated astonishing wealth until they experienced a mysterious demise around 1200 B.C.

A new form of political organization, the *polis*, came into being in Greece in the eighth century B.C. Roughly translated as "city-state," the polis was an independent entity, trading and colonizing in its own name throughout the Mediterranean world. Early on, Corinth was the preeminent city-state, succeeded by Athens in the sixth century, with its nascent democracy.

The internal struggle for power between Athens and Sparta left Greece vulnerable to conquest, and it fell to Philip II of Macedon. Under his son Alexander's rule, Hellenistic Greek culture spread throughout the Mediterranean and the Middle East and reached as far as India. Even the Romanizing of the ancient world over the next 300 years did not erase this deep-seated Greek influence.

In the northern part of the Italian peninsula, the Greeks had encountered the Etruscans, who lived in Tuscany. Eagerly the Etruscans absorbed Greek culture while pursuing territorial gains, starting with Rome in the eighth century B.C. Etruscan expansionism eventually was thwarted by Greek opposition and a Roman uprising.

As the Romans gained control of the Italian peninsula, they set a course that would take the notion of empire farther than even Alexander had dreamed. Their republican form of government ended when Julius Caesar's heir, Augustus, became the first Roman emperor. He amassed the territorial holdings that would place Rome at the center of the ancient world. From Scotland to Iran, the Romans united tribal and civilized peoples under one standard and, eventually, one citizenship. By the fourth century A.D., administrative pressures had split the Roman Empire. Invasion soon ended the western empire, while the eastern endured for another millennium.

Some recent discoveries underscore this breadth of empire. Kourion, a Roman town on Cyprus buried by an earthquake in A.D. 365, has yielded finds rivaling those of Pompeii and Herculaneum. But, far to the north, excavations indicate that Romans did not always manage to impose their culture on conquered peoples. A site near Melrose, Scotland, shows that the local people successfully fended off Roman ways.

CK SEA

TOLIA

Issos

Cyprus

SYRIA

Kourion

JUDAEA

Minoans

2000 to 1450 B.C.

Europe's first advanced civilization sprang not from a well-watered continental plain but from the craggy landscape of the Aegean island of Crete. The farmers, herders, and artisans who lived there some 4,000 years ago in scattered inland villages had probably originated in lands to the east.

Skilled metalworkers, they built shrines on mountaintops and buried their dead in communal graves. Gradually, the people moved to the coast, and towns grew up there. Only in the early 20th century did the island's subsequent history come to light.

In 1894, Arthur Evans, a wealthy Englishman with a passion for antiquities, traveled to Crete to investigate the source of some engraved gems and seals he had found in Greek bazaars. Pottery sherds on the ground persuaded him to buy a six-acre site at Knossos, where he embarked on full-scale excavations in 1900.

Within months, Evans and his crew uncovered the remains of an elaborate palace. Terraced into a hillside for protection against earthquakes, the multistoried palace was built around a large open courtyard and contained two floors of underground chambers and passageways. Thousands of artifacts identified the functions of various rooms: kitchens, residences, workshops, ceremonial rooms, storerooms, and even bathrooms with toilets. Pottery, stone- and metalwork, and colorfully frescoed walls attested to the skill of the builders and artisans.

Evans called these ancient people Minoans, after Minos, the legendary king who kept the half-bull, half-man Minotaur trapped within a labyrinth. Mazelike Knossos, it turned out, was the most important of the four largest Minoan palace-cities. First erected about 2000 B.C., Minoan palaces were rebuilt and enlarged after probable earthquake damage around 1700. Soon after, palace culture reached its zenith.

Minoan history is still not fully understood. We know they were great sailors, plying the Aegean and eastern Mediterranean, trading timber, pottery, and farming products for gold, ivory, and gemstones, and establishing outposts. Minoan influence is evident in remains at Akrotiri on the island of Thera, 70 miles north of Crete. An immense volcanic eruption in the 17th century B.C. buried the town under layers of ash, pumice, and rock, preserving its Minoan heritage. Vivid frescoes include one of a young fisherman bearing a catch of mackerel (left). Another (below), 16 inches high, ran 20 feet along the walls of a Theran house. Remarkable for its nautical detail, it depicts landscapes and architecture of what some think is Thera, some the Libyan coast.

Minoan grandeur ended abruptly with the fiery destruction of palaces and towns throughout Crete in 1450 B.C. Until recent worldwide ice-core and tree-ring dating placed the eruption on Thera much earlier, at 1628 B.C., some archaeologists attributed the Minoan disappearance to the effects of that cataclysm. The evidence now points to conquest by the warlike Mycenaeans of the Greek mainland.

Faience figurine, Knossos, 11.6 in

Fisherman fresco, Akrotiri, Thera

Nautical fresco, Akrotiri, Thera

Palace of Knossos

Bull's-head
pendant, Zakros,
1.9 in

Double-headed ax,
Arkalochori,
3.3 in

Royalty and Ritual

Once the hub of a vigorous, populous city, the 1,500-room palace of Knossos sprawled across five acres in northern Crete. Discoverer Arthur Evans reconstructed this section, guided by a careful analysis of the finds. He drew criticism, however, for using concrete and steel and for rehabilitating entire frescoes from tiny fragments. Evidence of ritual found in shrines and caves includes two symbols that reverberate throughout Minoan culture. A bull's-head pendant from the palace-city of Zakros recalls tales of the bull-man Minotaur in its labyrinth. And, from the frequency of its appearance, the double-headed ax—such as the gold one here, found in a sacred cave at Arkalochori—represents the supreme Minoan symbol. The snake-wielding faience figure may be priestess or goddess. She wears the flounced skirt and low-cut bodice of a wealthy Minoan woman.

Mycenaeans

1550 to 1100 B.C.

Archaeologists have set the beginnings of the first mainland Greek civilization, the Mycenaean, in the mid-16th century B.C. At that time, numerous small chiefdoms dotted the southern peninsula, which is known as the Peloponnese. Each warrior-chief held sway over a walled town and the agricultural lands surrounding it.

These war-loving people traded wine, olive oil, and pottery throughout the Aegean and eastern Mediterranean, but were not above resorting to piracy and pillage to get what they wanted. Visiting Crete and its out-posts, they imported aspects of Minoan culture—especially art and religion—to the mainland.

Mycenae (opposite), a fortified town built on a rise in the Argos Plain, became their chief stronghold. Its strategically recessed Lion Gate forced invaders to pass through an alley created by the town's 26-foot-wide walls. Mycenae's excavation in 1876 by amateur German archaeologist Heinrich Schliemann created worldwide excitement, as had his dig at Homer's Troy in Turkey.

Schliemann had come to Mycenae looking for the graves of the Greek heroes of the Trojan campaign. Once inside the Lion Gate, he did not have to look far. A stone circle yielded five vertical shaft graves that clearly held the remains and riches of Mycenae's aristocracy.

Sixteen or more skeletons were entombed with jewels, crowns, weapons, and gold death masks. Schliemann was certain that he had found the Homeric King Agamemnon and his followers. He soon uncovered the ruins of a palace.

Fragments of a script known as Linear B, deciphered in 1952, show that the Mycenaeans used a vast bureaucracy, as well as warfare, to exert their control. Linear B, most experts agree, is an early form of Greek, making the Mycenaeans full-fledged Greeks.

Mycenaean civilization lasted only until about 1100 B.C. Then, mysteriously, its power ended, plunging Greece into a 300-year-long dark age.

Plaster head, 6.6 in

Inlaid bronze dagger, length 9.4 in (above); restored drawing of battle fresco, height 19 in (below, right)

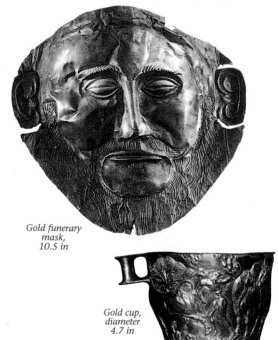

Gold funerary mask, 10.5 in

Gold cup, diameter 4.7 in

Warlike Pursuits

Mycenaean art extolled warriors and hunters. Clad as if for battle, hunters spear lions on an exquisite bronze dagger blade inlaid with gold and silver, found in a shaft grave at Mycenae. With a superior show of strength, warriors massacre skin-clad enemies in a fresco from the palace of Pylos. At first sight of the powerful visage hammered into a gold funerary mask, Mycenae's excavator, Heinrich Schliemann, believed he looked on the face of Agamemnon, the warrior-king immortalized by Homer. In reality, the mask predates Agamemnon and the fall of Troy—around 1250 B.C.—by at least three centuries. Found near

Sparta, a hammered gold cup worked in repoussé depicts the capture of a bull—a Minoan motif. One unwarlike image, a serene plaster head from Mycenae, may be that of a goddess.

Greeks

800 to 30 B.C.

At the beginning of the first millennium B.C., Greece was immersed in a dark age, yet poised for cultural regeneration. Some of the seeds of renewal were gleaned from the fallen Minoan and Mycenaean civilizations, others from the Cyclades, a group of islands between Crete and the Greek mainland. Cycladic figures, such as the one below, some dating back to 2500 B.C., bear precise head-torso proportions that foreshadow the precision of classical sculpture.

Archaeologists refer to this rebirth, beginning around 800 B.C., as the archaic period. It saw independent Greek city-states settle the mainland, the Aegean islands, the islands and coasts of the eastern Mediterranean, and Sicily and southern Italy. Greek language and culture, especially religion, gave the scattered populations a common identity.

Warrior-kings ruled some of the city-states. In others, oligarchies or tyrants exercised power. It would be many years before reforms instituted the system of democracy deeded by Greece to the Western world.

On the Greek mainland, Corinth rose to prominence in the eighth century B.C. A trading city situated at the base of a natural rock stronghold, Corinth controlled the isthmus between Attica and the Peloponnesian peninsula.

In the mid-sixth century, Athens began to overtake Corinth in trade and maritime achievement. The rise of a mercantile middle class in Athens and in other city-states

Cycladic stone figurine, ca 2000 B.C.

Painted wooden plaque, Pitsa, ca 500 B.C. (lower); Temple of Apollo, Corinth, 6th century B.C. (upper)

Pioneers in Art

The Doric Temple of Apollo, standing amid the ruins of ancient Corinth, preserves an architectural tradition established earlier. Corinth pioneered Doric monumental architecture in the seventh century B.C. A temple to Poseidon excavated nearby has been declared the earliest known peristyle, or colonnaded, temple in mainland Greece. Other art forms included a rare painted plaque showing a group of figures in a votive procession. From Corinth, too, came the technique for producing black-figure pottery, which rival city-state Athens adopted. Fine-quality Attic, or Athenian, clay produced an amphora that depicts a black-figure Achilles slaying Amazon queen Penthesilea. This episode appeared in one of the stories surrounding the Trojan War that were attributed to Homer. Most scholars agree the Homerian epics were composed in the eighth century B.C. But there is dispute over whether the blind poet Homer ever existed—whether one or several voices created the tales of the Iliad and the Odyssey.

Black-figure detail from Attic amphora, mid-6th century B.C.

blurred some of the distinctions between noble and commoner and set the stage for further social, economic, and military changes. At the same time, the city-state of Sparta began to institute government reforms and flex its muscles for the power struggles that would shape Greece's classical age—a period beginning about 500 B.C.

The fifth century was framed by conflict at beginning and end. Athens angered the Persians when it helped Greek cities in Anatolia revolt against Persian-backed tyrants in the 490s. Retaliatory Persian invasions culminated in the destruction of Athens, but the Greek navy roundly defeated the Persians at the Battle of Salamis in 479.

The lingering Persian threat enabled Athens to organize and lead a coalition of Greek city-states, which was known as the Delian League. Athens entered a period of unprecedented devotion to the arts,

Acropolis with classical buildings, middle distance, and Roman-era theater, foreground (above); fragment of a krater painted by Pronomos, ca 400 B.C. (right)

84

architecture, religion, philosophy, and the establishment of democracy.

This golden age was guided by the city's preeminent orator, general, and statesman, Pericles. Emerging as leader after the Persian troubles, he appropriated tribute collected by the Delian League and used it to pay for restoring Athens. The rebuilding proceeded on two fronts: on the Acrop-olis, a rocky citadel-turned-sacred-ground, and in the Agora, the Athenian market and meeting place. On the Acropolis, Pericles masterminded the building of the Parthenon—the exquisite temple to patron goddess Athena—and other monuments.

In the Agora, Pericles built colonnaded stoas, where philosophers, politicians, generals, and lawyers held forth and where the state minted its money.

As Athens grew, rivalry mounted with the militaristic regime of Sparta. By 431 B.C., the two city-states were at war—a conflict that would last until Athens surrendered in 404. During this time, plague wiped out one-third of Athens' population, carrying off Pericles among the victims.

In Pursuit of Excellence

Athens stood at the forefront of the Greek classical age. Athenian coinage, with its portrait of Athena and, on the obverse, her owl companion, was accepted currency throughout the Mediterranean. In the seventh century B.C., Lydians had been among the first to strike coins. Athenian statesman Pericles began a massive building program that included the marble Parthenon, at left, center, and a monumental gateway, the Propylaea, farther left. Around 1800, British diplomat Lord Elgin persuaded the Turkish occupiers of Athens to let him remove many sculptures from the Parthenon. Today they are on display at the British Museum. Sculpture had

Discus thrower, Roman copy of Greek original

reached its peak. The Greek idealized depiction of the human body was much admired by the Romans. All that survives of sculptor Myron's bronze discus thrower is this Roman copy in marble. During the classical period, Greek drama, with masks and costumes, was a popular art motif, as shown in this painting on a krater.

The Spartans could not maintain their hold on Greece. In 371 B.C., Thebes took control, followed by the Macedonians under Philip II. Greek independence ended with Philip's victory at Chaeronea in 338.

In the following Hellenistic age, which lasted until the Roman conquest in 30 B.C., Greece exchanged the provincialism of city-state identity for the cosmopolitan notion of world citizenship.

Alexander, son of Philip II of Macedon, explored Greek philosophy under the tutelage of Aristotle. Taking command of the army on his father's death in 336 B.C., Alexander spent the next 13 years consolidating his Greek empire and systematically defeating the Persians and their satraps. At the insistence of his exhausted troops, he halted at the Indus River. In 323, he died of a fever in Babylon at the age of 32.

In Alexander's lifetime, a mantle of Greek, or Hellenistic, culture had spread over what Greeks called the *oecumene*, the inhabited world. Greek was the language of trade and communication. Greek art, architecture, and town planning became models of their kind. Science and learning were extolled around the civilized world. The great library at Alexandria in Egypt became a third-century research center as well as a repository. Yet Alexander's successors were unable to sustain his legacy, and the rising fortunes of Rome dictated the next chapter of Greek history.

Detail of mosaic of Alexander the Great, Pompeii, probably 2nd century B.C.

Hellenistic Heritage

Larger than life, Alexander the Great locks gazes with the unseen Persian king Darius III at the Battle of Issos. Little Hellenistic painting survives; this detail of a floor mosaic found at Pompeii is a Roman copy of a fourth-century Greek work. Alexander inherited his plan of conquest from his father, Philip II of Macedon. A sumptuous Macedonian tomb, discovered at Verghina in 1977, may have held Philip's remains. This wreath of gold oak leaves and acorns covered charred bones in a golden casket. During the Hellenistic age, sculpture became more naturalistic, and remarkable achievements resulted. A winged Victory adorned the prow of a warship—a commemorative statue from Samothrace. Artists also depicted everyday subjects—the old, the inebriated, and here, young women engaged in a game of knucklebones.

Marble winged Victory, ca 200 B.C.

Gold wreath from Macedonian tomb, 4th century B.C.

Terra-cotta knucklebone players, late 4th century B.C.

Demons Charon (left) and Vanth in tomb, Tarquinia

Detail from tomb painting of hunt, Tarquinia

Bronze chimera,
Arezzo, 30 in

Life and Afterlife

*Though heavily influenced by the
Greeks, Etruscan art displays a unique
worldview and virtuosity of
technique. Joie de vivre and celebration
of nature leap from a sixth-century
B.C. tomb painting at Tarquinia.
Its soaring birds and playful dolphins
swarm around robust youths engaged
in hunting and fishing. Found at
Arezzo during the Renaissance, a fifth-
century bronze chimera attests to*

Etruscans

800 to 200 B.C.

Few ancient cultures are so wrapped in enigma as the Etruscan, Italy's first civilization. Spreading widely over the area known as Etruria—modern-day Tuscany—the Etruscans wrested the hill towns of Rome from the less advanced Latins in the eighth century B.C., creating there a city-state, one of 12 major settlements in what came to be a loose-knit federation.

About the same time, the Greeks were making vigorous colonization efforts in Italy. Contact with the Greeks provided inspiration to the emerging Etruscan culture and opened lucrative avenues of trade. Demand for their wine and olive oil, as well as the rich local deposits of iron and copper, allowed the Etruscans to broaden their market to include central Europe, the Aegean, and the eastern Mediterranean. In exchange, they sought pottery and gold, silver, and ivory—precious resources for their artisans to fashion into wondrous objects.

Etruscan city-states were governed by wealthy families who controlled the labors of slaves, serfs, and artisans. Members of the ruling class lived pleasure-filled lives, attending lavish banquets, parading in large processions, and consulting sooth-sayers for personal guidance.

This love of life permeated, too, the Etruscan way of death. Despite the density of Etruscan settlements, little domestic architecture—which was constructed of wood and terra-cotta—survives. For centuries, however, archaeologists have unearthed hundreds of stone-and-earth tombs, some forming vast cities of the dead. Wealthy Etruscans were buried with their most prized possessions in tombs that often mirrored their homes. Elaborate frescoes painted in a vivid, naturalistic style depicted scenes of feasting and merriment. As Etruscan power began to wane—because of Greek resistance to further expansion and a successful Roman uprising—the gaiety of tomb paintings was tempered with renderings of underworld demons (left). By 200 B.C., Etruria had fallen to the Romans, with whom the Etruscans merged in culture and citizenship.

The Etruscans took with them the interrelated secrets of their origin and language. Whatever its source, Etruscan culture bequeathed to the Romans such hallmarks as a writing system based on the Greek alphabet, the reading of omens, the triumphal procession, the toga, and the purple robes and scepters favored by Roman emperors.

Etruscan metalworking magic, combining a lion's head and body, a serpent for a tail, and a goat's head on its spine. Etruscans also mastered terra-cotta sculpture, a major element of domestic and temple architecture. In this fifth-century, Greek-inspired temple roof ornament from Satricum, a satyr and maenad mirror the enjoyment of life's pleasures, shared by both sexes. Nearly four feet tall, a pair of winged horses adorned a Tarquinian temple.

Terra-cotta horses, Tarquinia

Terra-cotta satyr and maenad, Satricum

Romans

753 B.C. to A.D. 476

Tradition places the founding of Rome in 753 B.C.—on April 21, to be exact. On that date, Romulus, having killed his twin, Remus, who had been suckled at his side by a she-wolf, founded the city on a series of hills on both sides of the Tiber River.

Archaeology confirms that the area was inhabited in the ninth century B.C., when tribes of Latins and Sabines, mostly farmers and herders, settled there. Kings ruled Rome in the early days, those dating from the late seventh century being Etruscan. Etruscan culture provided many of the traits now considered particularly Roman, and their engineering prowess created lasting public works such as the Cloaca Maxima, the main sewage drain to the Tiber.

Around 509 B.C., the Etruscans were deposed and a republican form of government replaced the monarchy. Two consuls, elected by an assembly, shared power. Under the republic, the customary laws passed down by oral tradition began to be codified and written down.

Society became segmented into aristocratic patricians and commoner plebeians—class differences that would cause uprisings and plague Roman life for many centuries. Gradually, plebeians gained equal rights and were admitted to politics and public office. Roman life differed vastly for rich and poor. The rich built houses with large, airy courtyards; the poor lived in crowded tenements three to five stories tall. Slaves provided labor for the wealthy.

The later years of the republic saw a building boom that gave Rome its enduring character. The Forum, the civic center on low ground between the Palatine and Capitoline Hills, already held a number of significant buildings, including the Temple of Castor and Pollux. Rome was by then on its way to becoming the capital of the ancient world, and the Forum was its heart.

Julius Caesar, marble, 1st century B.C.

Imperial City

The ambition of Julius Caesar, shown here in the uniform of a Roman general, brought an end to the Roman republic. Returning victorious from his Gallic campaigns, he routed political opposition in a civil war and had himself declared dictator. Suspected of designs on a king's crown, he was assassinated in 44 B.C. Caesar's grandnephew and heir, known as Caesar Augustus, became Rome's first emperor. Under his auspices, the Temple of Castor and Pollux in the Forum (right) was restored. The Colosseum, at left rear, was built by later emperors Vespasian and Titus, whose victories over Judaean rebels in A.D. 66-70 are commemorated in the triumphal arch in the background.

Roman Forum: center, columns of Temple of Castor and Pollux,

5th century B.C.; background, Colosseum and Arch of Titus, 1st century A.D.

Last Days of Pompeii and Herculaneum

In a two-day eruption in A.D. 79, Mount Vesuvius sealed the fate of Pompeii and Herculaneum, leaving a legacy of Roman provincial life that archaeologists still are unearthing 19 centuries later. Vesuvius before the eruption and the wine god, Bacchus, are depicted in this wall painting—one of many from Pompeii's 160-acre site. The volcano's truncated profile (below) tells the dramatic story. Pompeii, then a town of more than 10,000 people six miles to the south, was buried slowly by ash, letting many residents flee before deadly gases overcame the rest. In 1860, archaeologist Giuseppe

Fiorelli pioneered stratigraphic digging at Pompeii and made ingenious casts of the impressions left in hardened ash by decayed bodies and objects. Herculaneum, a resort town on Vesuvius's west flank, suffered a different fate. Surges of gas and pumice inundated the town and killed and buried many of its 4,000 residents. A female victim (opposite), her teeth clenched in agony, was one of scores of skeletons discovered by Giuseppe Maggi in the 1980s. Herculaneum's human remains, preserved by their muddy shroud, tell much about health and disease in Roman times. Scientists point out, for instance, that sound teeth such as this woman's confirm a low-sugar diet.

Ruins of Pompeii, with two theaters, foreground, and forum, open space left of center (lower); wall painting, Pompeii (upper)

Classical Rome showed many Hellenistic influences. The Greek deities of Mount Olympus were renamed and worshiped in Roman temples derived from Greek forms. Art, especially sculpture, followed Greek models. But the Romans soon developed their own unmistakable style, marked by their use of the arch, their transformation of the column from structural element to ornament, and their method of combining cement—made by mixing volcanic ash with lime and crushed stone—with water to form concrete.

The Romans called the Mediterranean *Mare Nostrum*—Our Sea—and so it became. After gaining control of the Italian peninsula, they began a systematic conquest of lands bordering the Mediterranean.

Achieving their regional aims by 100 B.C., the Romans expanded into the Hellenized east, into North Africa, and north and west across Europe, encountering tribes with less advanced cultures. These lands were used as a

vast commissary from which to stock the needs of the imperial city.

Roman expansion surged during the reign of Emperor Augustus, who ruled from 27 B.C. to A.D. 14; the empire reached its farthest extent under Trajan a century later.

Augustus' respect for religion—and a desire to have himself considered close to the gods—led him to repair 82 temples already in existence and to build many of his own. Near the spot on the Forum where his great-uncle Julius Caesar's body was burned, he erected the Temple of the

Hadrian's Wall, England (above);
amphitheater at Leptis Magna, Libya (below)

Remains of Empire

Impressive Roman ruins, scattered the length of the former empire from Scotland to Iran, reflect both military and cultural inspiration. In northern England, Emperor Hadrian ordered construction of a wall to keep barbarian invaders out of Roman Britain. Begun in A.D. 122, Hadrian's stone defense reached nearly 74 miles from coast to coast. Protective towers and forts rose along its length. Where Roman armies went, Roman peacetime culture usually followed. Imperial settlements quickly acquired the hallmarks of Rome itself. The amphitheater at Leptis Magna, built in A.D. 56, was one of the largest in the empire, seating some 25,000 people. A prosperous Punic town on the Libyan coast, Leptis Magna became part of Rome's southern empire in 46 B.C. Emperor Trajan made it a Roman colony in A.D. 110, and it grew into the third largest city in Africa after Carthage and Alexandria. Opulent buildings included temples, baths, triumphal arches, a theater, a forum, and a magnificent basilica. Some of the construction was underwritten by wealthy Punic citizens, but the grandest additions were made by Emperor Septimius Severus, native son of Leptis Magna, in the second century A.D.

Divine Julius, as well as temples to the imperial family's other divine ancestors, Mars and Venus. Not far away he also built a pantheon, known today for its subsequent reconstruction by Emperor Hadrian. Hadrian's builders used concrete and the vaulted arch to construct a dome that needed no internal support.

As a center of commerce as well as politics, the Forum also housed shops and services. In recent years, archaeologists excavating the stairway of the Temple of Castor and Pollux uncovered the remains of a dentist's "surgery," identified by 86 decayed teeth discovered in a drain.

Emperors after Augustus continued building to enhance their own power and prestige. Triumphal arches celebrating various victories rose throughout the city. It took a decade to complete the 50,000-seat Colosseum, the largest Roman amphitheater. Romans gathered here to watch savage clashes between gladiators or between armed men and animals—and unequal contests between starved wild animals and members of the new and imperially mistrusted faith, Christianity. With floor flooded, the Colosseum was also used to stage mock naval battles.

Despite all the attention paid to the glorification of Rome, the focus of the empire was on its frontiers. As

Fruits of Legion Labor

In the wake of conquest, Roman armies brought the infrastructure of civilization to the empire. Engineers provided plans, and legionnaires (opposite) constructed roads, bridges, waterworks, fortifications, and tunnels. This winding stretch of road in northwestern Syria formed part of the 50,000 miles of major roads that linked the empire. Roman roads— usually arrow straight—seldom meandered like this. The two-tiered supporting arches of a functioning Roman aqueduct soar 90 feet above a valley near Segovia, Spain. Romans equated civilization with water—for gardens, pools, fountains, and public baths. The legions obliged by building this aqueduct to carry water ten miles from mountain sources.

the defense and administration of these vast territories became more unwieldy, imperial control weakened. Emperor Constantine ended the persecution of Christians in A.D. 312. By the end of the century, Christianity had become the state religion. Constantine moved his capital from Rome to Byzantium, which he renamed Constantinople, setting the stage for the division of the Roman Empire into eastern and western halves. Rome, in the west, weakened by the repeated invasions of Germanic tribes, was ripe for sacking by the Visigoths in A.D. 410. Its final defeat came in 476, when the German chief Odoacer deposed the last emperor of the western empire.

As Rome developed into a modern city, little effort was made to spare its ancient treasures from construction needs, pollution, the rumblings of traffic, and other agents of deterioration. The tremendous effort to preserve the treasures of Rome's past is a task that now involves the archaeologists of at least six nations.

Roman road, northwestern Syria (lower); aqueduct, ca A.D. 100, near Segovia, Spain (upper); Roman legionnaires, sculptural relief, 2nd century A.D. (opposite)

Ravenna

Rome

Sicily

M E D I T E R R A

Crossroads of Faith

2000 B.C. to A.D. 750

The Middle East, which saw the first stirrings of Western civilization, also witnessed the birth of three great monotheistic religions. Half the world's people would one day inherit the legacy of Judaism, Christianity, and Islam.

Monotheism—the concept of a single, all-powerful God—was brought from Mesopotamia into Canaan by Abraham, patriarch of the pastoral Hebrew tribes. The Hebrews' God, Yahweh, of whom they were the Chosen People, demanded total devotion from them. In Canaan, they established the kingdom of Israel, which flourished under the leadership of Saul, David, and Solomon in the first millennium B.C. After Solomon's death, the kingdom divided and was overrun by Assyri-

ans and Babylonians. The Jews, as the Hebrews were also called, were sent into exile. Though restored to Israel in the sixth century B.C., they suffered lengthy foreign domination. In A.D. 135, after Jewish uprisings against Roman rule, Jerusalem was laid waste. The Jews were banished and began a worldwide diaspora.

Prophets were active during Roman times, and within Judaism there was much talk of the imminent coming of the Messiah. The ministry of Jesus in the first century A.D. attracted many followers. Originally a sect within Judaism, Christianity became a secretive religion during 300 years of Roman persecution. Only after Christianity was sanctioned as an official religion of the Roman Empire did the infrastructure of churches and hierarchy fully emerge.

Islam's founder, Muhammad, was born into Arabia's nomadic and polytheistic tribal society. Sometime around A.D. 610, he embraced monotheism after revelations from the God he called Allah. Allah was the God of Abraham, and the prophets of the Judeo-Christian tradition were precursors in a line of prophets ending with Muhammad himself. At first, he made worshipers face Jerusalem during daily prayer. He thought that Jews and Christians would accept Islam as monotheism's natural outcome. When that did not happen, Muhammad changed his focus to Mecca and used the power of the sword to aid his proselytizing. Jihad, or holy war, became the method by which Islam spread throughout southwest Asia and far beyond within 120 years of his death.

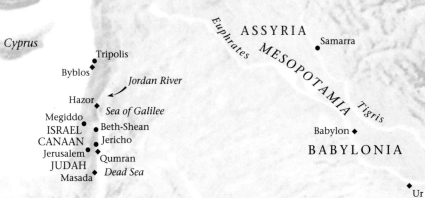

BLACK SEA

CASPIAN SEA

Constantinople
(Byzantium)

ANATOLIA

CAPPADOCIA

Tarsus

Haran

ASSYRIA

MESOPOTAMIA

Samarra

Crete

Cyprus

Euphrates

Tigris

NEAN SEA

Tripolis

Byblos

Jordan River

Hazor

Sea of Galilee

Megiddo

Beth-Shean

Babylon

ISRAEL

CANAAN

Jericho

Jerusalem

JUDAH

Qumran

Dead Sea

BABYLONIA

Masada

Ur

EGYPT

PERSIAN
GULF

Nile

Medina

ARABIAN

RED SEA

PENINSULA

Mecca

● Ancient and modern town site

◆ Archaeological site only

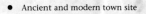

0   300 mi

0   400 km

99

Land of Canaan

2000 to 900 B.C.

The name Canaan may come from an ancient Semitic word for "reddish-purple." By 2000 B.C., Canaan extended from Gaza northward to Tripolis. Coastal waters there yielded the murex sea snails that were the source of the rich purple dye prized throughout the ancient world.

The Canaanites lived in villages and walled cities such as Hazor, Megiddo, and Jericho. They worshiped a multitude of gods. Unlike Mesopotamia or Egypt, Canaan lacked a life-giving river system. Farmers and shepherds had to rely on seasonal rains for their water needs. When too much rain fell, flooding produced disastrous erosion; when too little fell, crops withered and died. In either case famine often resulted.

At the beginning of the second millennium B.C., pastoral nomads entered Canaan from the east. Among them, according to tradition, came the Hebrew patriarch Abraham. God had made a covenant with Abraham that he and his people would receive a land of their own—the Promised Land—in return for devotion to one God, whom the Hebrews called Yahweh. Abraham had left his home city of Ur in Mesopotamia with his tribe and flocks and traveled north beside the Euphrates River. He stopped along the way to graze his animals and occasionally to plant crops and wait for the harvest. After spending some time at Haran, in the north, he headed west, then south along the Mediterranean coast to Canaan.

Abraham and his people brought monotheism to Canaan, confronting

Diversity

The Philistines, one of the "sea peoples," often buried their dead in anthropomorphic sarcophagi. This clay head served as the lid of a full-size coffin. Found at a 12th-century B.C. site near the Jordan Valley, the coffin shows Egyptian influence in Philistine burial practice. The Canaanites themselves created elaborate burials, both during and after the time of Hyksos rule. A drinking cup in the form of a man's head was placed with other luxury items in a 15th-century B.C. tomb near Jericho. Throughout ancient Canaan, modern archaeology has confirmed many stories set down in the Bible. Yigael Yadin, an eminent Israeli archaeologist, wrote that he found it helpful to

Canaanite drinking cup, Jericho

the Canaanite pantheon led by the powerful god Baal. The Hebrews remained in Canaan until famine sent them into Egypt, probably in the 17th century B.C. There they lived in relative peace and prosperity under the rule of the Hyksos, an Asiatic power then controlling both Egypt and Canaan. But, under restored Egyptian rule, they suffered probable enslavement. Tradition places the beginning of their exodus from Egypt under the leadership of Moses in the 13th century B.C.

Having made their way across the Sinai, the Hebrews proceeded to conquer the cities of Canaan. Their success was short-lived; soon after, the Philistines—one of the Aegean "sea peoples"—attacked Canaan.

The Hebrews were ill-equipped to handle the Philistines, who carried off the sacred Ark of the Covenant that held the Ten Commandments received by Moses. Saul, the first Hebrew king, fought to recover the Ark, but he died in a crushing defeat at the hands of the Philistines. In time, David succeeded him, emerging victorious—and king of a unified Israel. Seeing a fitting capital in

Urusalim, a Canaanite city, he conquered it and brought the restored Ark to the city he had renamed Jerusalem. David succeeded in vanquishing the Philistines and other enemies. In his old age he named Solomon as his heir.

Solomon transformed the kingship of Israel, preferring to reign in opulence and style. He also transformed the economy, revitalizing agriculture and establishing maritime trade. He is best known as a builder of palaces, fortresses, and the first Temple of Jerusalem.

Limestone horned altar, Megiddo

begin a dig with a spade in one hand and a Bible in the other. Baal, here shown in his form as Reshef, god of war, was the most formidable Canaanite deity. The Hebrews, enjoined to monotheism, encountered his pantheon of gods upon arrival in Canaan and occasionally forsook Yahweh for participation in Baal's ritualistic cult. Another lapse into idolatry occurred during the exodus from Egypt; the priest Aaron fashioned a golden calf, which was worshiped by the wandering Hebrews. This earlier example from Byblos was buried in a Canaanite sanctuary around 1800 B.C. Hazor (below), which was the largest city in Canaan in the 12th century B.C., shows evidence of being razed to the ground, perhaps by Joshua. Solomon rebuilt Hazor during his building campaign. Horns decorate the four corners of a 10th-century B.C. Israelite altar from Megiddo. In Solomon's time, grasping the horns was a method of seeking sanctuary.

Golden calf, Byblos

Bronze Baal-Reshef figurine

Israelites and Judaism

900 B.C. to A.D. 135

By the ninth century B.C., the brief heyday of Israel as a political power had passed, yet a firmly planted Judaism endured in a divided Israel. The Israelites held an abiding belief in the God of Abraham and the covenant that sealed the relationship between nation and deity. The Promised Land, though split into the kingdoms of Judah and Israel since Solomon's death, was still theirs. The Ark, the dwelling place of Yahweh, rested in Jerusalem, the sacred center of the faith. It was enshrined in Solomon's magnificent Temple, the focal point of the holy city.

The God of Israel demanded absolute fidelity from his followers. His worship departed radically from the polytheistic religions of the ancient world, and the Israelites sometimes found themselves backsliding into the worship of other gods. Yahweh was fierce and just. His word rested in the Torah, the first five books of the Bible. These were attributed to Moses and contained the Commandments and other prescriptions for living a moral life. The Torah came to be supplemented by other books of the Bible and by the Talmud, a voluminous collection of moral tales and commentary.

A divided Jewish nation fended off many enemies until the late eighth century B.C., when Assyria conquered the northern kingdom, Israel, and deported its inhabitants. In 587 B.C. the Babylonians invaded Judah, sacked Jerusalem, and carried off its inhabitants to Babylon.

During these exiles the Jews established strong communities of faith, centered around assembly places called synagogues. After Persian ruler Cyrus the Great conquered Babylon, he freed the Jews to return

Entrances to Cave 4, Qumran

Isaiah scroll from Cave 1, Qumran

Dead Sea Treasures

The Old Testament Book of Isaiah speaks from a pieced-together scroll of leather almost 25 feet long. Longest of the Dead Sea scrolls discovered in caves near Qumran in 1947, Isaiah is written in a style of Hebrew dating to 100 B.C. Cave 4 contained the richest store of scrolls. Qumran's caves served as hideaways for members of the ascetic Essene sect of Judaism.

to Jerusalem in 538 B.C. Those who came back began immediately to rebuild the Temple. Jerusalem remained under Persian control for two centuries—until Persia fell to Alexander the Great in 333 B.C.

Alexander and his Greek successors brought a strong Hellenistic influence to the Promised Land, as they did throughout their realm. Greek customs were enforced. Jewish rites were outlawed, and the Temple witnessed Greek sacrifices and the worship of Greek gods. The Jews regarded this as sacrilege, and Judas Maccabaeus led a revolt, recapturing Jerusalem in 165 B.C. The Jews' cleansing of the Temple and its rededication formed the basis

of the Jewish festival of Hanukkah.

There followed a period of Maccabean rule under the control of the Seleucid Empire, centered in present-day Syria after Alexander's death. Then the Romans, seizing on a power vacuum in Israel, attacked under Pompey, who captured Jerusalem in 63 B.C. He called the province Palestine, a name associated with the Jews' traditional enemy, the Philistines.

Palestine, also known as Judaea, became a client-state of Rome, greatly reduced in size. Roman oppression stirred up rebellion among the Jews. The first strike, in A.D. 66, was met with Roman ferocity and the destruction of Solomon's Temple in 70. Three years later, the

surviving Jewish zealots perished at the hilltop fortress of Masada (below).

Afterward, Jews exiled from the city of Jerusalem clamored for its freedom from Rome. In A.D. 135 a second revolt, led by Simon bar Kokhba, briefly drove the Romans from Jerusalem. Bar Kokhba's papyrus dispatches, found in a desert cave, were a celebrated archaeological find of 1960. The retaliatory destruction of Jerusalem by Emperor Hadrian forced the Jews into a diaspora that would persist until the creation of the modern state of Israel in 1948. Bereft of homeland, Temple, and priests, Judaism nonetheless survived through its synagogues and teachers called rabbis.

Birth of Christianity

A.D. 1 to 400

The essence of Christianity lies in the life, teaching, and death of Jesus, a Jewish carpenter from Nazareth. Many scholars place the birth of Jesus in the year 6 B.C., during the time of a Roman census and a year or two before the death of King Herod.

Sometime in his thirties, Jesus

Fresco from Cappadocia, Turkey

Christian Imagery

Scenes of Jesus' life permeate Christian art. A map dated 1500 (left) is filled with Christian iconography, including a sword-wielding Herod the Great and the Three Kings bearing gifts. A fresco depicting the birth of Jesus adorns the domed ceiling of a church cut into a rock face in Turkey. In a mosaic from a sixth-century Italian basilica, Jesus calls brothers Simon Peter and Andrew to become his first disciples. Archaeology attests to crucifixion in Jesus' day with the discovery of this nail-pierced heel bone near Jerusalem.

Mosaic from Sant'Apollinare Nuova, Ravenna, Italy

began a public ministry in the vicinity of the Sea of Galilee with the aid of 12 handpicked disciples. His message espoused the love of God and the promise of salvation for all people, while his observances were firmly rooted in Jewish tradition.

Jesus attracted a devoted following who believed he was the Christ, a Greek term for the Messiah. Perceived as a troublemaker, he was arrested outside Jerusalem. After his death by crucifixion around A.D. 33, his followers reported seeing a resurrected Christ. Soon after, in their presence, he ascended into heaven. The resurrection of Jesus became a cornerstone of the Christian faith.

The disciples continued Jesus' ministry. The greatest gains were made by Saul, or Paul, himself a convert from Tarsus in Asia Minor. Paul traveled widely throughout the towns of the Jewish diaspora. When many Jews resisted the notion of Christ's divinity, Paul focused on non-Jews; he eliminated conversion to Judaism as a preliminary requirement for Christian baptism.

Early Christians ran afoul of their Roman rulers for rejecting Roman deities, including the divinity of the emperor. When Rome burned during Emperor Nero's reign, he placed blame on the sect and began a persecution that would last 250 years.

Christianity was based in Jerusalem until the city was conquered in A.D. 70. Rome itself then became the nucleus; it was already the seat of the Apostle Peter, Jesus' designated successor. Early Christians met in homes where they prayed, sang, and shared a communal feast commemorating the last supper of Jesus with his disciples.

Heel bone, 1st century A.D.

Under Emperor Constantine, Christianity grew, churches were built, and a hierarchy of leadership evolved. By A.D. 400 it was the official religion of the Roman Empire.

Jerusalem, Holy City

To the three great monotheistic faiths that took root in south-western Asia, Jerusalem is a place of great reverence. Where the glistening Dome of the Rock stands today (middle left), the biblical patriarch Abraham prepared to sacrifice his son—an act of faith in God recognized by Jews, Christians, and Muslims alike. Some 3,000 years ago, King Solomon built his Temple on Abraham's Mount Moriah. Nothing remains of it or succeeding structures except for a portion of the Western Wall of the Temple platform (near left), now regarded as Judaism's most hallowed site. Christians also venerate Jerusalem as the place where scenes of the final days, death, and resurrection of Jesus Christ unfolded. Islamic conquerors built the Dome of the Rock in the seventh century A.D., principally to commemorate the spot from which Muhammad is said to have ascended into Allah's presence in heaven.

Pilgrim crosses, Church of the Holy Sepulcher

Religious Witness

Centuries of pilgrim-carved crosses etch the walls of the Church of the Holy Sepulcher, at the site of Jesus' crucifixion and entombment.

Spread of Islam

A.D. 600 to 750

In the sixth century, the Arabian Peninsula was inhabited by tribesmen and traders worshiping gods whose images rested in shrines such as the Kaaba at Mecca.

When Muhammad was born in Mecca about A.D. 570, it was already a pilgrimage site as well as a major center for caravan trade. Orphaned at an early age, Muhammad worked as a shepherd before becoming a wealthy merchant. He often meditated in caves outside the city, where he had a series of revelations that finally identified him as the prophet who would lead the polytheistic Arabs to the one true God, Allah.

Known as Islam, or "submission," Muhammad's faith built onto the Judeo-Christian tradition but considered Muhammad himself the ultimate Prophet. The revelations from God to Muhammad form the basis of the Koran, Islam's holy book.

Muhammad began his ministry in Mecca, then moved to Medina. Muslims, adherents of Islam, figure their calendar from the year 622, the date of that hegira, or emigration. Eventually he gathered support, returned to Mecca, and united most of the Arab world under Islam.

Succession disputes after the Prophet's death in 632 challenged the nascent religion. Some Muslims supported the leadership of elected caliphs, while others wanted succession to remain in the line of Muhammad and his son-in-law Ali. The division persists today in the differences between the Sunni and Shiite sects.

Islamic conquest sped through the Middle East, into Africa and Europe, and to the borders of India and China under the Umayyad caliphs. Its boundaries reached a zenith about 750 as the Abbasids came to power, and attention turned to art, architecture, and scholarship.

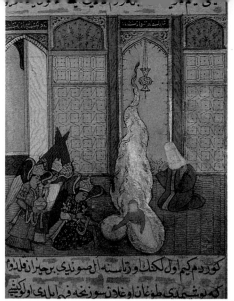
Miniature of birth of Muhammad, 14th century A.D.

Muslim Symbolism

At Samarra, Iraq, worshipers ascend the spiral minaret of a ninth-century mosque (opposite), built during Islam's golden age under the Abbasid caliphs. An Iraqi lusterware bowl of that period features a lute player. In Mecca, pilgrims circle the Kaaba, holiest Islamic shrine in that holy city. Miniaturists depicted Muhammad's life but avoided the sacrilege of showing his or his mother's face. The flame symbolizes spiritual power.

The Kaaba, Mecca

Lusterware bowl, 10th century A.D.

GREENLAND

ICELAND

SCANDINAVIA

Oseberg

Birka

Gotland
Sea

BALTIC SEA

Orkney
Islands

BRITISH
ISLES

BRITAIN

Lindisfarne

NORTH SEA

Gundestrup   Lindholm

Tollund   Grauballe

Newgrange

Limerick

Dublin

Sutton
Hoo

Waterford

Avebury   London

West Kennet   *Thames*

Cerne Abbas   Stonehenge

Jersey

La Hougue Bie

NORMANDY

BRITTANY

Carnac
Gavr'inis

GAUL

ATLANTIC

OCEAN

Rhine

Danube

La Tène   ALPS   Hallstatt

IBERIAN

PENINSULA

Rome

M
E
D
I
T
E
R
R
A

Malta

● Ancient and modern town site

◆ Archaeological site only

0   400 mi

0   600 km

Europe: Into the North

6000 B.C. to A.D. 1100

Novgorod

Volga

Gnezdovo ◆ ● Smolensk

Kiev ●

Dnieper

BALKAN
PENINSULA

BLACK
SEA

THRACE ● Constantinople
(Byzantium)

N E A N   S E A

Long before Egyptians raised the first pyramid or Greek statesman Pericles began planning the Parthenon, Neolithic farmers in western Europe were building tombs and temples of their own. These great stone monuments—or megaliths—are the most conspicuous reminders of prehistoric Europe. Who were these megalithic tomb and temple builders, and where did they come from?

Early peoples moved into northern regions of Europe as Ice Age glaciers receded. Farmers spread northward and westward from the Balkan Peninsula and by 6000 B.C. had settled central Europe. Craftsmen acquired experience in working metals into tools and ornaments.

By 5000 B.C., farming had spread into present-day France, reaching Britain by 4300 and Scandinavia by 3500. In large parts of western Europe, farming entailed clearing fields of boulders dropped by retreating glaciers. About 4700 B.C., some farmers began raising those boulders to form durable markers and tombs. Much of our knowledge of these megalithic peoples comes from artifacts found in their tombs.

Remains of other ancient cultures have been preserved in coastal wetlands, inland bogs, and freshwater lakes. Recent discoveries include remnants of pile dwellings built on the shores of Alpine lakes up to 6,000 years ago. But the region's most startling find was made high in the Alps in 1991, when hikers discovered the frozen body of a 5,000-year-old man, dubbed the Iceman.

About 1190 B.C., a group of related tribes with a common culture and burial practices arose in central Europe. Called the Urnfielders because they cremated their dead and buried them in large urns, these tribes began to move farther afield as the population north of the Alps increased. Four groups probably emerged from the Urnfield culture—Celts in the west, Slavs in the north, Italic speakers in the south, and Illyrians in the southeast.

The Celts had originated north of the Alps about 800 B.C. Their mastery of iron metallurgy enabled them to expand until conquered by the Romans. Germanic peoples, a loose alliance of tribal groups, succeeded the Celts in central Europe.

Known as "barbarians" to the Romans, the Germanic peoples battered the western empire for centuries, sacking Rome in A.D. 410. By the sixth century, Germanic tribes had established kingdoms in Europe. The large holdings of the Franks gave rise to the empire ruled by warrior-king Charlemagne, whose statesmanship and guidance have earned him the epithet "Father of Europe."

Charlemagne successfully defended his empire from Scandinavian raiders called Vikings, but they terrorized the rest of Europe for more than 250 years, beginning in the late eighth century. They invaded the British Isles about A.D. 790, moved on to Iceland, and from there reached Greenland and other sites in North America. Viking traders also established settlements in present-day Russia. Local populations outside Scandinavia assimilated the Vikings, but they, like the many peoples who preceded them, made a significant contribution to the cultural identity of the European continent.

Megalith Builders

4700 to 1500 B.C.

Scattered throughout Europe, from the Mediterranean island of Malta to Scotland's Orkney Islands, the immense stone monuments known as megaliths are the legacies of early farming communities. These ancient megalith builders left few other clues to their way of life.

The establishment of farming in Europe was gradual, beginning about two thousand years after the rise of agriculture in the Middle East. But by 3500 B.C., farmers had cleared much of the forest that blanketed western Europe, and agriculture became widespread. Using the undressed boulders they found while clearing their fields, Neolithic farmers erected various kinds of stone structures, most of which seem to have played a part in burial rituals or in rites involving ancestor worship.

Some of the earliest farming communities built communal burial chambers, the most common type of European megalithic monument. As many as 50,000 survive. Many had a stone-slab entrance passage and were covered by large earthen mounds called barrows, or piles of rock called cairns. West Kennet long barrow, a 300-foot-long mound with burial chambers in southern Britain, was in use for more than a thousand years. Newgrange, in Ireland, dates

Stone figurine, Malta

Temple, Hagar Qim, Malta

from about 2500 B.C. There, a narrow passage some 60 feet long leads to a burial chamber at the center of the mound. Instead of using a simple capstone to support the roof of the chamber, the skilled builders of Newgrange stepped stones upward and inward from the walls to create a vaulted ceiling nearly 20 feet high.

Neolithic builders also raised menhirs—standing stones. The Brittany region in western France is home to the largest concentration of megaliths in Europe. At Carnac, near the coast, 3,000 menhirs from 3 to 18 feet tall form parallel avenues of stone nearly four miles long.

Temples of Malta

Still standing after 5,000 years, limestone walls at Mnajdra (opposite), on the Mediterranean island of Malta, affirm the skill of megalithic temple builders. This temple and some 30 others on the island suggest that a priestly cult practiced ancestor worship there as early as 3500 B.C. Archaeologists have recovered numerous obese female figurines from a temple there at Hagar Qim. Many early peoples of Europe and Asia crafted such statues. Associated with fertility cults, they probably represent mother goddesses.

By 3200 B.C., ancient builders had constructed circles of stone in Britain and Ireland. Some, ringed by ditches and embankments, are called henges. John Aubrey, in the 17th century, was the first to recognize that the remains of about a hundred menhirs at Avebury in southern England formed a circular Neolithic enclosure. Avebury and Stonehenge, on the Salisbury Plain of southern England, were built in stages over many centuries.

Examples of another type of megalithic structure—temples—are found mostly on the islands of Malta and neighboring Gozo in the Mediterranean. These temples, such as Hagar Qim and Mnajdra, once contained cult objects and were used solely for rituals. The first ones date from the fourth millennium B.C., which makes them the oldest freestanding structures in the world.

Early, unscientific excavation stripped many of the temples of Malta as well as other European sites. Detailed studies of some sites are fairly recent. The first archaeological dig at Stonehenge was not mounted until 1901, and major excavations did not begin until 1919. For centuries, experts assumed that megaliths were younger than they are and had been inspired by structures found in more advanced societies such as those of the Mediterranean.

In the 1960s, technical advances in radiocarbon dating proved that the oldest megaliths were raised about 6,000 years ago and suggested they were the independent creations of Neolithic peoples. Archaeologists had to revise their assessment of Neolithic communities. They must

Temple, Mnajdra, Malta

Carved stone ball,
Scotland

Geometric carvings in a tomb on Gavr'inis, an island off Brittany, France

Legacies of Stone

Rough-hewn menhirs—standing stones—file through fields at Carnac (opposite), in Brittany; a few have fallen since farmers began erecting them some 6,000 years ago. Brittany, in northwestern France, contains the largest collection of megaliths in Europe—and some of the oldest stone structures in the world. Carved slabs support the roof of a 5,000-year-old tomb on the island of Gavr'inis. Similar patterns etch a stone ball of the same period found in Scotland. Farmers shaped England's Stonehenge —most famous of megalithic monuments—for some 1,500 years.

Stonehenge, England

have been complex societies with artisans capable of quarrying and transporting the huge stones.

Further study provoked more questions. Were some structures astronomical observatories? What do the patterns carved on stones at a few monuments mean? And does a religion connected to a mother goddess explain the "fat lady" figurines found throughout Europe? Most experts agree that a powerful significance must have imbued these ancient monuments.

Recent excavations at Brochtorff Circle, a burial complex in Malta, and La Hougue Bie, a cairn on the British island of Jersey, are providing additional insights into death rituals and lifestyles of the megalith builders.

The Iceman

3000 B.C.

In 1991, when German hikers Helmut and Erika Simon discovered a shriveled body at 10,530 feet in the Alps, they thought they had found a discarded doll. Authorities assumed the corpse—since nicknamed the Iceman—was one of many accident victims found each year in those mountains and began trying to wrench him from the grip of the ice. Rescuers worked with axes, ski poles, and even a jackhammer. No one suspected that the corpse was that of a prehistoric man.

Five days later, Austrian archaeologist Konrad Spindler examined the body. The style of the Iceman's ax, which he thought was bronze, caused Spindler to estimate that the mummy was 4,000 years old. The

Bronze Age in Europe began about 2200 B.C. Later chemical analysis, however, proved that the ax was copper. The Iceman was from the Copper Age, which predated the Bronze Age and lasted from about 4000 to 2200 B.C. Radiocarbon analysis indicated that the mummy, one of the best preserved and oldest humans ever found, was 5,000 years old. The Iceman died about 3000 B.C.—more than 1,600 years before Egypt's boy-king Tutankhamun was born.

Sadly, his well-meaning rescuers had mangled the Iceman's corpse as they hacked him from the ice. His clothes were shredded, and the jackhammer had gouged his left hip. A small horde of people trampled the site, scattering artifacts. The Iceman's left arm snapped as his body was packed for shipment, and a contaminating fungus quickly began to grow on his skin.

The location of the find—on the border between Austria and Italy—inspired a political dispute. Austrian

*Reconstruction
of the Iceman*

police recovered the body, but surveyors soon determined that the Iceman had died some 300 feet inside the Italian border. Three political entities—Austria, Italy, and the autonomous region in Italy where the Iceman was found—lay claim to the remains. The custody battle slowed research. Nevertheless, scientists have managed to amass a lot of data in the short time since the find.

Copper Age villagers in central Europe raised wheat and barley, using plows and wheeled carts.They ate domesticated dogs, cattle, sheep, goats, and pigs. Traders and prospectors traversed the Alps exchanging goods and ideas. Perhaps the Iceman was a shepherd or a trader.

What researchers have learned is that the man was short—only five feet two inches tall—had dark, wavy hair, and was between 25 and 40 years old when he died. His clothing and equipment were suitable for life in the mountains. The design of his garments suggests that he probably came from a nearby village. Traces of grain on some items could mean that he had recently helped bring in the harvest. There have also been some surprising discoveries.

Strands of hair only three and a half inches long and tattoolike markings on the Iceman's back suggest that haircutting and tattooing were practiced much earlier than anthropologists had thought. And the Iceman's "first-aid kit" of antibiotic fungus, his flanged copper ax, grass knife sheath, and deerskin quiver all indicate a degree of sophistication not commonly thought to be typical of Copper Age people.

Because of the way he died, the Iceman tells us much about how he lived. He was not found buried in a tomb amid grave goods placed there by others. He died surrounded by the personal possessions he needed for living— for surviving a journey in the Alps.

Imprisoned by Ice

Frozen for 5,000 years under an Alpine glacier, a Neolithic man, now known as the Iceman, surfaced in September 1991. He lives again in a bust created for the NATIONAL GEOGRAPHIC magazine by anthropologically trained artist John Gurche. Two German hikers discovered the mummified corpse near the boundary between Austria and Italy. Found at an elevation of 10,530 feet, it is among the oldest and best preserved of all prehistoric corpses. Radiocarbon dating has proved that the Iceman lived during the Copper Age—4000 to 2200 B.C. in central Europe—the time of the introduction of the plow and the wheeled cart. The condition of the mummy leads scientists to think he fell asleep and froze to death. The moving ice in glaciers crushes and tears bodies frozen in them, but the Iceman lay in a hollow, and the glacier flowed above him. His eyeballs and internal organs remain intact. Artifacts preserved with the corpse shed new light on Copper Age society and force archaeologists to reevaluate their assumptions about the technology of those times. The Iceman carried a thong threaded with lumps of tree fungus that had

Fungus on leather thong

antibiotic properties, suggesting that he might have used it as a first-aid kit. The Iceman's ax, oldest found in Europe with binding and handle intact, has an advanced design similar to those crafted centuries after

Copper ax with yew handle, leather binding

his icy burial. A deerskin quiver found near the mummy astounded scientists, who had not seen its like before. It contained two complete arrows and twelve unfinished ones. His six-foot longbow had not been notched or fitted with string. Archaeologists can only wonder why the Iceman was wandering alone in the mountains with unfinished bow and arrows. Flint knives have been recovered at other Copper Age sites, but no intricately woven grass sheath like the one that held the Iceman's. His shoulder cape, of plaited grass, was found near his body; it failed to provide enough warmth to save the Iceman's life.

Deerskin quiver with 2 complete and 12 unfinished arrows

Grass sheath and ash-handled flint knife

Plaited-grass shoulder cape

Celts

800 to 50 B.C.

A group of tribes linked by religion and language, the Celts left behind richly equipped burial sites, great works of art, and the remains of huge fortresses. The Celts began to emerge in central Europe before 800 B.C. At its peak, Celtic culture reached from the North Sea to the Mediterranean and from the Black Sea to the Atlantic. Celtic warriors—women as well as men—were feared throughout the continent.

Most Celts relied on farming for their livelihood. Above farmers in the intensely stratified society were craftsmen, who excelled in metalworking and technological innovation. Highest in the hierarchy were the chieftains and the priests, or Druids. Druids performed the rites that were an integral part of Celtic life and provided access to the supernatural world that pervaded it.

The Celts are closely associated with ironworking. The first part of the Celtic Iron Age, from 800 to 500 B.C., is named the Hallstatt culture after a cemetery discovered near that town in Austria in 1846. Graves of chieftains unearthed at Hallstatt, along with the artifacts found in them, are the oldest archaeological evidence of the Celts. Archaeologists found there abundant evidence of the spread of iron use in Europe. Swords, crucial to Celtic superiority, were among the first iron objects crafted; plowshares came later. With iron tools and weapons, the Celts shaped the culture of the continent.

Celts abandoned their Hallstatt fortresses in the fifth century B.C., and the center of Celtic culture moved to the west. That shift marks the second phase of the Iron Age in Europe, called the La Tène culture after the Swiss region where, in 1857, artifacts representing it were first found. Abstract geometric designs and stylized animal forms characterize the expertly crafted artwork of the La Tène period. Art, central to Celtic life, manifested itself in every aspect of existence—from battle swords to ceremonial shields.

Celtic culture reached its peak in the fourth century B.C. By the mid-second century, princes were building large, walled settlements that the Romans called oppida. These would fall later to Roman armies. Somewhat arbitrarily, Julius Caesar, in 58 B.C., designated the tribes east of the Rhine River Germanic and those west of the Rhine Celtic. Gaul, the home of more than 60 major tribes, had become the center of Celtic culture. Caesar concentrated his troops there between 58 and 52 B.C. and succeeded in conquering it. Defeated but unbowed, the Celts held on to many of their traditions and left western Europe a rich legacy that survives today in language, art, and custom.

Bronze helmet, diameter 8 in

Silver panel from the Gundestrup cauldron

Gilded bronze shield, 32 in

Cerne Abbas giant, Dorset, England

Bronze figurine, 6 in

Bronze sculpture, 9.7 in long

Arts and Artistry

Age-old outline of the 180-foot Cerne Abbas giant, a Celtic god of fertility and the hunt, etches a chalk hillside in southwest England. Celts, a loose alliance of peoples united by religion and language, emerged in Europe about 800 B.C. Celtic religion, with its strong belief in the afterlife, inspired metalsmiths to craft weapons, jewelry, and other goods that accompanied the dead to their graves. A horseman and his dog pursue a wild boar on top of a bronze cart. The rare sculpture of a female dancer may depict a ritual. Celtic women, as well as men, attained fame as warriors. A bronze, horned helmet dredged from the Thames in London dates from the first century B.C. A shield of hammered and gilded bronze reflects the expertise of Celtic craftsmen; its delicate decoration leads scholars to believe it served a ceremonial function. Warriors line a panel of the silver Gundestrup cauldron, one of the most famous of Celtic relics. Found in pieces in a Danish peat bog in 1891, the vessel, 27 inches in diameter, consisted of 14 panels shaped by silversmiths some 2,000 years ago. Recent research suggests that the Celts may have commissioned it from Thracian master smiths.

Germanic Peoples

500 B.C. to A.D. 650

About 500 B.C., a large group of people with cultural characteristics distinct from the Celts and their other neighbors began to emerge in northern Europe. Called the Germanic peoples, their origins are lost in time, but there is evidence that their ancestors first settled along the eastern shores of the North Sea in the second millennium B.C. During the late Bronze Age and early Iron Age, they spread over southern Scandinavia and Germany, establishing numerous small farming villages. The Germanic peoples separated into different subgroups, or tribes—among them Sueves, Goths, Vandals, Teutons, Burgundians, Franks, Jutes, Angles, and Saxons.

Bronze neck ring, Denmark, diameter 8.2 in

Experts suggest various reasons for the spread of Germanic culture. Around 500 B.C., the climate in northern Europe grew cold and damp; perhaps it forced farmers to seek warmer, drier lands. Another possibility is that the Germanic tribes wanted to share in the iron technology that had developed and spread in central Europe.

A growing population certainly helped drive the Germanic tribes to migrate over time to new lands. Cimbrian and Teutonic tribes moved south from Denmark, and Goths from Sweden. By 200 B.C., Germanic tribes had reached the lower Danube River. The Sueves roamed the regions of central and southern Germany, causing the Celts to retreat to Gaul.

In 102 and 101 B.C., Roman soldiers repelled Teutonic and Cimbrian warriors from the edges of the Roman Empire. Julius Caesar, intent on defeating the Celts, at first seemed to ignore the Germanic threat, but in 58 B.C. he stopped another advance. Roman armies kept the Germanic peoples at bay for a while, but by A.D. 200 the Goths had reached the Black Sea. Soon after, the Alemanni and Franks moved toward Gaul and Italy. Romans fortified their towns, including Rome, against the fearful onslaught.

Greek as well as Roman historians wrote of "barbarians" who took part in pagan rituals and practiced human sacrifice. Evidence that Germanic peoples sacrificed humans to their gods is ample. Some 2,000 mummified corpses have been recovered from European bogs—particularly those of Denmark and northern Germany—since the first authenticated discovery of a bog body in 1773. Many of these, including Tollund man and Grauballe man, appear to have been ritualistically murdered as sacrificial offerings.

In A.D. 375, when Huns from Central Asia attacked eastern Europe, Goths, Vandals, and other Germanic tribes fled in terror. Waves of barbarians poured into the Roman Empire, which was no longer powerful enough to repel them. Finally, in 476, Rome and the western empire fell. Barbarian leaders took control until Justinian, ruler of the Eastern Roman Empire, reconquered much of the west in the mid-sixth century.

The Germanic tribes had brought their own institutions as well as oral and artistic traditions into the Roman Empire, but by the sixth century, many of them had adopted Christianity and Roman customs. Outside the empire, small kingdoms emerged, and Germanic states became established in western Europe. The kingdom of the Franks grew to be the largest of those states, stretching through most of present-day France, the Low Countries, and part of Germany. The Franks had a deep and lasting impact on the culture of western Europe.

Angles and Saxons, sea-roving plunderers from lands near the North Sea, left their mark in Britain, which was finally abandoned by the Romans in A.D. 410. By the sixth century the Anglo-Saxons had established wealthy and powerful kingdoms in southeastern Britain. The 1939 discovery of an Anglo-Saxon burial ground at Sutton Hoo provided evidence of a cosmopolitan society existing there by A.D. 625. Archaeologists excavated a wooden ship

Drinking horns, Sutton Hoo, England

Inlaid bronze fibula, Spain, 4.3 in

containing the burial chamber of an Anglo-Saxon king. They unearthed luxurious items, including bowls from Egypt and Constantinople and gold coins from France—evidence of extensive trading.

By the seventh century A.D., a number of small, prosperous Germanic kingdoms were trading with one another throughout Europe. In their wanderings, the Germanic tribes had distributed the peoples of modern Europe, and laid the foundations of future nations.

Buried Evidence

Victim of a violent death, the Grauballe man had his throat slit from ear to ear before being deposited in a bog pool 2,000 years ago, probably as a sacrifice. Scholars named him after the village near the Danish peat bog where he was found in 1952. The highly acidic peat, which tanned his skin, reddened his hair, and decalcified his bones, also helped preserve the corpse. Some 2,000 bodies have been discovered in European boglands. Also preserved in a Danish bog, Tollund man wears a peaceful expression—but his third-century B.C. killers had tied a noose of braided leather around his neck. Artifacts as well as human remains found in wetlands shed light on the Germanic peoples. A swamp in Denmark yielded a heavy bronze necklace (right) dating from the third century B.C. The crown-shaped circlet, probably a votive offering, opens at a hinged joint. The intricate and flowing curves of another bronze neck ring (opposite), found in a Danish bog, reflect the artistry of Germanic peoples. Scholars associate a garnet-inlaid bronze fibula discovered in Spain with the Visigoths, one of the most important of the Germanic tribes. Such brooches were used to fasten clothing. From a ship burial at Sutton Hoo in Suffolk, England, two drinking horns bear mounts of gilded silver. They date from about A.D. 625, when Anglo-Saxons held sway in England. Seagoing Germanic invaders—Angles, Saxons, Jutes, and Frisians—raided Roman Britain. By A.D. 410, the Romans had withdrawn their legions, and Germanic peoples began settling the island.

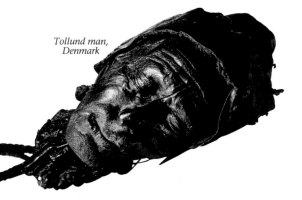
Tollund man, Denmark

Grauballe man, Denmark

Bronze necklace, Denmark, diameter 7.5 in

Vikings

A.D. 790 to 1100

The word "Vikings" evokes an image of fierce, flaxen-haired Scandinavian warriors brandishing axes and swords as they stream from a curved sailing ship with carved prow to plunder an abbey or a village. That picture, embellished by story and song, is based on historical fact. The Vikings—or Norsemen—of Scandinavia were the most terrifying and efficient raiders in northwestern Europe from about A.D. 790 to 1100. They owed part of their triumph in war to their long ships, which were easy to maneuver yet spacious enough to carry big cargoes. But a large measure of the success of the Vikings lay in their skill and character. They were master mariners, quick and cunning, who shared a fatalistic outlook toward life and death that rendered them fearless.

Although many people think of the Vikings as seafaring warriors, most of the population farmed in

Viking stone carving, Gotland, Sweden

Seafaring Warriors

Mariners to the death, Viking raiders erected ship-shaped monuments to mark burials; hundreds of graves dating from A.D. 400 to 1000 fill a field in Lindholm, Denmark (right). The rich were interred in boats; symbolic ships marked the tombs of the less wealthy. Curved at prow and stern, like the one above, carved in stone on a Swedish island, Viking long ships could reverse direction without turning. Battle gear included an iron helmet with bronze head panels and noseguard, found in a Swedish chieftain's boat grave. A Viking battle-ax could fell a horse with one blow; silver inlay decorates the head of an ax from a Danish grave.

Iron and bronze helmet, Sweden

Iron axhead with silver wire inlay, Denmark

122

their Scandinavian homelands. They raised rye, barley, and oats and herded cattle, supplementing these food sources by hunting, fishing, and trapping. Trade in locally mined iron expanded between A.D. 700 and 800.

The profits to be made from foreign trade in iron, furs, and amber prompted some Vikings to leave their native lands. Another stimulus for travel was the desire for fertile new terrain to sustain a growing population. Yet a third incentive was the fast wealth available through plunder. About A.D. 790, Viking ships began attacking Britain. For the next 250 years or so, the maritime raiders ravaged villages and monasteries throughout Europe. In 793, Norsemen sacked Lindisfarne monastery in England; they raided Britain and Ireland regularly for several decades.

By the end of the ninth century, Viking warriors were plundering continental Europe and northern Africa. Danish Vikings controlled much of northern and eastern England, an area that became known as the Danelaw, and Norwegian Vikings held parts of Ireland and Scotland. Norsemen voyaged into the western seas, and in 874 colonists began settling along the coast of Iceland. From

there they sailed west to Greenland and Newfoundland. The remains of a Norse settlement discovered at L'Anse aux Meadows in the extreme northern part of the island of Newfoundland date to before A.D. 1000.

While Danish and Norwegian Vikings voyaged westward, many Swedish Norsemen sailed east across the Baltic Sea, portaged to the Dnieper and the Volga Rivers, and traveled south on them through the lands of Slav, Balt, and Finno-Ugric tribes to the Black and Caspian Seas. Those Vikings, known as Rus, wintered in towns along the Russian rivers and traveled inland to trade in spring and summer.

They began dominating trade in the area about A.D. 800. Exchanging amber, iron, and furs for silver, gold, and brocades at trading centers such

Runic stone, Sweden, 5.4 ft

as Baghdad and Constantinople, Viking chieftains grew rich and powerful and created the first Russian state. They took control of the Slavic cities of Novgorod, Smolensk, and, finally, Kiev. By the 11th century, Kievan Rus exerted commercial power from the Baltic east to beyond the Ural Mountains and south to the Black Sea.

The kingdom of the Franks, one of the largest states in temperate Europe, had evolved into the Carolingian Empire, a well-run and well-defended political unit that successfully repelled Viking raids starting in the eighth century A.D. By about 900, however, the Vikings had gained a foothold in northwestern France, where they founded the Duchy of Normandy. Norman descendants of Scandinavian raiders would conquer England in 1066.

In the 10th century the provinces of Scandinavia evolved into states ruled by powerful kings. At the same time, the Vikings began converting to Christianity, which had been brought to them by English and Saxon missionaries. The Vikings gradually ceased their roving and receded in power and importance. Outside Scandinavia they were absorbed into local populations.

The achievements of the Vikings survived long after they faded from the European scene. Besides founding the first Russian state and settling Iceland, they established the towns of Dublin, Waterford, and Limerick in Ireland. By fostering trade, they revitalized flagging urban centers throughout Europe. As evidenced by Danish King Canute, whose kingdom stretched from Norway into the British Isles, the Norsemen were able administrators. Archaeologists have extracted from graves, such as the Oseberg ship burial in southeastern Norway, intricately carved wood sculptures and finely wrought jewelry made by skilled Viking craftsmen.

Although their alphabet consisted of only 16 symbols called runes and their written records are few, the Viking oral tradition became an art form. For centuries Viking bards retold Norse poems—called Eddas—and narratives—called sagas—keeping them alive until they could be transcribed for posterity by monks during the 13th century.

Those vivid stories of seagoing warriors who relished danger and destruction have immortalized the Vikings. Their maritime expertise and their maneuverable long ships made the Norsemen successful raiders and conquerors. Their days of glory were comparatively short—only about 250 years—but their daring, confidence, and disregard for personal peril have earned them a large place in history and legend.

Wooden head carved on sledge, Norway

Glass gaming pieces, Sweden

Colonists and Traders

Shaded and serene, grassy knolls (below) in the woods of Gnezdovo near the city of Smolensk, Russia, mark the graves of Vikings who settled here in the tenth century A.D. The remains of a fortified settlement on the Dnieper River, the site contained some 3,000 grave mounds and a wealth of artifacts known as the Gnezdovo Hoard. Among the riches found there were pendants expertly crafted in silver. Vikings, eager to trade amber and furs from the Baltic region for Arabic silver and Byzantine gold, navigated south on Russian rivers to reach the Black and Caspian Seas. Known as Rus, the Viking overlords settled along the trade route, creating Russia's first organized state and giving their name to the modern nation. In their Scandinavian homeland, Vikings erected thousands of runic stones that commemorate places, events, and people. Many of the thousand-year-old inscriptions record the deaths of kinsmen; this one, on a 5.4-foot-tall limestone memorial in Gotland, Sweden, honors a son killed in Romania. Glass gaming pieces, including a "king" figure, excavated at Birka, Sweden's oldest town, probably arrived as trade goods from the east, but they also suggest the possibility of glasswork here as early as the ninth century. Viking craftsmen also excelled in working with wood. They built sturdy ships that carried them as far as North America. A ship burial in Oseberg, Norway, contained a wooden sledge decorated with a monstrous head at each of its four corners.

Silver pendant, Gnezdovo Hoard

Silver pendant, Gnezdovo Hoard

Site of Gnezdovo Hoard, Smolensk, Russia

125

Sub-Saharan Africa

SAHARA

LOWER
NUBIA

UPPER
NUBIA (KUSH)

Nile

RED SEA

ARA
PEN

Napata
Jebel Barkal ← Nuri
El Kurru

Meroë
Naqa

Nile

Atbara

Aksum
Qorqor
Lalibela

Timbuktu •   SONGHAI

Niger

SHARA

Jenne-jeno

MALI

YORUBA

Tada   Nok
Oyo • Ife   NOK
Benin   Igbo-Ukwu
AKAN   IGBO

ATLANTIC

OCEAN

Congo

Lake
Victoria

Kongo

KONGO

SHONA
Great Zimbabwe
Sabi

KALAHARI

DESERT

• Ancient and modern town site

◆ Archaeological site only

0   800 mi

0   1200 km

Ancient Kingdoms

1050 B.C. to A.D. 1650

Across the vast breadth of the African continent lie clues to humanity's greatest story—that of the evolution from hominids to city dwellers. Nowhere else on earth is the range of human history and activity as long or as complex. Despite this heritage, Africa has remained one of archaeology's greatest puzzles. Only since the 1920s has the sub-Saharan part of the continent become the focus of serious archaeology. Huge tracts of land remain unstudied, and large gaps pepper the chronological record.

One reason for this was the European colonialist attitudes of many 19th-century archaeologists and historians, who believed that innovations such as agriculture, metalworking, and animal domestication must have been introduced from areas outside sub-Saharan Africa.

Recent discoveries and sophisticated dating techniques have dispelled these assumptions. The city of Jenne-jeno, in Mali, for example, unearthed in 1977, was an urban center that thrived through trade—probably in agricultural products and later in metal items—long before contact with the outside world.

The logistics of studying Africa's past, however, remain difficult for other reasons as well. The continent's great size, climatic extremes, and immense rain forests make archaeological surveys a problem.

The lush equatorial forests of Nigeria, for instance, obscure virtually all signs of previous human occupation. The rich treasures of Nigeria's Igbo-Ukwu site were uncovered only because a villager dug up strange objects in his backyard. The humid forests also have claimed nearly all the wooden sculptures created by ancient cultures in western Africa. Archaeologists are left to reconstruct some cultures only through sparse and fragmentary artifacts.

In desert localities, such as the Kushite city of Napata in present-day Sudan, drifting sands mask clues to the past. Archaeologists have turned to aerial photography and other remote-sensing techniques to search for signs of human activity.

Scholars are hindered, too, by the lack of written records south of the Sahara. Few accounts by early explorers provide complete records of the nature of ancient societies. In Benin, however, bronze plaques outside palaces take the place of written records, presenting a symbolic chronicle of court life.

In recent years, archaeologists have begun to view African prehistory through African eyes. Instead of relying on scant written sources, they have begun to find clues in oral traditions, which provide continuity between living and long-gone societies. At Jenne-jeno, for instance, native workers immediately identified clay figures as children's toys, even though they were a thousand years old.

With these new perspectives, scholars are exploring the varied cultures of early sub-Saharan Africa and examining the means by which people have adapted to their environments. These insights have made Africa a challenging and fascinating scene of recent archaeological effort.

PRECEDING PAGES: Sudanese camel drivers pass the 2,000-year-old tombs of their royal ancestors. Kushite kings were buried beneath these pyramids in a sacred complex at Jebel Barkal.

Kush

1050 B.C. to A.D. 350

Amid the stark desert lands of present-day Sudan, in northeastern Africa, stands a massive red sandstone butte known as Jebel Barkal. Not far from it rose the city of Napata, the capital of the Kingdom of Kush and the site of the first high civilization in sub-Saharan Africa.

Today, sand engulfs the temple complex at Jebel Barkal, and time shrouds the achievements of these people, who were wealthy traders in gold and iron. The history of Kush remained obscure until early in the 20th century, when Harvard Egyptologist

George Reisner excavated the tombs of some six dozen Kushite kings and clarified their chronology.

The people of Kush occupied this once fertile region, known later as Nubia, for thousands of years. Stretching south from the first cataract of the Nile to Khartoum, Nubia lay at the crossroads between the rich cultures of Egypt and other parts of Africa.

For a long time, Egyptian traditions dominated Kushite culture, although Kush maintained a degree of political independence. By 750 B.C., the Kushite kings had grown strong enough to conquer Egypt itself. A succession of five Kushite kings ruled over Egypt and Kush during the 25th Egyptian dynasty.

In 663 B.C., Assyrian invaders forced the Kushites out of Egypt, and Egyptians regained control. During the following century, the Kushites relocated their capital from Napata southeast to a fertile floodplain near the confluence of the Nile and Atbara Rivers. Gradually, the new Kushite capital of Meroë developed into a

Rock-crystal ball, El Kurru, 2 in

Egyptian Echoes

Recumbent rams, symbols of the Egyptian god Amun, line the approach to his temple at the base of Jebel Barkal (right). Kushites borrowed Egyptian gods, language, and the practice of building burial

pyramids. Found in the tomb of a Kushite royal wife, this rock-crystal ball bears a gold head of Egyptian goddess Hathor. A phalanx of Egyptian-style figurines known as ushabtis—answerers— *filled the burial chamber of King Taharqa, ready to serve him in the afterlife.*

Stone ushabti *figurines from the tomb of Taharqa, Nuri, 7 to 23.5 in*

Gold cylinder, tomb of Aspelta, Nuri, 4.3 in

busy urban center, made prosperous by an extensive trade in copper, gold, iron, ivory, and slaves.

From Chinese-inspired bronzes and a Roman sculpture found in the ruins of Meroë, archaeologists confirm a far-reaching trade. In addition, the discovery of sizable slag heaps and brick furnaces suggest that Kushites mastered ironworking.

More may be gleaned about this culture when scholars succeed in deciphering the Meroitic written language. Kushites developed their own script from Egyptian hieroglyphics. Their mysterious symbols cover numerous stone stelae and votive plaques at Meroë.

Meroë's prosperity declined rapidly in the second century A.D., partly because of environmental degradation produced by overgrazing and deforestation. In A.D. 350 the powerful Kingdom of Aksum destroyed Meroë, and Kush's long history came to an end.

Kushite Capitals

Outlines of the great Kushite religious center at Jebel Barkal, near Napata, emerge from an aerial photograph (opposite). A huge temple dedicated to the Egyptian god Amun stood here, made resplendent by King Piye, who conquered Egypt in 724 B.C. Jebel Barkal remained a religious center even after defeat at the hands of Assyrians and Egyptians led the Kushites to establish a new capital at Meroë, 300 miles up the Nile, in the sixth century B.C. The cylinder decorated with ornamental friezes may have belonged to sixth-century King Aspelta and perhaps contained sacred papyrus scrolls. The ruins of Meroë include pyramids, large walled enclosures, temples, palaces, and royal baths. A distinctive "kiosk" at Naqa, a major ceremonial center south of Meroë, is a third-century A.D. hybrid—Roman architectural style blended with Meroitic decorative features. The bronze sculpture of an unknown ruler of Kush reveals the sophistication of Kushite metalwork in the first century A.D. Reflecting the legendary skill of his country's archers, the king wears a thumb ring, used for drawing a bowstring.

Bronze statue, 19.5 in

Aksum stela, about 68 ft

Pre-Christian and Christian Monuments

A massive granite stela soars 68 feet into the sky of northern Ethiopia—the most dramatic surviving monument of the pre-Christian period of the Aksum

Fallen Aksum stela, 49 ft

Aksum and Lalibela

1000 B.C. to A.D. 1200

In the early centuries A.D., a thriving trade in African ivory and animal skins fueled the explosive growth of the Kingdom of Aksum, in present-day Ethiopia. By the fourth century, its armies had crushed the Kushite capital of Meroë in Sudan and its navy controlled military and mercantile interests in the Red Sea.

Archaeologists trace the roots of Aksum to the first millennium B.C., when settlers from the southern part of the Arabian Peninsula began to cross the Red Sea and settle in the Ethiopian highlands. These Semitic-speaking migrants brought with them many cultural and architectural traditions from their homeland, including a written script and the practice of worshiping a moon god. By 500 B.C. they had established a literate, urban culture, which slowly began to influence the indigenous Kushitic-speaking farmers.

By the first century A.D., the peoples had commingled extensively and created a trading power with its capital at Aksum. The state traded with the Roman Empire through its port of Adulis on the Red Sea. Aksum reached its pinnacle in the fourth century, when its conquest of Meroë gave it control over the ivory trade originating in the Nile Valley.

During this time, Christianity became the state religion, an event archaeologists partly inferred from the change in symbols on Aksumite coins—from the pagan moon god's crescent and disc to the cross of Christianity.

By the seventh century, Muslim Arabs had destroyed the Aksumite

fleet and taken control of Red Sea ports. Deprived of much of its trade, the Kingdom of Aksum went into decline. Continued Muslim conquests cut Ethiopia off from the rest of the Christian world.

In the late 12th and early 13th centuries, King Lalibela of the Zagwe dynasty attempted to reestablish a strong Christian Ethiopia in the tradition of Aksum. This "new Jerusalem" saw the construction of 11 churches hewn out of solid rock in Roha—later renamed Lalibela. The churches and the towering obelisks built by earlier Aksumites are dramatic reminders of these once great kingdoms of ancient Ethiopia.

St. George at Lalibela (above and below)

Mural, St. Mary at Qorqor

kingdom. Carvings on this and a toppled 49-foot stela imitate Aksumite buildings of masonry with a timber framework. The monuments were believed to mark royal graves, and in the 1970s archaeologists uncovered a series of tombs underneath them that run as deep as 25 feet. Christianity became Aksum's state religion but declined after Muslim conquest in the 7th century. In the late 12th and early 13th centuries, Ethiopian king Lalibela reestablished Christianity in the area. He commissioned the building of St. George and ten other churches. Hacked out of volcanic rock, these churches still are used today for worship. In creating St. George, workers chipped a 40-foot-deep trench into the rock, then carved the remaining block into the shape of a Greek cross. Painstakingly hollowed out, the churches were decorated with murals of biblical scenes, such as this one of Eve and the serpent in St. Mary at Qorqor.

West African Kingdoms

500 B.C. to A.D. 1650

While digging in his backyard one day in 1938, Isaiah Anozie, of the small town of Igbo-Ukwu in southeastern Nigeria, happened upon some strange metal objects. Unknowingly, he had stumbled upon the remains of a long-forgotten African culture that dated from the ninth century A.D.

Later excavations revealed bronze vessels inscribed with

Nok terra-cotta head, 10.25 in

Bronze shell, 8.1 in

filigree patterns, together with jewelry, furniture, headdresses, daggers, and swords. Decorative motifs included a menagerie of bronze beetles, grasshoppers, frogs, snakes, monkeys, elephants, and leopards. Nearby, a grave site contained a corpse richly arrayed in bronze crown, breastplate, and anklets. More than 100,000 glass beads also adorned this dignitary. Seated on a stool, he held a bronze staff or fan, topped with the figures of a horse and rider; at his feet lay ivory tusks and a bronze leopard skull.

Such chance discoveries characterize the archaeology of the forest cultures of Nigeria. Here, in the thick tropical woodland, undergrowth and trees obscure the telltale signs that might alert archaeologists to the presence of lost cultures. No written history existed here before Europeans arrived, and early European accounts seldom shed light on how people lived. Also, towns have occupied the same sites for many centuries. It is difficult to undertake archaeological excavations in places where people still live.

Despite these problems, Igbo-Ukwu and other Nigerian sites have revealed the existence of a number of rich cultures, such as those of Ife and Benin. But little remains of these peoples except their exquisite sculptures, chiefly in bronze and clay.

Beginning in 1944, workers in the tin mines of central Nigeria found hundreds of pieces of sculptured clay figures. These were produced by the Nok culture, so named after a nearby mining village. Nok sculpture is the earliest known in sub-Saharan Africa, with some pieces dating back to about 500 B.C. The art of the Nok people may prove to be ancestral to other local art traditions.

By the fourth century B.C., Nok farming communities occupied large areas in central and eastern Nigeria. Some 100 years earlier, iron artifacts had made their appearance, which suggests that the Nok people were among the first iron users in tropical Africa. Evidence indicates that the Nok culture ended around A.D. 200.

Four centuries later, a people known as the Yoruba established several city-states in the forests of southwestern Nigeria. The Yoruba kingdoms of Oyo, Ijebu, Ife, and Ketu were bound together by a common language and a complex religion based on the cult worship of hundreds of gods. By A.D. 1000, Ife

Nigerian Sculpture

Sculpture began to appear in the West African region of Nigeria around the fourth century B.C. Early pieces include a terra-cotta head from the Nok culture, possibly once part of a full figure. Nok farmers probably placed such figures in shrines in their newly cleared fields to ensure the land's fertility. Later West African cultures perfected metalworking skills. Around A.D. 900, artisans in the eastern Nigerian city of Igbo-Ukwu created a lost-wax bronze casting of a leopard perched upon

an intricately filigreed shell. Between the 12th and 15th centuries, the Ife culture brought this metalworking technique to a high art, casting numerous lifelike heads of their *onis*, or leaders, in bronze by using the lost-wax process. The meaning of the vertical striations

Life-size Ife bronze heads

remains uncertain; perhaps they represented ritual scarification or simply were used to soften the surface of the casting. Holes around the mouth and lower face probably held an artificial beard. The seated copper figure from the Nupe village of Tada, just north of Ife, is the only known example of a human figure in the style of the Ife heads. It may indicate commercial ties with Ife. Its sensual naturalism is rare in early African art. A lack of archaeological evidence still shrouds much of African prehistory. Scholars can only guess from the style of workmanship that the bronze figure of a hunter with his dog at his side and an antelope slung across

emerged as the cultural and commercial center of the region; it remains a holy place to the Yoruba people today. Ife's prosperity as a trading power enabled it to develop art for the royal court and to establish a number of cults and shrines.

In the early 20th century, German archaeologist Leo Frobenius's excavations brought Ife to the attention of Europeans for the first time. Frobenius heard of the wonders of Ife from a Yoruba sailor he met on the docks of Hamburg. The sailor told him that Ife was the center and origin of humankind and the world. The ruler of Ife, the *oni,* outranked other Yoruba kings and approved all coronations. The sailor also mentioned that "heads of ancestors turned to stone" were buried at Ife.

Upon his arrival at Ife in 1910, Frobenius found little to suggest that it was once the capital of a mighty empire. The city itself lay abandoned, ravaged by a long civil war. Yet, while visiting a nearby shrine, Frobenius discovered two pieces of terra-cotta embedded in the earth. Remarkably, they were finely wrought

pieces of a human face. With great excitement, he and his assistant sank shafts into the earth in a grove dedicated to Olokun, the Yoruba goddess of wealth and the sea. Eighteen feet beneath the surface, they found pottery and "exquisitely life-like terracotta heads, with clear-cut features and purity of style."

Since then, numerous heads have been discovered, many forged from bronze and representing Ife leaders. These are thought to have been funerary effigies. The realism and sophistication of the sculptures that he uncovered and the complexity of the Yoruba religion reminded Frobenius of classical Greece. With the typical Eurocentrism of his

Brass figure of Akan warrior, 4.25 in

Bronze figure of hunter, 14 in

Copper figure, Tada, 21.1 in

time, he declared that such a high culture must have originated in Europe. Ife, he decided, represented the last vestiges of the lost Greek colony of Atlantis. Despite Frobenius's fanciful, erroneous theories, his collections did acquaint the outside world with the remarkable art of Ife.

Europeans were far more familiar with the sculptures of the Benin culture than with those of Ife, because of contacts dating back to the 15th century. Extensive trading had begun with the Kingdom of Benin after the Portuguese first made

his shoulders comes from the lower Niger River region. Both the meaning and the date of this casting remain a mystery. However, the hunter is known to play an important role in African myth and song. The figure shows a masterly appreciation of the dynamic energy conveyed by deliberate distortion. The equally vigorous brass casting of a galloping Akan warrior comes from an area in the southern region of present-day Ghana where gold dust, the universal currency, was mined extensively until the 19th century. The figure probably served as a counterweight for measuring portions of gold dust in the possession of an Akan treasurer.

landfall in 1486. A wealthy mercantile power that may have borrowed many cultural traditions from the Ife people, Benin reached its pinnacle between the mid-15th and mid-17th centuries.

The Bini people of Benin lived in a collection of farms protected by walls and a ditch. Each clan paid tribute to a ruler, known as the *oba*. With the arrival of the Portuguese, the oba of Benin grew more powerful. He exercised a monopoly in foreign trade, particularly the slave trade; in addition, he demanded half of all proceeds from the sale of ivory obtained by hunters.

With this immense wealth, the obas established a number of artists' guilds that worked in bronze, brass, ivory, and wood. Metalworkers used the lost-wax process to create ceremonial busts and the plaques that covered the pillars of royal palaces, providing a symbolic chronicle of court life and pageantry. First, the subject was

Bronze flute player, 24.9 in

Detail from ivory salt cellar, 11.75 in

modeled in wax around a core of clay—and metal for big castings—then encased in layers of clay. A tubelike wax channel connected the model to a funnel opening. Firing the clay mold produced an exact impression and melted the wax, which was "lost" as it was poured out. Next, the mold was sealed in further layers of clay, with a crucible of metal fitted to the funnel opening, and heated. When the whole thing was upended, molten metal poured into the void left by the wax. Finally, after the metal hardened, the clay casing was smashed, the clay core reamed out, and the tubelike channel filed off.

Benin tradition claims that its artists learned metalworking from the Ife people. Even when the political power of the Ife declined, custom dictated that they receive the severed head of a Benin oba after he died. Ife bronzesmiths then created a commemorative head for placement in the ancestral shrine.

Around the turn of the 15th century, it is said, the sixth oba of Benin, Oguola, asked the oni of Ife if he would send an expert metalsmith

to teach Benin artisans how to craft these bronze memorial heads. The oni sent him the Ife master smelter Iguegha, whose memory is still honored by the bronzesmiths' guild in this region.

In coastal forest lands farther south—in southwestern Zaire and northern Angola—the Portuguese made contact in 1482 with the well-established Kingdom of Kongo. European knowledge of Kongo art dates from this time. It included intricately woven, plaited, and knotted textiles, as well as ivory carvings and funerary figures sculptured in stone to be placed on graves. Among the latter were idealized representations of rulers wearing a distinctive cap of office, and mother-and-child figures. Other Kongo art forms were sacred fetishes—wood figures often embedded with mirrors and nails.

Despite the discovery of exceptional sculptures and other artwork, archaeologists still know very little about the prehistoric cultures of the West African forest kingdoms. Aided by oral traditions, historians are beginning to fill in the picture.

Art of Benin

Sophisticated techniques of Benin metalworking are evident in a bronze plaque (opposite) that details the common ritual sacrifice of a cow. Hundreds of these plaques adorned the palace of the Benin oba, or king. Wherever he went, the all-powerful oba was accompanied by royal musicians. Benin metalsmiths immortalized one such performer, dressed in a leopard-skin kilt and playing an ivory flute. The wealth and power of the Benin kings grew in part from a lively trade with Portugal—which encouraged some Benin artisans to craft European subjects in their own traditional styles. This ivory salt cellar portrays two Portuguese dignitaries with their attendants.

Bronze plaque
from a Benin palace, 20 in

Jenne-jeno

250 B.C. to A.D. 1400

While reviewing aerial photographs of Mali's Niger Inland Delta in 1975, two American graduate students made an exciting discovery. Nearly two miles southeast of the thriving city of Djénné were the remnants of an ancient town, revealed by a series of unmistakably man-made mounds.

Susan and Roderick McIntosh of Rice University in Texas eagerly visited the site in 1977, finding the barren soil littered with beads, pieces of pottery, fragments of stone bracelets, and bits of corroded metal. In addition, they discovered numerous mud-brick house foundations and the remains of a massive city wall. As is frequently the case in archaeology, a little luck and a great deal of skill had converged at the right moment. Radiocarbon dating confirmed suspicions that this was the oldest known city in sub-Saharan Africa.

Jenne-jeno—ancient Jenne—first emerged in the third century B.C. as a tiny cluster of modest houses. By A.D. 800, the city had grown large enough to support perhaps 10,000 or more inhabitants and to serve as the center of trade and commerce in West Africa. The early date of the city contradicted prevailing theories that urban communities arose in West Africa only after the arrival of North African Arabs who traveled there in the ninth century to set up trading centers.

The central mound at the site measured more than one mile in circumference and rose to a height of 23 feet—beyond the reach of annual floods. Digging into it, the McIntoshes discovered evidence of 1,600 years of human habitation. The deepest—and consequently the oldest—layers revealed that the earliest inhabitants lived in circular houses fashioned from bent poles and woven reed mats daubed with mud. Pottery styles suggest that these early herders and fishermen migrated from the Sahara as the region gradually grew more arid.

In the second phase of life at

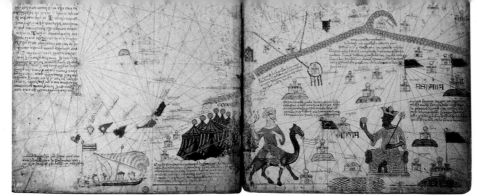
Detail from The Catalan World Atlas of the Year 1375

Jenne-jeno, between A.D. 300 and 800, the inhabitants used mud from the floodplain to build houses. Shapely red burial urns were discovered in this layer. The McIntoshes also found iron fishhooks and bracelets, as well as ceramic pots and bowls designed only for decorative use. Perhaps the most exciting find of all was a single gold earring, beautifully crafted from gold that was mined hundreds of miles to the south.

In the third period, from A.D. 800 onward, the archaeologists found terra-cotta statuettes and ceramic flasks, glass beads from North Africa, and an abundance of round and rectangular houses. It appeared that when one house fell, another quickly replaced it.

From these artifacts and observations, a picture of life at Jenne-jeno

began to emerge. The finely crafted pottery indicated a society sophisticated and affluent enough to support workers dedicated solely to making pottery. The craftsmanship evident in iron and copper work also suggested specialized artisans. To support these workshops, copper was brought from 600 miles away and iron ore from 30 miles—evidence of a powerful merchant culture.

Yet, the archaeologists asked, what could this area, which lacks natural resources, offer for these goods? They had only to look to modern Djénné, whose major export for the past six centuries has been food. The annual flood of the Niger River deposits rich silt on fields in which rice and other crops are grown. In the river, Nile perch and several kinds of catfish are plentiful.

Jenne-jeno perhaps provided the famed desert city of Timbuktu, 220 miles to the northeast, with home-grown food and gold traded from the south in exchange for salt, copper, and other goods from the caravan trade in the north. Goods traveled between the two cities in large canoes or were carried on foot.

Mysteriously, Jenne-jeno was abandoned around 1400; there was a move to the site of modern Djénné. Perhaps the old city symbolized pagan ways that displeased the new Muslim elite. Fortunes shifted, and Timbuktu bloomed as the center of trade and Islamic culture in the Mali Empire.

Three-headed figure

Niger River Traders

The great mosque in Djénné, Mali (opposite), dates back to the 14th century, though the mud walls have needed regular repair. Protruding studs provide footholds for workmen. Near Djénné, archaeologists have unearthed evidence of a thriving ancient culture at the city of Jenne-jeno. Terra-cotta statuettes found in the area, such as this enigmatic, three-headed figure, may have had religious significance. Snakes wrapped around some figures perhaps relate to origin myths. By the 14th century, neighboring Timbuktu was a wealthy trading post. European audiences reveled in Timbuktu's fabled riches, as shown in a Spanish map of 1375 portraying King Mansa Musa holding up a large nugget of gold.

Figure with snake around neck and arm

Figure with snake around torso

Great Zimbabwe

A.D. 1200 to 1550

In the late 19th century, word spread of vast stone ruins rising in the grassy highlands of present-day Zimbabwe in southeast Africa. This site, now known as Great Zimbabwe, was once the capital of an African state that stretched west from the Indian Ocean to the Kalahari Desert and five hundred miles south from the Zambezi River.

In 1871, German geologist Karl Mauch visited Great Zimbabwe and viewed the monumental stairways and columns topped with soapstone carvings of unique birdlike figures. Inspired by fanciful accounts passed down from Portuguese chronicles, he attributed the buildings to the Queen of Sheba.

The complex, covering an area of 100 acres, includes a hilltop structure containing many rooms and cut by a maze of passageways. In the valley below, an elliptical building, its outer wall surmounted by a chevron frieze, encloses a mysterious conical tower with a solid core. About a million blocks form the outer wall. None of the stonework was cemented with mortar, and much of it shows sophisticated masonry techniques.

Great Zimbabwe sits on the southeastern edge of a great granite plateau, averaging between 3,000 and 5,000 feet in height. Surrounded by inhospitable land, the plateau is fertile and mineral-rich, the beneficiary of moist trade winds that blow in from the Indian Ocean. The Shona culture may have developed here. Predecessors of the Shona people are thought to have built Great Zimbabwe and some 200 other sites scattered across the plateau—smaller zimbabwes. The word "zimbabwe" probably comes from the Shona words for "venerated house" or "house of stone" and is still used to describe a chief's dwelling or grave. Zimbabwe was the name chosen by the African nation when it shed its colonial name of Rhodesia in 1980.

Mauch was followed to Great Zimbabwe by a string of adventurers and amateur archaeologists. Employees of the colonial administration of Cecil Rhodes, who founded Rhodesia, performed often destructive excavations, muddying the waters for later archaeologists and looting gold artifacts and other treasures.

Excavations by David Randall-MacIver, in 1905, and Gertrude Caton-Thompson, who made careful studies in 1929, gradually shed light on this mysterious site. An extensive survey was conducted by Peter Garlake in the 1960s. Through radiocarbon dating and other procedures—such as cross-dating native objects with Chinese, Persian, and Arab imports found with them—a chronology was compiled.

The fertile grasslands probably attracted Bantu-speaking farmers to this region in the fourth century A.D. The Shona people who eventually settled here used iron hoes to cultivate sorghum and millet. By the 11th century, the time of the first permanent settlement at Great Zimbabwe, herds of long-horned cattle had become a symbol of prestige and power. Miniature cow figurines and evidence of ceremonial burial of cattle horns underscore the economic and social importance of cattle.

In addition, gold was mined locally in small veins and panned in rivers. By the 14th century, Great Zimbabwe, strategically positioned near the head of the Sabi River Valley, controlled much of the gold trade passing from regional goldfields to the east coast for export to Arabia, India, and elsewhere. These riches enabled rulers to muster the large

Curved stairway

labor force and specialized stonemasons needed to build the elaborate stone structures.

Great Zimbabwe became a center for both sacred ritual and industry. Here gold, copper, and iron were fashioned into a variety of objects. A cache of iron hoes was found, together with copper ingots and jewelry, gold wire and beads, and thin sheets of gold for covering wood carvings. Craft items, gold, and ivory were traded for foreign items ranging from Chinese celadon to engraved and enameled Syrian glass.

By the mid-15th century, Great Zimbabwe was in decline. This may have been the result of a dynastic dispute, or perhaps intensive farming and grazing exhausted the soil. The abandoned ruins remained sacred to later generations of Shona.

Heritage of a Nation

Stone ruins cluster at the heart of Great Zimbabwe (below), site of a southeast African culture that thrived between the 13th and 15th centuries. Its most prominent feature, an elliptical building now known as the Great Enclosure, has walls as tall as 32 feet and was built without the use of mortar. Archaeologists believe that the structure served not as a fortification but as a shelter and symbol of the power of the ruling elite, who controlled a lucrative foreign trade in local gold. The term "zimbabwe" probably comes from the Shona words for the residence of a leader. Centuries of experience in stonework at Great Zimbabwe are evidenced in the fluid lines and originality of this curved stairway

built into a wall's thickness. Skilled masons worked with the native rock, a type of granite that fractures easily into cubelike blocks, and incorporated chevron-patterned friezes and other design details into their work. Craftsmen fashioned from soapstone seven birdlike figures that stand on columns. Sporting sturdy legs and toes instead of claws, these stylized figures probably represented revered ancestors or gods. Today, one such figure is the symbol of the modern nation of Zimbabwe.

Soapstone birdlike figure, 12 in

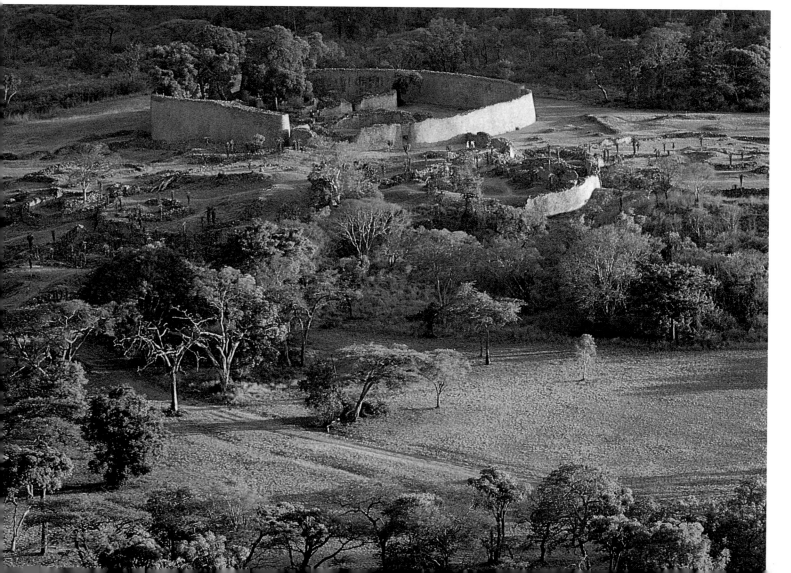

Gold platelets, Afghanistan, 1st century A.D., about 0.5 in square

Metal Ages

For some 2.5 million years early humans looked to stone as the underpinning of material life. Stonework, the first true technology, provided humankind with tools, weapons, amulets, and likenesses of gods and goddesses. Then, about 11,000 years ago, people in the Middle East began working other natural substances—gold, silver, and copper—and the Stone Age gave way to the Metal Ages.

Today, ancient metallurgy is an important facet of archaeological research. More durable than textiles, pottery, or other relics, metalwork records technological advances. Consequently, archaeologists have designated broad eras of human development as the Copper, Bronze, and Iron Ages. These "ages" occurred at different times in different areas, and not all civilizations proceeded through them in the same fashion. In spite of such variables, the Metal Ages chronology serves as a useful dating tool. In 1991, for example, an ax discovered near a body high in the Alps helped date the find to the European Copper Age.

Gold also caught the attention of early peoples. Found free in nature, in streambeds and hillsides, it is virtually indestructible and superbly malleable, as evidenced by the 2,000-year-old stamped platelets shown at left. Exactly when the first nugget was cold-hammered is unknown, but the oldest significant trove of gold artifacts dates from before 4000 B.C. It was discovered in 1972 by a tractor operator digging a trench in Varna, Bulgaria. The grave site he uncovered predated the major hoards of the Middle East by several centuries. And the find reinforced an

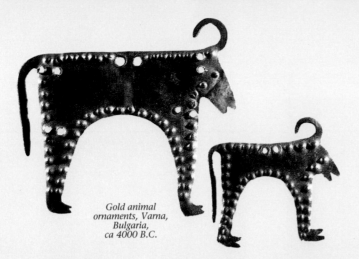

Gold animal
ornaments, Varna,
Bulgaria,
ca 4000 B.C.

Sumerian gold
helmet, Ur,
3rd millennium B.C.

idea that has recently gained prominence among archaeologists: that metal technologies often sprang up independently of one another in various parts of the earth.

Finds of gold and silver often help substantiate the stuff of legend. When the British archaeologist Sir Leonard Woolley began uncovering tombs of Sumerian royalty in 1927, he found elaborate gold headdresses, jewelry, and other treasures, which helped prove that the legendary First Dynasty of Ur had been a reality. The objects also indicated that by the third millennium B.C. most of the goldworking techniques used today were already known.

Several hundred years later, during Egypt's Middle and New Kingdoms, goldsmithing reached unmatched heights. The Egyptians called gold the "body of the gods," and they considered their stewardship of it a sacred trust. Using criminal and captive labor, they worked a chain of a hundred mines in the mountains of Nubia. Their master smiths then turned the gold into pieces fit for the gods, which their pharaohs were considered to be.

Because Egypt's pharaohs were entombed with a wealth

Viking mold
with silver
castings, 10th
century A.D.

Gold and Silver

Worth far more than their weight in gold, a pair of horned animals (upper) came from the earliest trove of gold yet discovered—6,000-year-old graves found outside Varna, Bulgaria. Early metallurgists there may have links to the fabled Thracian smiths who inhabited the same region 3,000 years later, creating such masterworks as an elegant eight-inch stallion (opposite). Also master craftsmen, Sumerian goldsmiths could work a 110-pound sheet of gold into a ceremonial helmet enlivened with repoussé hair and furnished with earholes. Providing their own telling details, the inscriptions on ancient coins often feature the crops or concerns of the societies that minted them. Metal artifacts help trace the spread of religions as well, as in these Viking pendants and a stone mold depicting both the hammer of Thor—the god of

thunder—and the Christian cross. Golden burial gloves found in a Chimu grave attest to the wealth of the New World. According to some estimates, more than half of all the gold and silver ever mined came from the corridor stretching from Mexico to Peru. Gold-hungry conquistadores arrived in the New World in the 16th century, seeking the riches of the Aztec, the Inca, and neighboring peoples. Today, little remains of their sophisticated metalwork, as the Spaniards melted down most of the artifacts. Rapacious adventurer Francisco Pizarro exacted a ransom of 24 tons of gold and silver for the life of Inca ruler Atahuallpa. With the treasure firmly in hand, Pizarro ordered the king publicly strangled.

Chimu gold
gloves, Andes,
about 21 in

*Gold coin,
Etruria*

*Silver "barley" coin,
Metapontum, Italy,
5th century B.C.*

of gold objects, most of their graves were plundered long ago. In 1922, however, British archaeologist Howard Carter discovered the virtually intact tomb of Tutankhamun. Desert sands and rubble had obscured the entrance to the boy-king's burial chamber, thus saving for posterity the gold-sheathed wooden throne and other exquisite furnishings that have come to epitomize Egypt's golden age.

Another fabled kingdom of gold, that of Croesus, King of Lydia from 560 to 546 B.C., is credited with minting the first gold coins of guaranteed value. Located in present-day Turkey, Lydia was renowned for the alluvial gold in its Pactolus River. The legendary King Midas was said to have given the river its golden character when he bathed in it to rid himself of a blessing that had turned into a curse—the power to turn objects into gold.

Gold and silver have continued to be both blessing and curse to humankind. The desire for the metals helped fuel the conquests of Alexander the Great, as well as the spread of the Roman Empire. By the second

*Silver and gold stallion,
Bulgaria*

Copper raven,
Ohio,
300 B.C.-A.D.
500

century A.D., every gold and silver mine known to the ancient world lay under Rome's control.

Fourteen hundred years later, the search for El Dorado drew Spanish adventurers to the New World. Though the Gilded Man remained only a dream, explorers did encounter the magnificent cultures of the Maya, Aztec, and Inca. The Inca's predecessors in the Andes had practiced goldsmithing since about 1500 B.C. Among the first cultures to work platinum, Andean people in what is now Colombia perfected a technique for laminating gold with platinum by the first century B.C. Though their knowledge of precious metals was extensive, and they also used copper and bronze, New World peoples remained ignorant of ironworking techniques until Europeans arrived.

Copper tools,
Kalibangan,
India,
2500 B.C.

Copper tool,
Danube Basin,
ca 4500 B.C.

While the quest for gold and silver has changed the political face of the earth, the development of more utilitarian metals has eased everyday life.

People in the Middle East began to make the transition from hunter-gatherer societies to agricultural communities about 11,000 years ago. As life became more settled, people produced more material goods. Among these were the metal objects that would usher in the Copper Age.

Like gold, copper can be found free in nature and is easily worked by cold-hammering. Also like gold, copper was first used for ornament or display. The oldest piece of worked copper ever found is an 11,500-year-old pendant from the Shanidar cave in northeastern Iraq. The first simple tools made from the metal appeared in the Middle East around 9,000 years

ago. Soon after, people realized that they could subject copper-bearing ores to high heat and extract the metal. No longer would they be limited to random finds of pure deposits. Archaeologists speculate that potters firing copper oxides in their kilns may have chanced upon the techniques for smelting. Crucibles found at the sites of Sialk and Tal-i-Iblis, near the copper-rich Zagros Mountains in Iran, attest to early smelting, a pro-

Sumerian copper cudgel, Luristan, ca 2450 B.C.

cess that requires temperatures greater than 1500°F and a closed, oxygen-starved furnace.

Smelting in turn led to casting, and early smiths of the same period began pouring molten copper into stone molds to make weapons, vessels, and tools. About 3200 B.C., smiths in Elam and Mesopotamia developed lost-wax casting, a technique in which molten metal is

Copper and Bronze

The trail of copper leads to sites throughout the Old and New Worlds. Tools uncovered in the Danube Basin date from the seventh millennium B.C., indicating that coppersmithing techniques developed independently in central Europe, even as they were developing in the Middle East. On the Indian subcontinent, simple copper weapons and tools from Kalibangan, in the Indus Valley region, bear the undeciphered script of the Harappan civilization, whose smiths were the earliest metallurgists in southern Asia. In Sumer, metalworkers used the lost-

wax technique to create the intricate designs on this copper cudgel. In a 4,000-year-old Sumerian text, copper debates silver, accusing the precious metal of impracticality. "Like a god, you don't put your hands to useful work," copper rails at silver. As useful as copper was, it too was often put to decorative purposes. A pearl-eyed copper raven typifies the hammered metalwork of the Hopewell people of the Ohio River Valley. New World metallurgy began about 1500 B.C. in the central Andes, where metal implements were used in an early form of brain surgery. A socketed bronze spearpoint exemplifies the skills of

ancient craftsmen in Southeast Asia. The first metal to be worked in this region, bronze appeared on Thailand's Khorat Plateau around 2000 B.C. Smiths there quickly mastered smelting, alloying, and casting techniques, producing sophisticated vessels and weaponry. Over time, bronze weapons changed the face of warfare throughout the world. Blades of bronze maintained a killing edge, while bronze body armor, shields, and helmets offered new protection. As late as the 15th century A.D., Islam's formidable Mamluk slave-soldiers carried into battle bronze axes like this one, incised with the blazon of a

poured into a void left in a clay mold by a wax model that had been melted earlier and drained out. This innovation allowed smiths to create more intricate designs.

Copper became a prized commodity, and archaeological evidence indicates that trade routes formed between copper-rich mountainous areas and the early cities of the Fertile Crescent. The ancient name of the Euphrates River, a vital corridor for this trade, actually meant River of Copper.

Most early copper objects were owned by the wealthy or by the state. Archaeologists analyzing a cache of fourth-millennium B.C. copper tools found near the Dead Sea speculate that they were "issued to agricultural workers seasonally and recalled when necessary for checking and repair by a central authority. Such tools were not only functional, but also repositories of wealth."

By the middle of the second millennium, the techniques of coppersmithing had spread across Europe, carried in part by an itinerant group of merchants, tinkers, and potters called the Beaker People for the distinctive pottery they left behind. But metalsmiths in the Middle East remained far ahead of their European counterparts. Before 4000 B.C., they were casting the first bronzes from a natural alloy of copper and arsenic. Pure copper does not cast well. Bubbles form, resulting in a porous product. Copper-arsenic bronze, however, is less porous and therefore stronger; but fumes produced during casting can be deadly. At some point, early metalsmiths replaced arsenic with tin to create an alloy that would reshape the world. Copper-tin bronzes made more durable tools and formidable weapons, gave rise to new artistic traditions, and led to elaborate trading networks.

The height of European bronze making occurred from about 1500 to 1200 B.C. In the Aegean, the seafaring Mycenaeans established a wide trading network and asserted hegemony over the region. Using

Mamluk bronze ax, 15th century A.D.

Bronze spearpoint, Southeast Asia, ca 2000 B.C.

Greek bronze figurine of helmet maker, 8th-7th century B.C.

sultan. Extolling the craft of metalworking, a Greek figurine depicts a smith at work on a Corinthian-style bronze helmet. Covering the entire head, these helmets were hammered from a single piece of bronze. The Thracians, enemies of the Greeks, admired the helmet design and adapted it to their own uses. Fortified by bronze armor and weapons, Greek hoplite soldiers, attacking in phalanx formation, dominated Mediterranean battlefields for almost 500 years.

Thracian bronze helmet, 6th century B.C.

149

bronze armor and weapons, their leaders inspired the epics of Homer. In the 1870s, Homer's heroes became more than legends when archaeologist Heinrich Schliemann uncovered the sites of Troy and Mycenae, and the wealth of a warrior elite.

The record of East Asia's movement into the Metal Ages is cloudy. About 2000 B.C., peoples of the Khorat Plateau of present-day Thailand, the Red River region of Vietnam, and the North China Plain appear to have moved directly from the Stone Age into the Bronze Age. China's Shang dynasty produced some of the world's most sophisticated bronzes. Shang smiths perfected techniques that achieved very hot temperatures. They also developed a casting method in which parts of an object were cast sep-

arately and then joined into one piece.

Meanwhile, villagers in Southeast Asia began using lost-wax casting to fashion elaborate containers. Now called Dong Son drums, for the Vietnamese village where they were first found, these bronzes were traded throughout Southeast Asia.

About 1500 B.C., one of civilization's most important discoveries was made: how to work iron. The Hittites of Anatolia may have been the first ironmasters and could have spread the technology to surrounding cultures. Unlike copper and tin, iron ore is abundant in nature. Once iron-working was mastered, iron tools quickly became commonplace.

In the first millennium B.C., the Hallstatt Celts of central

Bronze horse and wagon towing gilded sun, Denmark, ca 1400 B.C.

Akkadian bronze head, Nineveh, 2350-2150 B.C.

Bronze head, Benin, Africa, 16th century A.D.

Bronze and Iron

Emboldened by bronze, a noble visage presumed to be that of Naram-Sin of Akkad survived 43 centuries before being uncovered amid the ruins of Nineveh. His grandfather Sargon founded the first Mesopotamian empire.

From West Africa the elegant bust of a queen mother of Benin, crowned by a peaked headdress and wearing a stylized choker of beads, bespeaks that culture's talent for working bronze. Benin metalsmiths may have learned their craft from neighboring Ife metalworkers around 1400 A.D. In the 16th century, trade with

Portugal gave the Kingdom of Benin greater access to metals. Using lost-wax casting, Benin smiths created their renowned art primarily to depict rituals performed at the court of their sacred king. A diminutive bronze horse pulling a gilded sun probably depicts a ritual surrounding the solar fertility cult of prehistoric Denmark. Known as the "sun-chariot," the piece came to light in 1902 when a Danish peat bog was plowed. Such bogs served as sacred sites, where devotees propitiated their gods by throwing gold and bronze treasures, including lurs— magnificent golden horns—into the murky waters. With the arrival of metal technology around 1500 B.C., the sun and fire gained increasing spiritual status. The horse, a powerful

Europe began moving west, spreading the knowledge of ironworking as they went. Their master smiths fashioned plowshares, tire rims, and swords from the metal. It would be 1,500 years before the technology crossed the Atlantic to the Americas.

China entered the Iron Age about 600 B.C., when Zhou dynasty smiths learned to smelt iron. By the second century A.D., the Chinese had perfected what they called the "thousand refinings" technique, which allowed them to forge iron into steel.

In Africa, the Metal Ages appear to have begun in earnest with iron. Furnace remains and slag heaps from Meroë in the Kingdom of Kush and from West Africa's Nok Valley date from the first millennium B.C.

The mastery of metals was a seminal event for almost all of the world's cultures. The Dogon people of West Africa trace their origins to a mythical blacksmith who pilfered a piece of the sun from the celestial forge and escaped the angry gods by sliding down a rainbow. He also brought back seeds that spilled across the earth, thus sowing the almost magical knowledge of metallurgy.

new means of transport, also assumed religious significance. To the fractious and pagan Celts, whose fortified

towns dotted the European landscape during the first millennium B.C., the horse was a divine creature, revered for its prowess in battle. Fine craftsmen, the Celtic metalsmiths often molded images of the animal as adornments. This small bronze horse's head may have ornamented a warrior's chariot. Another warlike group, the Vikings of Scandinavia, staged their raids from the sea, relying on expertly built boats to carry them long distances. Iron rivets from a Viking boat discovered near Ellesmere Island indicate that the far-ranging Norse landed in Arctic Canada hundreds of years before other Europeans arrived. A testament to the propitious marriage of metals and

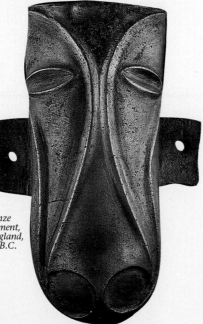

Celtic bronze chariot ornament, Yorkshire, England, 1st century B.C.

Ax with bronze and gold mount, iron blade, Syria, ca 1400-1300 B.C.

warfare, this battle-ax unearthed at Ras Shamra in Syria features a blade of iron and a socketed bronze mount decorated with gold inlay and open-mouthed animal figures.

Viking iron rivets, Canada, ca 12th-14th century A.D.

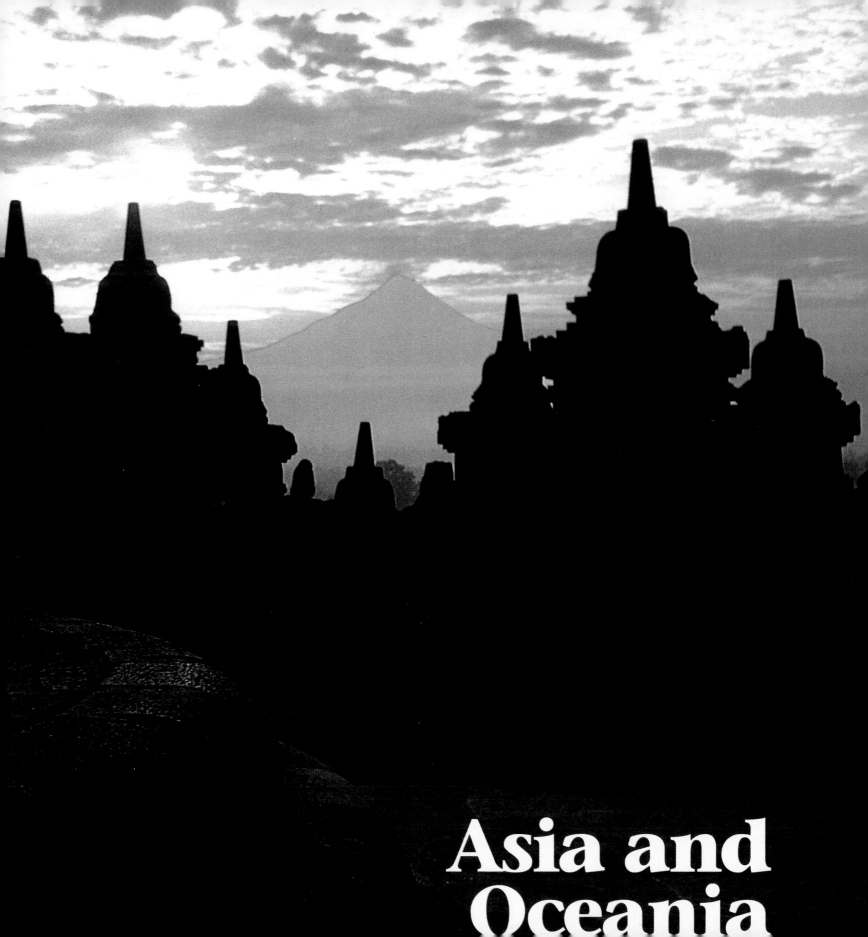

Asia and Oceania

PERSIA

SUMER

The Indian Subcontinent

6000 B.C. to A.D. 1500

As early as 6000 B.C., farmers were growing barley and wheat on the western margins of the Indus River Valley, today part of Pakistan. These agricultural settlements provided the basis for the civilization that emerged in the Indus Valley around 2500 B.C. By 1500 B.C., about the time that Aryan tribes began entering the Indian subcontinent from the northwest, the Indus civilization had collapsed.

For the next thousand years Indian history is veiled in obscurity. Virtually no monuments or archaeological remains have come to light. By 600 B.C. the pastoral Aryans had settled in agricultural communities. Rudiments of the Indian caste system had come into existence, dividing society into hereditary classes ranging from priests to outcasts. Elaborate rituals replaced the worship of nature gods. By the mid-sixth century B.C., when Buddhism's founder was born, Hinduism had developed its basic concepts, such as a belief in reincarnation regulated by one's accumulation of good and bad deeds.

Buddhism inspired an artistic flowering, which was abetted by the emperor Ashoka, who ruled in the third century B.C. After Ashoka's reign, new waves of foreigners invaded India from the northwest. Greeks from Bactria, Parthians from Persia, and Scythians and Kushans from Central Asia carved out kingdoms that influenced the culture of the north. The south, however, was isolated from the turmoil.

Under the Guptas, who forged an empire in the north from A.D. 320 to 467, art, literature, science, and philosophy flourished, becoming a model for later generations. This period saw a revival of Hinduism, although Buddhism inspired some of the greatest Gupta art.

After the Guptas, invaders from Central Asia ushered in another turbulent period in the north, a region divided into petty kingdoms ruled by Rajput warriors. In the south and east, where long-lived dynasties thrived for hundreds of years, Hinduism and its temples became the focus of cultural life until most of India fell to Muslim conquest in the 14th century.

PRECEDING PAGES: At Borobudur, the world's largest Buddhist monument, in Java, Indonesia, a stone Buddha sits amid ancient bell-shaped stupas.

ARA

BACTRIA

HINDU KUSH

K U S H A N

Indus

Harappa

Mohenjo Daro

H I M A L A Y A

Mathura

Ganges

GANGES PLAIN

Sarnath

Khajuraho

Lothal

Sanchi

Ajanta

I N D I A

Konarak

BIAN SEA

BAY

OF

BENGAL

Thanjavur

Anuradhapura

Sigiriya

Polonnaruva

Sri Lanka

● Ancient and modern town site

◆ Archaeological site only

0   400 mi

0   600 km

155

Indus Valley

2400 to 1500 B.C.

Bronze dancer, 4 in

More than four thousand years ago, one of the mysterious peoples of antiquity forged a great civilization in the Indus Valley in what is now Pakistan. Its two major cities, Mohenjo Daro and Harappa, about 400 miles apart, emerged full-blown, with no evidence in their stratified layers for their beginnings and development.

Masterworks of town planning, they both had crisscrossing straight streets laid out on a grid. Urban planners also provided the cities with indoor wells and baths and an elaborate public sanitation system, whose earthenware pipes discharged wastes from homes into brick sewers beneath the streets.

The number of well-built brick houses suggests a strong middle class—probably merchants who traded in wheat, barley, dates, melons, and cotton. Barrack-like structures suggest that the population also included slaves or near-slave workers.

The Indus, or Harappan, civilization left behind no royal tombs, no palaces, and no temples, although scholars believe the Great Bath at

Mohenjo Daro, 2nd millennium B.C., topped by ruins of a 2nd-century A.D. stupa

Mohenjo Daro may have had a religious function, perhaps a precursor of the ritual ablutions of later Hinduism. Other evidence of religious life consists of family altars, terra-cotta goddess figurines, and phallic or circular stones that may have symbolic significance.

Beautifully carved seals, made chiefly of steatite and one to two inches square, are considered the outstanding achievement of Indus artists. Most seals have animal motifs depicted with remarkable realism. Possibly used in commerce, these seals have been unearthed by the thousand in the Indus Valley. They have also turned up in ancient cities of Sumer, enabling scholars to give a rough date to the Indus civilization.

Steatite seals, about 1 in square

Unlike the Sumerians and the Egyptians, the Indus people left only a scant written record, and it remains undeciphered. The inscriptions, mostly on the seals and their impressions, contain about 400 symbols, but scholars have few clues to their meaning. The seals probably bear the names of the owners and identify their wares.

No one suspected the existence of this civilization until Sir John Marshall began his excavations in 1921. Since then, archaeologists have found evidence for about 300 communities, including the seaport of Lothal.

Scholars are puzzled by the mysterious demise of the two cities. Mohenjo Daro shows a progressive deterioration. Skeletons scattered in the streets during its final stage, when buildings were mere hovels, suggest that the final blow to the city was delivered by invaders—perhaps the Aryans, who entered the Indian subcontinent about 1500 B.C. On the other hand, Harappa shows no sign of a slow decline or violent ending. The city was just abandoned.

Art and Everyday Items

Striking a saucy pose, a bronze figurine of a dancing girl from Mohenjo Daro wears only a necklace and bangles. She is among the best-known works of art from the Harappan culture. Above a network of excavated streets in Mohenjo Daro's residential district stands the walled upper town that contained the city's public buildings. Experts estimate the city's population at some 40,000. A Buddhist shrine, built in the second century A.D., towers over the citadel's brick structures, which included a huge granary, an assembly hall, and a public bath. The systematic layout of the streets and the uniformity of the two major centers, Mohenjo Daro and Harappa—which are some 400 miles apart—imply that a strong central authority regulated life and organized a public workforce. The extensive use of baked brick masonry required immense outlays of labor and fuel. Square seals incised with intricately carved animals

display symbols of the still undeciphered Harappan script. One seal depicts a human figure in a yogalike pose. A playful terra-cotta pig may have served as a toy. Harappan craftsmen also used clay to make fine wheel-turned pottery. This bearded figure carved in steatite bears the proud countenance of a priest or ruler. Found in the ruins of Mohenjo Daro's residential section, the stylized bust shows a formality also characteristic of Sumerian sculpture. The flourishing trade with Sumer may explain some of the similarities between the Indus and Mesopotamian civilizations.

Steatite bust, 7 in

Terra-cotta pig, 3.75 in

East gateway of the Great Stupa, Sanchi

Buddhist Legacy

550 B.C. to A.D. 1000

The founder of Buddhism, Siddhartha Gautama, was born into a royal family in the mid-sixth century B.C. in the Himalayan foothills. He renounced a worldly life at the age of 29, seeking salvation as a mendicant and ascetic. He attained enlightenment at 35, and for the next 45 years he traveled through northern India, preaching a code of behavior called the Eightfold Path. He became known to his followers as the Buddha, or the Enlightened One. His doctrines showed the way to escape a cycle of rebirths and to thereby end suffering and achieve salvation.

Although Buddha made no claim to divinity, he came to be regarded as a god by many of his followers. According to tradition, relics, such as strands of his hair and ashes from his funeral pyre, were interred in large, dome-shaped shrines called stupas. In later years, stupas were built to contain relics of other revered Buddhists or religious texts.

When the emperor Ashoka converted to Buddhism about 260 B.C., his missionary efforts popularized the faith throughout his realm and beyond. His edicts, engraved on rocks and on freestanding stone pillars, are among the earliest monuments of Buddhism and contain some of the earliest Indian writing. Of some 30 original monoliths, about a third survive. They are the oldest major archaeological relics after those of the Indus Valley civilization. Other Buddhist monuments include monasteries and sanctuaries hewn out of rock.

In early Buddhist art there were no images of Buddha. He was represented by symbols such as a footprint; a wheel, representing his teaching; and the *bodhi,* or bo, tree, under which Buddha found enlightenment. The Buddha figure was first produced about A.D. 100, appearing in Gandharan sculpture in northwestern India, where Greco-Roman influence was strong, and in the more indigenous school of art that evolved on the Ganges Plain around the city of Mathura.

Although Buddhism began to decline during the Gupta dynasty, which began in A.D. 320, art continued to be commissioned for Buddhist monasteries, resulting in such masterpieces as the Ajanta cave murals. Gradually Hinduism reasserted its hold over the population. By the time Muslim conquerors began their raids into India around A.D. 1000, Buddhism had all but disappeared from the land of its birth.

Inspired by Faith

Richly carved gateway (opposite) to the Great Stupa at Sanchi in central India records episodes from the Buddha's life. Four such ornate toranas, 34 feet high, lead to the massive masonry shrine, built to house a relic of the

Buddha. A tiered umbrella, symbol of royalty, crowns the monument. A colossal figure of a reclining Buddha in cave 26 at Ajanta depicts the Master's death and his entry into nirvana, a state of bliss. Thirty caves were quarried out of a rock scarp at Ajanta, in western India, to create

monasteries and sanctuaries. In an Ajanta mural, a celestial nymph wears jewels and finery that illustrate the opulence of the Gupta age. Four lions crown one of the pillars erected by the emperor Ashoka to promulgate his faith. Found in 1904, the capital has become a symbol of India.

Reclining Buddha, Ajanta, length 23 ft

Lion capital, Sarnath, 6.8 ft

Mural of celestial nymphs, Ajanta

Hindu Revival

A.D. 600 to 1300

The seventh century marks the beginning of a Hindu renaissance, and for the next 700 years Hinduism was the major source of inspiration for Indian art. During this era, usually referred to as the Hindu medieval period, temples became principal centers of artistic activity. Architecture and sculpture, as well as dance and literature, reflected the upsurge of faith and devotion to the myriad gods of the Hindu pantheon.

However, two deities in their many guises, or aspects, grew in importance and were venerated above all others. Vishnu, the preserver and protector, who had descended to earth in various incarnations, shared power with Shiva, god of destruction and restorer of life. Scholars detect in Shiva aspects of a god of the earlier Indus civilization, as well as traits of the wrathful god Rudra of the early Vedic hymns. By the medieval period, most Hindus had become devotees of either Shiva or Vishnu.

As the deities were anthropomorphized, their images became objects of worship, replacing the fire altars of the early Aryans. By medieval times, temples had become residences and shrines of the gods. Their images were attended by a powerful Brahman priesthood, who bathed and anointed the idols and presented them with offerings of flowers and fruit.

Politically, India was divided into numerous warring kingdoms, ruled by a succession of dynasties who enhanced their prestige by building temples and patronizing the arts. In the north the major powers were the Palas and the Pallavas. The Chalukyas dominated the central region. In the south the Cholas emerged triumphant around A.D. 900 after a long struggle for power.

Less than a hundred years later, the Chola kings, who were prolific builders, erected a great temple at Thanjavur, its highly decorated towers rising to a height of 190 feet. This structure, considered by many a triumph of southern Indian architecture, established the artistic reputation of the Cholas.

This style continued to evolve in the south, where Islam had little influence, until the time of Muslim conquest in the 14th century. In the north, the vigor of Hindu culture had been undermined earlier by Turkish conquerors, who began to set up Muslim states in the 13th century. Their soldiers destroyed many temples of the "infidels." Other centers, such as the one at Khajuraho, were deserted for centuries and rediscovered only in the 1800s.

Bronze Shiva, Chola period

Apsara, *Parshvanatha Temple, Khajuraho*

Temples and Gods

Images of the gods and their consorts crowd the central tower (left) that rises above the shrine of the Kandariya Mahadeva Temple at Khajuraho, an abandoned Hindu religious complex in north-central India. A total of 85 temples, built between A.D. 950 and 1050, once stood at the site, but only a quarter of them survive. A voluptuous apsara, *who dances and sings in heaven, adorns one of these, a Jain temple built in Hindu style. The Jain religion, which worships some of the same gods as Hinduism, received patronage from the city's tolerant royalty. In eastern India, guardian creatures flank the stairway to the 13th-century Temple of the Sun at Konarak. The god Shiva as Nataraja, Lord of the Cosmic Dance, tramples a dwarf representing evil in a tenth-century bronze from the Chola period in south India. His rear hands carry the flame of destruction and the drum of creation, symbolizing the cosmic cycle of death and rebirth.*

Sri Lanka

250 B.C. to A.D. 1300

Buddhism shaped the ancient civilization of Sri Lanka from the time the Indian emperor Ashoka sent missionaries to the island in the third century B.C. Following his conversion, King Devanampiya Tissa and succeeding Sinhalese monarchs expressed their

invaders from southern India overran the island. One of the largest archaeological sites in the world, sprawling over about 25 square miles, the ancient city had more than 3,000 monastic structures.

Little remains of these buildings and palaces, which were constructed largely of wood, but archaeologists have uncovered stone platforms, sculptured guard stones, columns, and finely carved, semicircular "moonstones." The latter have been found at the bottom of stairways leading to temples or shrines.

Sinhalese rulers moved the seat of government to Polonnaruva, which had intermittently been the capital. The fortified city, with its towering buildings of durable brick, is better preserved than Anuradhapura.

Reservoirs and remnants of canals, relics of a sophisticated irrigation system found all over the island, attest to the engineering skills of the Sinhalese. But the giant statues of Buddha, hewn from a granite cliff, perhaps best convey the splendor and spiritual vitality of this ancient civilization.

Stone statues, Gal Vihara, Polonnaruva

religious zeal and sought to earn merit for their future lives by building monasteries and massive, domed shrines that embellished the capital of Anuradhapura. These shrines, called dagobas, were dazzling white with their coating of plaster. Like their stupa counterparts in India, they contained sacred relics.

Monumental dagobas, some taller than Menkaure's pyramid at Giza in Egypt, dominate Anuradhapura—center of the island's Buddhist civilization until the 11th century, with brief interruptions when

Huge stone troughs that held the daily rations of rice for thousands of monks have also survived. Rows of square-cut pillars are vestiges of the fabled Brazen Palace, which housed several hundred monks and held a great pillared assembly hall. A fifth-century chronicle describes the building, with perhaps some exaggeration, as having nine stories, a copper roof, and "pillars consisting of precious stones, on which were figures of lions, tigers, and...shapes of goddesses."

In the 11th century, the Buddhist

Fortress-palace, Sigiriya

Royal Capitals

Isolated stronghold of Sigiriya, crowned with palaces, temples, and gardens, provided either a refuge or a retreat for King Kassapa I, who reigned from A.D. 477 to 495. According to ancient chronicles, Kassapa fled to this 600-foot citadel fearing reprisal for usurping his brother's throne. Some scholars believe the record is biased and maintain the king sought to create a paradise retreat. Sigiriya's glory was brief; the city was abandoned when its founder was killed. Today its fame resides in its cliff paintings of jeweled celestial nymphs, shown rising from clouds. Several hundred of these figures once adorned the western face of the rocky outcrop, but only 18 survive. At Polonnaruva, a majestic statue of a reclining Buddha reflects the glowing faith of the kings who made this city their capital in the 11th century. Recent scholarship suggests that the upright figure may be a monk, perhaps the Buddha's disciple. The prosperous walled city also included hospitals, palaces, parks, and artificial lakes.

Cliff painting of celestial nymphs, Sigiriya

Southeast Asia

5000 B.C. to A.D. 1500

Magnificent ruins of cities and shrines tell of the vanished glory of Southeast Asia and its parade of mighty kingdoms. Rice cultivation, which provided the economic basis for the great civilizations, probably originated in the area around 5000 B.C. However, it was not until later that most of the ancestors of the present people in the region arrived.

The first wave of migrations brought the Malays, who began filtering in from southern China around 2500 B.C. But most of the ethnically diverse groups that today make up Myanmar (Burma), Cambodia, Malaysia, Thailand, Indonesia, and Vietnam owe their origins to peoples driven from China in the first millennium A.D. by the Han Chinese and their successors.

Around the beginning of the first century A.D., Indians began to establish trading posts in Southeast Asia, introducing the local ruling elite to Indian civilization. The rulers invited to their courts learned Brahmans of the priestly class of Hindu India, who brought their knowledge of sciences, religion, arts, technology, and literature with them. This contact deeply influenced the early kingdoms of Southeast Asia. Missionaries who carried the Buddha's message also helped spread Indian culture. Indian religion left a great mark, for Hinduism and Buddhism played major roles in stimulating local creativity. The wealth of art and monuments in the great capitals resulted from periods of intense religious fervor.

Except in northern Vietnam, which China controlled until the tenth century A.D., Chinese influence played a lesser role in shaping the emerging civilizations. However, their rulers regularly sent envoys to China and paid tribute.

The fusion of Indian and local traditions created a flowering of art and a succession of dynamic kingdoms. The first was the Hindu maritime empire of Funan, known by the name appearing in Chinese records. Established around the first century A.D., its suzerainty extended from southern Vietnam to Burma, and its influence undoubtedly hastened the process of Indianization.

Treasures from Chen-La, a contemporary of Funan, include a life-size image of a god who combines aspects of the Hindu divinities Shiva and Vishnu. In typical fashion, the statue blends Indian elements and local artistic genius.

As Funan waned, the mighty Khmer, who built fabled Angkor, rose from the small state of Chen-La; by 1200 they ruled much of mainland Southeast Asia. Funanese descendants formed the Sailendra dynasty of Java, the builders of the great Buddhist temple at Borobudur. Another early maritime empire, the Srivijaya, ruled from Sumatra from the seventh to the thirteenth century.

To the west, the Burmans vanquished the Mon and Pyu kingdoms and, from their capital at Pagan, inaugurated Burma's golden age. All this changed when the Mongols invaded under Kublai Khan, ruler of China. As the empires of Pagan and the Khmer waned, the Thai expanded their domain.

Ever divided, this richly diverse region presents a kaleidoscope of civilizations that rose to great heights before falling into decline.

CHINA

PACIFIC

OCEAN

BURMA

PYU

Pagan

Mekong

Irrawaddy

MON

INDOCHINA

Sukhothai

PENINSULA

CHAMPA

CHEN-LA

Ayutthaya

Bangkok

Angkor

FUNAN

Mekong

SOUTH CHINA SEA

MALAY PENINSULA

SHRIVIJAYA

BORNEO

OCEAN

SUMATRA

SAILENDRA

JAVA

Borobudur

Prambanan

• Ancient and modern town site

◆ Archaeological site only

0   400 mi

0   600 km

165

Angkor

A.D. 802 to 1432

Sculpture, architecture, and engineering attained unrivaled heights in southern Indochina between the ninth and thirteenth centuries, when Khmer god-kings ruled an empire from their capital at Angkor, in central Cambodia. This cultural explosion owed its origins to the skills brought to Southeast Asia by Indians. Indian merchants began arriving in numbers by the first century A.D., seeking commerce with China and gold, gems, and spices for their trade with the Roman Empire.

The Indians introduced Hinduism and a concept of the universe and divine rule that inspired the construction of immense, lavishly carved stone and brick temples. These were intended to please the gods and glorify the god-kings by portraying their legendary feats.

Funan was the first powerful state to emerge in southern Indochina, the center of Indian expansion. By the

third century A.D., Funan had become a maritime power, virtually controlling the sea-lanes used in the Sino-Indian trade.

The arts flourished, influenced by Indian culture, religion, and technology. French conservator Bernard Groslier considers Funan the crucible in which native elements and Indian contributions were fused into a new civilization, which the Khmer then inherited and brought to its peak.

Alongside the Funanese in the basin of the Mekong River were Khmer who had established the kingdom of Chen-La. It had been a vassal state until it annexed Funan about 550 A.D. But in the seventh century, the fractious Khmer caused the disintegration of their kingdom into a number of petty states under the suzerainty of Java. In the last

Angkor Wat

Re-creating the sacred mountain of Hindu cosmology, the temple above represents Mount Meru, abode of the gods and center of the universe. Lively reliefs portray scenes from Hindu epics and myths, as well as events in the life of Suryavarman II, the 12th-century king who raised the monument as his observatory, shrine, and tomb.

years of the eighth century, Jayavarman II liberated his people, united Chen-La, and founded the first dynasty of Angkor. The empire's prosperity was based on a sophisticated irrigation system with enormous reservoirs and canals; this enabled farmers in the fertile plains around Angkor to produce two or three rice harvests a year and sustain a population of almost a million.

Angkor sprawls over a plain twice the size of Manhattan and includes a complex of 72 major monuments. A dozen kings constructed capitals here to glorify their lives. Each city had a nucleus of temples and palaces surrounded by cultivated fields. The only buildings constructed of brick and stone were the temples.

The largest temple and the culminating achievement in Khmer architecture was Angkor Wat, built in the first half of the 12th century.

The Bayon
at Angkor Thom

Surrounded by a time-weathered surface of gray stone, the giant faces sculptured on the massive towers of the Bayon temple (left) project an aura of serenity. Although the structure represents a temple-mountain and symbolizes the traditional Khmer cosmology, the Bayon is dedicated to Buddha. Most other temples at Angkor were symbolic abodes of Hindu gods. The Bayon stands in the center of Angkor Thom. This was the walled capital established by Jayavarman VII, who ascended the throne in 1181 and rallied the Khmer to defeat Cham invaders from present-day Vietnam. Fifty-two towers, carved on four sides with faces, surround the massive, pyramidal central tower, where two saffron-robed Buddhist monks sit in an open window. Exuberant heavenly dancers, the celestial apsaras, decorate the pediment below, from another part of the Bayon temple. Their steps and angular postures are duplicated in classical Khmer dance, which still holds an exalted place in Cambodia. Heavily carved surfaces along the gallery walls of the Bayon

portray the life story of the king, the Khmer in battle, and such scenes from everyday life as fishing and gambling at cockfights. A devout Buddhist, Jayavarman VII embarked on a feverish building spree, constructing 102 hospitals, 101 rest houses for pilgrims, and 20,000 shrines to promote Buddhism, which became the principal faith of Cambodia. In the frantic pace workmanship declined, making the monuments more vulnerable to deterioration. A ghostly, enigmatic smile hovers on the lips of a three-faced sculpture with a lotus crown, found within one of the four massive gateways to Angkor Thom. Bernard Philippe Groslier, French scholar and chief conservator of Angkor in the 1960s, observed that the faces, with their mystical, fleeting smiles, are the symbol and message of the art of the Bayon.

Three-faced stone sculpture, 2 ft

Stone relief of apsaras, height 2 ft

Reliefs ornament nearly every surface, creating a dramatic mix of small detail and massive architecture.

Ultimately, the burden of building enormous monuments and thousands of shrines drained the economy, contributing to the decline of the empire, which was also debilitated by bloody wars. The kingdom

won a brief reprieve under the strong rule of Jayavarman VII, who came to the throne in 1181; but when the Thai sacked Angkor in 1432, the Khmer abandoned their capital.

Although Buddhists continued to worship at Angkor, many temples were left to the jungle. Vines and trees rooted in the moldering struc-

tures, prying the stones apart. Introduced to the West in 1860 by Frenchman Henri Mouhot, Angkor became a model of conservation archaeology until war stopped most work in 1975. Eroded by the elements, scarred by bullets, and pillaged by thieves, Angkor endures, bearing witness to the grandeur of the Khmer Empire.

Pagan

A.D. 1057 to 1287

Whitewashed temple
Gilded Buddha, Ananda temple, ca 30 ft

Pagan's days of glory began in 1057, when King Anawrahta conquered the neighboring Mon kingdom. He brought back to his capital in central Burma the Mon's Buddhist relics and scriptures, as well as a large number of artists, craftsmen, and learned monks. Ancient chronicles claim the attack was inspired by religious zeal. Other motives also may have driven Anawrahta, whose conquest gave Pagan access to the sea and the lucrative trade with India, Sri Lanka, Malaya, and China. Anawrahta's military skill welded numerous ethnic groups, such as the Mon and Pyu, into an empire nearly the size of Burma, now called Myanmar.

As a devout convert to the Theravada branch of Buddhism, Anawrahta spent much of his wealth honoring Buddha by building religious monuments. Succeeding monarchs and their subjects continued this fervent patronage as they also sought to gain merit for their future lives. This obsession produced 5,000 temples and shrines in some 250 years, leaving a remarkable legacy of Buddhist architecture and art.

Although the monasteries and their congregation halls—built of ornately carved wood—have vanished and the Irrawaddy River has washed away part of the city, many of the religious buildings—constructed of baked brick—survive. These fall into two categories: temples and pagodas.

Early temples were dark and cavelike, with small windows. Later structures had larger interiors with larger windows that allowed light to fall on the images of Buddha. Murals adorned interior walls, while exterior walls were embellished with glazed terra-cotta tiles that depicted the Buddha's previous incarnations.

Pagodas, which entomb sacred relics, owe their origins to stupas in India and Sri Lanka. Pagan's architects varied the basic design, creating a range of styles from massive and ornate to austerely elegant.

Some shrines fell victim to neglect when Pagan was conquered by Kublai Khan in 1287 and the city was abandoned. Others have been places of worship for nearly 900 years. Today government archaeologists protect and preserve this spectacular site.

Temples and Shrines

Relics of a mighty civilization stud the plain of Pagan (below), the ancient Burmese capital. More than 2,000 brick-and-stucco temples and bell-shaped pagodas still stand, all differing in size and detail. Gilded spires crown one whitewashed temple and its many domes. Today, caretakers repaint only the most venerated monuments. While pagodas are solid structures, with room to house only a statue or holy relic, temples usually have vaulted interiors into which worshipers can enter. A 30-foot gilded Buddha, one of four in the Ananda temple, lifts its hands in the gesture of teaching. A detail from a frieze around the Abeyadana temple portrays a bodhisattva, a saint in the Mahayana branch of Buddhism, who postpones his own salvation to help others and is revered as a deity.

Detail of frieze, Abeyadana temple

Sukhothai and Ayutthaya

A.D. 1240 to 1500

Thailand, once known as Siam, became an independent kingdom in the 13th century, an era of cataclysmic political change in Southeast Asia because of the Mongol invasions. Thai had been migrating south from their ancient homeland in southern China into what was then the northwestern part of the Khmer Empire, ruled from Angkor. In the mid-13th century, the Thai set up new states in lands that had been formerly dominated by the Khmer.

Sukhothai was founded in one of the areas occupied by immigrant Thai. When King Ram Kamheng succeeded to the throne in about 1279, Khmer power was in decline. Using a combination of force and diplomacy, Ram Kamheng welded the numerous petty Thai states in the area into an extensive empire with Sukhothai as its capital. Known as the cradle of Thai civilization, Sukhothai was the birthplace of the script, religion, architecture, and art forms that created the cultural identity of the nation.

Theravada Buddhism, spread by monks from Sri Lanka, became the principal religion, and the city's large number of shrines, monasteries, and images of the Buddha attest to the piety of its inhabitants. The high, pointed spires and multitiered roofs that characterize Thai architec-

172

ture had their origins in Sukhothai.

A national historical park, established in 1978, contains nearly 200 monuments—temples, stupas, monasteries, congregation halls, and images of Buddha in stucco and bronze. With the help of UNESCO, the Thai Fine Arts Department is excavating and restoring throughout the city. This policy disturbs archaeologists and art historians who prefer to see monuments left as they are, as unaltered evidence of the past.

Archaeological research continues in the park, and new finds include stucco images of the Buddha, some of which were fashioned from a mixture of lime, sand, and sugarcane juice. These cruder sculptures contrast with the sleek bronze Buddhas of the late 14th century.

By the middle of the 14th century, many states under Sukhothai's suzerainty had broken their ties to the empire. Out of this welter of petty kingdoms, warlike Ayutthaya emerged as the regional power, conquering Sukhothai in 1438 and vanquishing the once mighty Khmer in the same century. Ayutthaya survived for another 300 years, until 1767, when Burmese soldiers put the city to the torch, destroying priceless art, libraries, and temples.

Ayutthaya represented a golden age to King Rama I, who established the dynasty that rules Thailand today. He had bricks to build modern Bangkok brought from the ruins of Ayutthaya. There, in 1957, scavengers found an untouched treasure of 15th-century murals, jewels, and votive objects in a royal crypt hidden within a shrine. Much of the cache disappeared into the art market before the government became aware of the find and saved the rest for the Ayutthaya National Museum.

Reclining Buddha, Wat Lokaya Sutha, Ayutthaya

Wat Yai Chai Mongkol, Ayutthaya

Sukhothai and Ayutthaya

Reclining in a Thai version of his traditional deathbed posture, a smiling Buddha image (opposite) evokes the serenity of relinquishing earthly passions and entering the state of bliss called nirvana. A disciple worships at the Master's feet. Placed temporarily within the sparse remains of the columned Wat Mahathat temple complex at Ayutthaya, the small statue, slightly more than 15 inches long, was found there but predates the temple. In the iconography of Buddhist art, one of the distinguishing features of the Buddha is the protuberance on the crown of the head, symbolizing enlightenment. A heavily restored head of another recumbent Buddha at Ayutthaya manifests the enigmatic smile and elongated earlobes that also characterize the Buddha image. Ruins of the massive, brick chedi, or reliquary shrine, at Wat Yai Chai Mongkol tower above fallen heads. Constructed just to the southeast of Ayutthaya at the end of the 14th century, the shrine was enlarged 200 years later to commemorate a Thai victory over the Burmese. In the Buddhist language of gesture, the upraised bronze hand at right promises protection. Part of a statue of the Buddha, it exhibits the sinuous grace of 14th-century sculpture from Sukhothai, the first Thai capital. Elongated and elegant Buddhas, often cast in bronze, are considered the crowning achievement of Sukhothai art. Embodying the joys of motherhood, a pottery female figurine clasps two children. The crude effigy may have served in rituals of propitiation to protect expectant mothers from the dangers of childbirth. In the late 13th century, Sukhothai artisans also produced fine pottery—often using Chinese motifs or imitating glazed Chinese ware—for export in the widespread and profitable ceramic trade.

Bronze hand of Buddha, Sukhothai, 7.8 in

Pottery figurine, Sawankhalok, Sukhothai, 6.2 in

173

Borobudur and Prambanan

A.D. 760 to 1050

Great stone monuments soaring in splendor above the lush rice fields of central Java attest to the Buddhist and Hindu heritage of the island. The fertility of this region provided the ancient kingdoms of Indonesia with the riches to create religious structures that rank among the masterpieces of Asian art.

Begun around A.D. 760 and completed some 80 years later, the Buddhist shrine of Borobudur was built around a low hill encased with stone blocks. The stepped monument rises in a series of terraces that symbolically represent the stages through which a person's soul must pass to achieve enlightenment. On the lower levels, wall reliefs portray the life of the Buddha as a young prince and episodes from sacred texts. Above these tiers are three plain circular terraces with latticed stupas, sheltering life-size figures of Buddha seated in contemplation. At the summit stands a larger, closed stupa. The circular terraces may represent the formless state of bliss, or nirvana.

The Hindu monarchs of the Sanjaya dynasty, which ruled Java after about 850, were equally devout patrons of religious architecture and sculpture. At Prambanan, the Sanjayas built a large temple complex. Its principal shrine, dedicated to the Hindu god Shiva, has a massive, heavily sculptured pinnacle that towers over the verdant countryside. This burst of creative energy lasted for more than 200 years and produced dozens of other religious structures before the Sanjaya rulers moved their capital to east Java.

These holy places lay abandoned, decaying, and shrouded in vegetation for more than 800 years. Some restoration work took place at Borobudur in the early 1900s. In 1972, a major effort to save the monument from collapse began; this involved marking, moving, cleaning, and repairing 800,000 stones.

Detail of sculptural panel, Borobudur

A Show of Faith

Elephant-headed Hindu god of wisdom and prosperity, Ganesha (opposite) presides over a shrine in the Shiva temple at Prambanan. A bell-shaped stupa crowns the immense Buddhist monument of Borobudur. In a detail from one of the 1,300 panels along its four galleries, a relief of a couple evokes a mood of tenderness.

Great Stupa, Borobudur

Map labels:

S I B E ...
T I A N   S H A N
Bezeklik
Dunhuang
SILK ROAD
Samarkand
Kashgar
TAKLIMAKAN DESERT
Merv
P A M I R S
SILK ROAD
C
Balkh
HINDU KUSH
H I M A L A Y A
P E R S I A
PLATEAU OF TIBET

East Asia

5000 B.C. to A.D. 1400

Almost one-third of the human race lives in East Asia. For most of its history, that vast region—which can be defined to include China, Korea, Japan, and parts of eastern Russia—has been dominated or profoundly influenced by Chinese culture and civilization. The East Asian world flourished in relative isolation for thousands of years before overland and sea routes to the West gradually connected it to Central Asia, India, and, finally, to Europe.

Isolation was the natural result of geographical barriers. The Pacific Ocean discouraged all but the most tentative exploration in an easterly direction. The Himalaya and the Tibetan Plateau loomed beyond the deserts to the west of China.

The mountains and forests to the south presented daunting barriers.

Human populations have shaped their lives there within three broadly defined regions: the arid grasslands of the north; the irrigated farmland of the Yellow and Yangtze River Valleys; and the wet-field farmland of the south. An imprecise but effective border separates the fertile south from the dry grasslands and deserts. It extends westward from the Gulf of Bohai, runs roughly along the route of the Great Wall to the lower reaches of the Tibetan Plateau, and from there turns sharply south. Until recent times, 95 percent of the people of continental East Asia lived in settled agricultural and urban settlements to the south and east of that boundary. But nomadic and pastoral "barbarians" from the northern

steppes, though relatively few in number, had a major impact on the history and culture of the region.

Persistent conflict between settled agricultural populations and horse-riding nomads in the amorphous border region tested the mettle of a long line of Chinese dynastic rulers. Han emperors twice conducted major campaigns against them and were victorious both times.

Later history reversed Chinese fortunes and produced several foreign dynasties—most notably the Mongol Yuan dynasty of the 13th century. The Mongols subdued the heart of continental Asia, making possible an exchange of ideas and information that introduced Europeans to this distant world—up to then beyond their imagination and beyond their reach.

R I A

Karakorum

Yellow

H   I   N   A

SILK ROAD

Chang'an
(Xi'an)   Anyang   Yellow
Lintong
Xianyang   Yangshao
Hao   Banpo   Luoyang

Yellow

Gulf of
Bohai

YELLOW
SEA

SEA OF
JAPAN

KOREA

CHOSUN
SILLA
Kyŏngju

JAPAN   Kanto
Plain

Nara
Kyushu   Tokyo Bay

Hangzhou   EAST
Hemudu   CHINA
SEA

Longshan

Yangtze

PACIFIC

OCEAN

S O U T H   C H I N A   S E A

● Ancient and modern town site

◆ Archaeological site only

0   600 mi

0   800 km

China

5000 B.C. to A.D. 800

Ancestors of the Chinese people living in widely separated agricultural settlements left tantalizing clues to the beginnings of organized society in the river basins of the East Asian mainland.

At least as early as 5000 B.C., timber houses raised on wooden pilings were being constructed in the marshes near present-day Hangzhou. In this region, at a village called Hemudu, archaeologists have discovered some of the earliest evidence of rice cultivation in Asia. While southern rice farmers pursued their way of life, farmer-hunters farther north in the central highlands built walls, villages, and roads out of the dusty earth. A rich site discovered near the city of Yangshao gave its name to the culture that rose in the central Yellow River Valley. Near present-day Xi'an, reconstructed houses in Banpo, a Yangshao-style village, reveal the self-sufficient life of its inhabitants. They

lived in reed-thatched, mud-plastered pole houses, often built partly below ground level, grouped together on a hillside terrace and surrounded by a protective moat. Villagers cultivated millet, and their diet included game, fish, and the meat of pigs and dogs that they had domesticated. They probably also grew hemp that could be woven into cloth for garments.

Widely separated communities developed distinctive styles of pottery, which were painted and decorated with geometric patterns and other designs characteristic of different regional cultures.

The Yangshao-style culture co-existed with, and eventually gave way to, that of Longshan sometime after 3000 B.C. Longshan villagers protected their settlements with pounded earth walls. They were

farmers, growing rice and millet. Village artisans also developed a knowledge of metallurgy, in particular bronze casting, as early as 2000 B.C. Society was stratified, with indications of specialized occupations.

Communities grew larger under the leadership of rulers who increasingly fortified their cities with walls. Traditional Chinese accounts of their early history tell of three dynasties of ruler-warriors who dominated the people of the central plains. These are known to the Chinese as the Xia,

Ancient Forms with Spirit

Painted ceramics, carved jades, and finely cast bronzes unearthed at widely scattered sites provide evidence of the technological skill, keen eye, and sense of beauty characteristic of the early ancestors of the Chinese. Styles and patterns differed. Eight-pointed stars ring a 5,000-year-old pottery basin discovered at a village site in the eastern province of Jiangsu. Fashioned

a thousand years later in the far northwest, a quizzical painted pottery head represents one of the earliest human images found intact in China. Perhaps the handle of a pot lid, it has two horns; the lump between them is the head of a serpent climbing up the back. The vessel may have served a ceremonial function. Shang and Zhou dynasty craftsmen cast bronzes exuberantly embellished with animal forms. Four rams guard the corners of

Jade dragon pendant, Zhou, length 6.5 in

the Shang, and, finally, the Zhou, who came to power about 1100 B.C.

In the 1920s the discovery of large quantities of inscribed animal bones and turtle shells led archaeologists to the site of what proved to be the last Shang capital, located near the modern city of Anyang. Since that time, much older Shang cities have been discovered.

In their great cities, the Shang raised ceremonial centers on pounded earth platforms and built substantial dwellings using the post-and-beam construction still used in China today. Anyang provided evidence of at least 53 such buildings. Inscriptions on tens of thousands of "oracle bones" and on bronze ceremonial objects give us certain information about the Shang: Their society was highly stratified; their warriors fought with chariots; their rulers were served by diviners and artisans; and the king played a priestly role in the community.

Among the most precious

emblems of status and rank among the emerging priest-kings and their minions were objects of finely wrought jade. Nephrite and many other beautiful stones had been carved for ritual and decorative purposes for thousands of years. Some have been dated back to 5000 B.C. By the time of the Shang and the Zhou, jade objects reflected social status and relationships. During religious rites, the ruler wore a jade emblem to show his authority. A set of ceremonial jade objects placed on an altar served as embodiments of the deities of the ancestors in whose honor the rites were performed. During the Shang and Zhou dynasties, jade objects were buried, burned, or thrown into rivers in honor of the prevailing spirits.

In the 11th century B.C., the warriors of Zhou, a Shang vassal state, conquered their masters. The Zhou preserved cultural traditions inherited from the Shang, increasing the observance of court ritual and ancestor worship.

The Zhou had acquired a huge domain, which they organized as a system of vassal states ruled by loyal regional lords. Three armies

enforced the king's central authority, and Zhou maintained its stability for more than 300 years. But by 800 B.C. royal prestige had deteriorated, and in 771 rebels sacked the capital city of Hao, near present-day Xi'an. The Zhou monarch retreated eastward to Luoyang. By 700 B.C. the great Zhou kingdom had splintered into many warring states, some of which built territorial walls.

During the chaotic period that followed, history still was written down and law codes were discussed. Two philosophers of the fifth century B.C. had a lasting impact on Chinese life: Confucius preached a code of virtuous behavior, while Laozi advocated harmony with nature.

By the end of the fourth century B.C., seven major states remained in

Bronze elephant vessel, Shang, 9 in

a wine vessel, and an elephant curls its trunk on another. Close inspection of either bronze reveals coiling snakes, dragons, and birds covering the surface. Many such treasures were found among rich goods buried in tombs; others were buried singly as offerings to mountains and rivers. These containers held liquid, probably wine used during ritual observances. Lustrous jade was associated with both strength and

Bronze vessel with rams, Shang, 23 in

purity. Perforated jade disks symbolized eternity, and Zhou rulers used them to commune with the cosmos. Jaunty dragons march around the edge of one example (opposite, top) found in Henan; another dragon adorns a jade pendant (above, left). So strong was the belief in jade's power, that a jade cicada placed in the mouth of the deceased was thought to preserve the body from putrefaction.

*Life-size
terra-cotta archer,
Qin Shi Huangdi
tomb complex*

Terra-cotta army site near tomb of Qin Shi Huangdi, near Xi'an

*Half life-size
reconstructed bronze
chariot and team,
Qin Shi Huangdi
tomb complex*

contention. Among these, the north-westerly Qin state had succeeded in building itself into a military power with an efficient bureaucracy. Qin soldiers, renowned for their discipline and ferocity, inspired terror. Before the end of the third century B.C., they had defeated all local rivals including, in 256, the kingdom of Zhou. In 221 B.C. the king, self-styled Qin Shi Huangdi—the First Emperor of Qin—declared total victory and prophesied that his empire would last 10,000 generations.

Qin Shi Huangdi, First Emperor of a unified China, was determined to rule as an absolute monarch. With the help of a small corps of able advisers, he broke up the old feudal system, replacing it with a strong, centralized government. He forced his former rivals, members of once powerful families in outlying regions, to move to his capital, Xianyang, where he could keep an eye on them.

At Xianyang, Qin Shi Huangdi embarked on an ambitious building program. Hundreds of thousands of conscripted laborers—convicts and prisoners of war—worked on his immense palace and, a few miles to the east, his imperial tomb.

Vast chambers excavated in 1974, less than a mile from the First Emperor's tomb, have lent credence to the stories that circulated in Chinese literature of the grandeur and great feats of the Qin. There, outside the village of Lintong, archaeologists have unearthed at least 7,000 life-size ceramic warriors, together with horses, chariots, and weapons. Continuing excavations promise to reveal other exciting finds, but so far no decision has been made to open the large tumulus that contains the First Emperor's tomb.

Changes instituted by the First Emperor transformed China. Systems of rewards and punishments and of taxation were installed. Currency was standardized throughout the realm, as were weights, measures, written characters, and even the length of wagon axles.

The Qin regime made vital contribu-

Buried Legions of the Qin and Han Dynasties

Exposed to the sun for the first time in more than 2,000 years, a six-foot warrior in Qin Shi Huangdi's ceramic legion is measured by archaeologists. Some 7,000 warriors—foot soldiers, archers, cavalry, and charioteers—have been located in pits uncovered in 1974 near the First Emperor's tumulus at Lintong, about 20 miles east of his ancient capital, Xianyang. Horses caparisoned in silver and gold pulling a chariot of bronze, discovered nearby in 1980, suggest a wealth of treasures to come. Workers who excavate anywhere near

Terra-cotta heads, Jingdi tomb complex

Terra-cotta army site near tomb of Jingdi, near Xi'an

Xi'an, the site of ancient Chinese imperial capitals, are trained to use caution. In the spring of 1990, a road crew working 12 miles north of Xi'an discovered a site that held closely ranked legions of two-foot-tall terra-cotta soldiers, buried near the tomb of Jingdi, fifth emperor of the Han dynasty. Socketed torsos have long since lost their wooden arms, and silk garments are turning to dust. Replication of human beings and animals, along with models of worldly goods, became common practice in burials as human and animal sacrifices of earlier times were all but abandoned.

181

Pottery drummer, Han

Pottery dancer, Yuan

Goods to Soothe the Soul

Encased in jade, Prince Liu Yan (opposite), half brother of the Han emperor Mingdi, was laid in his tomb in A.D. 90. Bi disks, such as the one on top of his head, were placed on head, chest, and other important parts of the body. According to ancient belief, one aspect of the human soul remained in the body while the other escaped to paradise. Relatives attended to the needs of both. The earthbound soul had to be made comfortable—and feel no temptation to return from the grave. The jade suit's life-giving power was thought to be so strong that the body would be protected from decay and its resident spirit would remain comfortable. Rich grave furnishings, weapons, food, and ceramic models of servants and courtly companions re-created life as the deceased had once known it. A leaping polo player and a court lady with her flute reflect aristocratic life during the Tang dynasty. A droll ceramic drummer from Sichuan province documents a local theatrical tradition as old as the Han. The much later Yuan dynasty dancer, unassociated with grave goods, reveals a growing Chinese taste for theater and for dance.

tions to Chinese government, but the people were worked to exhaustion. In an effort to unify and protect his empire, Qin Shi Huangdi ordered the construction of roads, canals, and other public works. He tore down the defensive walls of the old feudal states and ordered the construction of new frontier barriers, about which little is known. Modern scholarship has made it clear that Qin Shi Huangdi did not build an early version of the Ming dynasty Great Wall that stands today. Despite this, a persistent tradition in both China and the West continues to label him as a slave-driving Great Wall builder.

At his death in 210 B.C., the emperor bequeathed China the legacy of a strong, centralized bureaucratic state, which has remained the national ideal up to the present time.

During the imperial era that followed, beginning with the 400-year-long dynasty of the Han, the ancient practice of massive tomb burials continued. Miniature armies of warriors and legions of courtiers accompanied high-ranking patrons to the grave. In 1990, excavations near Xi'an led

archaeologists to the mausoleum of the Han emperor Jing—Jingdi in Chinese. This huge site, 23 acres in area, contains 24 pits holding up to 400 warriors apiece. Unlike those of Qin, these soldiers are only two feet tall; they were modeled without clothes and dressed in silk. Further excavations that year located a nearby kiln devoted to the production of such figures. Tombs themselves became increasingly elaborate under the Han—virtual underground palaces resembling the residences their owners had occupied in life.

The long years of the Han dynasty left a lasting heritage: Institutions by which China came to define itself—centralized authority, a professional civil service, and a Confucian political philosophy—all took shape under the Han. The majority Chinese population today is known as Han. Prosperity brought a flowering of technology, the arts, and religion. Part of the growth was related to the fruitful exchange of ideas and goods with Europe and southern Asia by land and sea routes known collectively as the Silk Road.

Glazed pottery polo player, Tang

Glazed pottery court lady, Tang

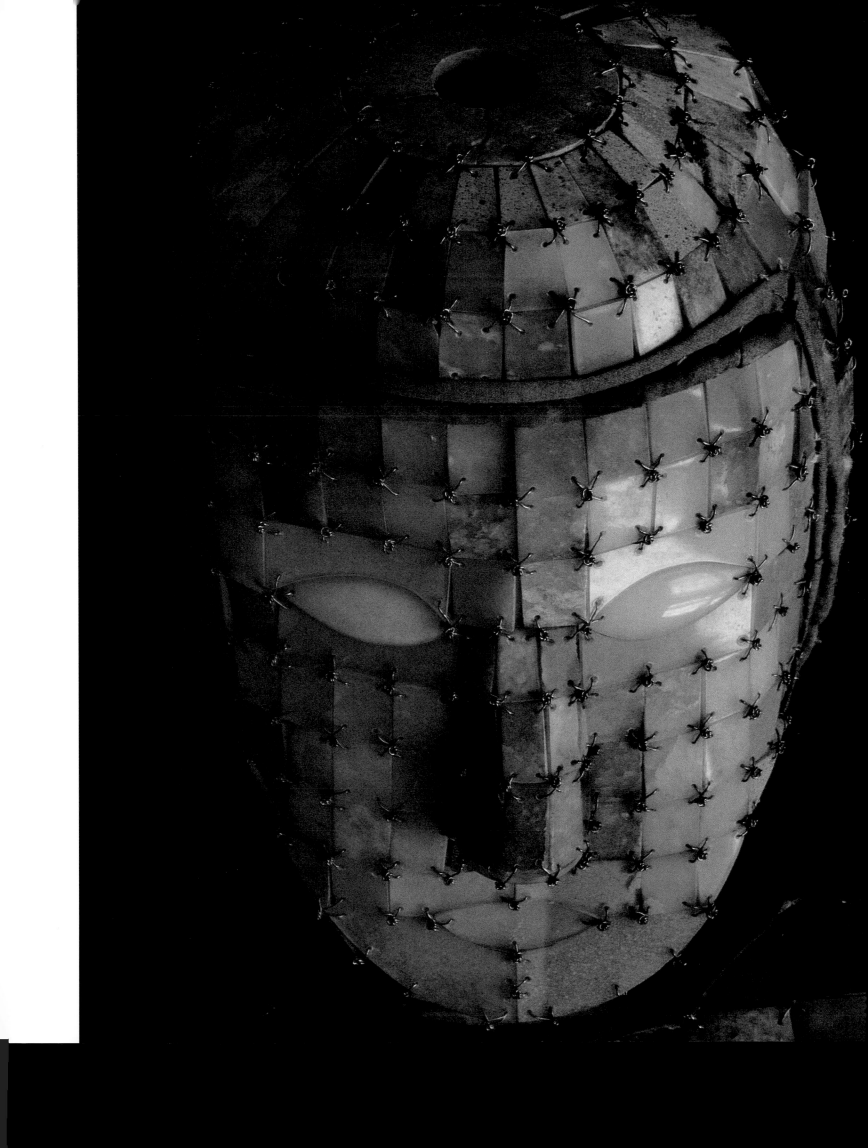

Silk Road

200 B.C. to A.D. 1400

In 329 B.C., Alexander the Great led his armies to the northeastern limit of the ancient Persian Empire—to the forbidding foothills of the Pamirs. Finding nothing left to conquer in that direction, he turned his armies south to India.

After his death, Persian satrapies flourished in relative isolation along with colonies that Alexander and his armies had left behind. Trading centers at Samarkand, Balkh, and Merv bought silk from traders in oasis settlements east of the Pamirs, but there is no record that westerners of that era had heard of China—nor the Chinese of them.

It was not until the second century B.C. that overland routes began to link the two worlds. That connection was initiated by the Chinese. Border skirmishes with nomadic warriors were a source of constant danger to the expanding Han Empire. Captive nomads brought word to China of flourishing kingdoms beyond the western mountains.

About 138 B.C., the Han emperor Wudi sent his emissary Zhang Chien to investigate the rumors and to seek political and military allies against mutual enemies. Zhang's journey, interrupted by ten years of captivity, brought back no alliances, but it did provide invaluable geographical information and very practical cargo. Among his treasures were alfalfa and seeds from western grapes. The journey piqued Chinese curiosity about the west and marked the beginning of an era of fertile exchange of goods and information.

Caravans rode northwest from Chang'an (now Xi'an), the ancient Chinese imperial capital, to the town of Dunhuang and the pass called the Jade Gate—then the outer edge of the Chinese world. Braving lands populated with thieves by day and ghostly noises by night, travelers chose one of several treacherous routes that skirted the fearful Taklimakan, described by modern travelers as one of the world's most appalling deserts. Between widely

Pilgrims and Traders

Melting snow from surrounding mountains provided water sufficient for settlements strung along the blistering northern edge of the Taklimakan. One of many centers devoted to religious studies and the translation of Buddhist scriptures brought there from India, the retreat at Bezeklik (right) commemorates the devotion of generations of pilgrims and scholars who braved the treacherous journey—

some of them on foot and some of them more than once. Musicians and entertainers also traveled the desert routes. A Tang dynasty artist portrays an itinerant troupe somewhat fancifully, seated atop a complaining camel. Tang wit and attention to detail depict the stance of an exotic western wine merchant, balancing his wineskin on his knee. Such Tang multicolor glazed pottery figurines were found in tombs.

Traveling musicians, Tang, 36 in

Pottery wine merchant, Tang, 14.6 in

spaced oasis settlements waited sandstorms, heat, cold, fatigue, hunger, and bandits. Finally, trails met at Kashgar and threaded high through the Pamirs, then west to Samarkand or south to the Hindu Kush.

Records show that, by the end of the eighth century A.D., nearly 200 monks had made the daunting journey to India and back. They founded monasteries along the way and ushered in a great Buddhist age during the early years of the Tang dynasty.

The last great era of overland exchange came from the mid-13th to mid-14th centuries, when Mongol armies stationed in Central Asia made the route relatively safe from thieves. Chinese culture and technology, including porcelain, textiles, gunpowder, paper money, and printing, spread throughout Asia and as far west as Persia, Mesopotamia, and eventually Europe. In turn, Arab culture made its way to China, and Islam took root and flourished in the north. The overland routes declined only after the Mongol Empire collapsed and maritime routes proved more efficient and more attractive.

Wall painting, Mogao Grottoes, near Dunhuang

Information Highway

Gouged foothills of the Tian Shan range enfold oasis centers to the south (right, at top). Monks and pilgrims found refuge and solitude in shrines carved into nearby cliffs. In a seventh-century Dunhuang cave painting, the founder of Buddhism guides his mount through a flower-strewn sky. In the 14th century, the Silk Road's last great era as an international highway, Marco Polo's family was depicted trekking along the desert route.

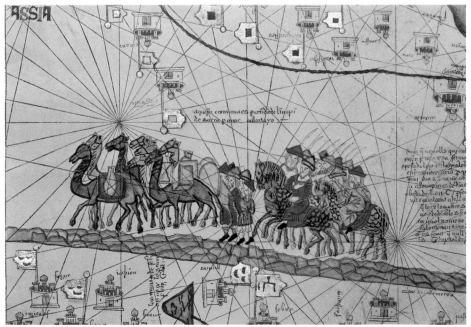

Detail from Catalan Atlas, *1375, printed upside down to show the Polo family caravan upright (note "Assia" in top left corner)*

Korea

3000 B.C. to A.D. 900

Korea, unlike insular Japan, shares an unobstructed common border with continental East Asia. Since the third millennium B.C., Korean culture has been enriched by wave after wave of eastward migration.

North Asian ancestors of the Koreans spoke an Altaic language, and their ceramic skills, burial customs, and bronze traditions were more like those of Siberia than of China. But China's influence was to become extremely strong.

In the second century B.C. the Han emperor Wudi, determined to defeat the nomadic Hsiungnu—who threatened China's northern border—and prevent any alliance between them and Korea, invaded the peninsula and destroyed the developing kingdom of Chosun. Korea thereupon became an outpost of Chinese civilization, adopting both Buddhism and Confucianism and acknowledging the hegemony of the Chinese emperor.

In the eighth century A.D., rulers of the Korean kingdom of Silla deliberately modeled their state and administration on ideas received from Tang-dynasty China. Chinese influence was never totally engulfing, however. Korean culture maintained an energy of its own, with its distinctive art, literature, and scientific traditions that have continued to thrive into modern times.

Celadon covered vase, 15.4 in

Chomsongdae observatory, Kyongju

Technology and Art

Study of the heavens developed early in Korea, as it did in many ancient agricultural societies. In an effort to chart the stars and to observe, predict, and attain harmony with the seasons, Queen Sondok of the southern Korean kingdom of Silla supervised construction of the Chomsongdae observatory (above) in A.D. 634. The tower served as the meridian for astronomical observations and the point of reference for measuring the cardinal points of the compass. It remains the oldest known observatory in East Asia. Royal tombs have yielded ornaments revealing the high level of Korean metallurgical skills during the Silla period. On a gold and jade crown (opposite), unearthed in 1974, the headband supports gold uprights fashioned in the shapes of trees and antlers. The motifs suggest north Asian rather than Chinese derivation. Skills of the Silla ceramicist blend with humor and an eye for detail in a stoneware vessel rendered as a sturdy horse and warrior. Korean accomplishment in the manufacture of delicate porcelain reached its peak with the famed green celadon glazes and inlaid decorations that Korean ceramicists perfected during the 11th and 12th centuries.

Stoneware mounted warrior, 9.3 in

189

Japan

10,500 B.C. to A.D. 800

A distinct hunting and gathering society, unlike any on the mainland, emerged in Japan in relative isolation. Coastal waters provided a year-round supply of fish, mollusks, and sea mammals. Thick forests yielded harvests of edible plants, roots, and nuts, as well as deer and boar. To take advantage of such abundance, early hunters needed only to fashion simple tools of stone, bone, wood, and rope. Small pit houses clustered along the deeply indented coast of present-day Tokyo Bay. Slanting thatched roofs supported by poles set into beaten earth floors provided shelter.

Modern scholars have named this early culture Jomon, or "cord pattern," after the manner in which potters decorated their ceramic vessels by pressing twisted cord into wet clay. In addition to elegant and prac-tical containers, the Jomon fashioned innumerable figurines—usually female—called *dogu*. Dogu probably had a ritual significance.

Physical evidence in the form of everyday tools—hoes, spades, harvesting knives, and rakes—provides proof of new technologies that were introduced into Japan from Korea and China between 300 B.C. and A.D. 300. The techniques and implements of wet-rice agriculture, as well as metal casting, weaving, wheel-made pottery, and forged tools, first appeared on Kyushu and eventually spread eastward beyond the Kanto Plain. The population

Clay haniwa *warrior, Yayoi, 51.4 in*

Earthenware dogu, Jomon

Emerging Japan

Talisman from a ten-thousand-year-old hunter-gatherer tradition, a small dogu *figurine assumes a squatting position. Characteristic of the Jomon ceramic culture, such figures may have been instrumental in ritual healing. Sword on his belt and arrows at the ready, a helmeted* haniwa *warrior encapsulates a millennium of change. Great chieftains marked their importance with* kofun, *huge burial mounds, often in a keyhole shape. Twenty thousand ceramic haniwa guardians in a variety of shapes once surmounted the tomb of the fifth-century Emperor Nintoku (left). Heralding a new direction in religion and culture, a ferocious celestial guardian (opposite) protects an altar in the Horyuji at Nara, one of Japan's earliest Buddhist temples.*

Wooden guardian figure, the Horyuji, Nara, 90 in

burgeoned. Villages began to appear, marked by rice fields and granaries. Gradually but decisively the new culture—known today as Yayoi—would come to dominate the land.

The origins of the Shinto religion—the way of the gods—seem to lie in this more settled society. Shinto recognizes life force—*kami*—in the sun, water, hills, and trees; in skillfully fashioned weapons and other objects; in all of the Japanese dead; and in the idea of Japan itself. It gives a feeling of unity to the Japanese people and their activities, including the arts. Even today, traditional wooden Shinto architecture resembles the building of the Yayoi period.

According to Chinese records of the third century A.D., a shaman named Himiko—Sun Princess—ruled certain regions of Japan. At her death, Himiko was said to have been buried under a great grave mound. The story of her interment suggests the beginnings of the construction of the *kofun,* or monumental tombs, that appeared in great numbers in later centuries.

By the end of the fourth century, horse-riding warrior clans, dominated by the Yamato tribe (who claimed descent from the sun goddess), had developed a military aristocracy capable of commanding the labor of countless subjects. Conspicuous among the works they ordered were the monumental tombs, often keyhole shaped, that gave their name to the Kofun period. Surrounding or surmounting the giant mounds were cylindrical clay statues—called *haniwa*—of men, women, birds, houses, weapons, tools, and other objects. Grave goods included swords, armor, and jewelry.

Society would change drastically again with the introduction of Buddhism from Korea in the sixth century. With it came the practice of writing in Chinese characters and the art, literature, and civilization of China, Korea, and Central Asia.

Chimu weaving, probably alpaca wool, Peru, 14th-15th century A.D.

Textile Treasures

Row upon row, the stylized human figures and fabulous felines that span this Peruvian weaving belong to a 4,000-year lineage of Andean textile making. Excavating Chan Chan, the capital of Peru's Chimu Empire, archaeologists Michael E. Moseley and Carol J. Mackey found caches of similar fabrics. They lay among other treasures and the skeletons of sacrificial victims in the burial chambers of a god-king—a sacred place.

Textiles have permeated human life for millennia. Some had simple, domestic, utilitarian purposes. Others—showing superior workmanship and rich decoration—served as royal apparel or sacred emblems. In their silent eloquence, textiles speak a symbolic language. They tell of the lives, customs, beliefs, and shared values of the men and women who made them, used them, and wore them in life and in death.

The oldest cloth that archaeologists have found is a 9,000-year-old, one-and-a-half-by-three-inch scrap, probably of linen. Discovered in 1988 in a dig at Çayönü in southern Turkey, it was wrapped around the handle of a tool made of antler. Because of the fragile nature of textiles, old fabrics are scarce. At Çayönü, calcium from the antler semifossilized the cloth and thus preserved it.

Another Turkish site, Çatal Hüyük, has yielded examples of linen textiles almost 8,000 years old, and pieces of felt—made by compressing fibers of wool rather than by spinning and weaving. In the Judaean Desert of Israel, the dry climate and the protection of caves have preserved rope, flax thread, and linen textiles, some dating from approximately 6500 B.C.

As a craft, basketry probably precedes cloth making by several thousand years.

Girl's dress, Egypt, ca 2800 B.C.

Coptic mattress cover fragment, 4th century A.D.

The Land of Egypt

A teenage girl of the third millennium B.C., in the reign of the Pharaoh Djet, wore this dress of fine white linen, the oldest pleated garment known. How the pleating was done is uncertain—perhaps by means of small wooden boards, perhaps with fingers and a stiffening solution. Pleated linen also appeared in kilts worn by nobility and kings. Centuries, dynasties, and conquests later, linen and wool

Experts see, in techniques by which the earliest fabrics were made, similarities to basket weaving. One scholar of ancient textiles, Dr. Gillian Vogelsang-Eastwood, has studied linen cloth from Çatal Hüyük and certain Israeli caves. She believes it was woven on a crude loom of four sticks. Threads were not spun but coarsely twisted. As the frame held the vertical threads under tension, the weaver interlaced double horizontal threads over and under.

For most of history, textiles were produced only from plant or animal fibers. Artisans used varying techniques to create a great diversity of fabrics. Important plant sources were flax for linen and cotton, as well as ramie, hemp, and other bast fibers. Animal fibers included silk from the cocoon of the moth *Bombyx mori* and wool from sheep, goats, and members of the camel family—llama, alpaca, guanaco, and vicuña.

Weaving produces fabric by interlacing two sets of yarns, usually at right angles. The lengthwise yarns are called the warp; the crosswise are the weft. One set of threads is held under tension on a loom. Weavers in ancient Egypt used a horizontal loom as early as 7,000 years ago, and vertical looms later, around 1900 B.C. Another ancient loom is the back-

medallions depicting a hunter and his dog typify textile art of the Copts, descendants of the pharaonic Egyptians. Cemeteries of this period have yielded fabrics used to cushion the head of the corpse. Mythological, rustic, and hunting scenes characterize Coptic tapestry, which created and emphasized design detail with a "flying shuttle," in which the weaver let a second weft shuttle guide the thread in unconventional diagonals and curves.

Silk coffin drape, China, ca 150 B.C.

Silk embroidery, China, 8th-9th century A.D.

strap, so-called because the warp, fixed to a firm beam at the far end, is, on the near end, fastened to a beam strapped to the weaver's body. Back-strap looms are still used in Central and South America and in Southeast Asia. In China, sometime after 2000 B.C., weavers worked at horizontal looms—perhaps equipped with treadles that assisted in lifting the warp and speeding the passage of the weft.

In the simplest form—plain weave, or tabby—the weft passes over and under the warp threads, with the order reversed in alternate rows. Weavers could vary the color or texture of yarns or use them in pairs. Twill weaves result when the weaver passes the weft threads over one and under two or more warp threads, which can create the appearance of diagonal lines. Archaeologists have found twill-woven fabrics in northern European bog burials of approx-

Oriental Silk

A silk fei i, *or flying garment (opposite, top), draped over the coffin of the highborn Lady Dai, bears designs that evoke the soul's ascension to heaven. Red leopards guard heaven's gates and flank a ramp leading to a portrait of the aged lady. Above her head, creatures symbolize immortality. It was the Chinese who discovered, around 3000 B.C., that the filament covering a silkworm cocoon—up to a mile in length—could be unwound and woven into fabric. Chinese embroidery probably began in the second millennium B.C. Artisans often used only one or two strands of floss and the most delicate needles, creating lifelike scenes. This fragment was found in 1907 in the Caves of the Ten Thousand*

Buddhas, near Dunhuang, a trading center on the Silk Road. China guarded the secret of sericulture until about A.D. 300. By then, through Korean weavers migrating from China, Japan had learned the techniques and soon mastered weaving and dyeing. In a dyehouse, workers produce sumptuously tinted and patterned silks for kosode—*thin, short-sleeved, inner kimonos. Silk cords even bound together the small metal plates of a samurai's armor.*

Dyehouse, Japan, 16th century A.D.

Samurai armor, Japan, 16th century A.D.

tries, more than 3,000 years old, were found in the treasure-filled tombs of Egyptian pharaohs.

Textiles ranged the ancient world through various contacts between cultures. Preeminent traders were the Phoenicians, whose ships carried embroidered garments from Mesopotamia, bales of linen from Egypt, and dyed wool from the eastern Mediterranean. Ur traded raw and spun wool, as well as finished garments, for copper and other raw materials.

The world's oldest known carpet, made of wool during the fifth century B.C., was found in a kurgan at Pazyryk, Siberia, but is thought to have come from Persia. The Persians imported silk, raw and woven, from China. When Alexander the Great made war against Persia, he seized rich textiles, including greatly coveted silk. In A.D. 652, when the Sassanid Persian empire fell before the

imately 800 B.C. and in late Stone Age Swiss lake dwellings—textiles perhaps 6,000 years old. In tapestry weave, the weft threads are packed so closely that the warp scarcely shows. The weft crosses over the warp only where its color may be needed for the design. The earliest known tapes-

Silk, gold, and silver fabric, Spain, ca 14th century A.D. (above); silk cloth, Spain, 13th-14th century A.D. (right)

Woman spinning,
Greece, ca 490 B.C.

sweep of Islam, Arab chronicles described magnificent bejeweled carpets captured from palaces.

Persians possibly possessed the Chinese secret of silk culture by the third century A.D. The Persian king Shāpūr employed Syrian prisoners of war as silk weavers, but there are no extant textiles to show their work; evidence lies in a contemporary inscription. A later Persian king, shown on a rock relief, wears clothing patterned with a mythical creature, half bird, half dog. The only documentation for this royal raiment is the carving. The patina or encrustation on bronze vessels has revealed the imprints of the silk they were once wrapped in, which is referred to by one scholar as "negative evidence." Knowledge about ancient weaving is also provided by illustrated ceramic vessels, or documents such as the papyrus that describes

work in an Egyptian textile mill.

Archaeologists have made a recent discovery that suggests that silk reached the West nearly a thousand years earlier than was once thought—perhaps smuggled in defiance of the Chinese strictures. Silk strands were found in the hair of a female Egyptian mummy from Dynasty XXI—1069 to 945 B.C. Silk thread also appeared in the sixth-century B.C. grave of a tribal chieftain in southwestern Germany.

Cotton had traveled westward from India, where it is native, by the seventh century B.C. to Nineveh, the capital of the Assyrian king Sennacherib. Around his palace Sennacherib grew exotic plants. One of them, the cotton plant, he boasted of as a "wool-bearing tree." Cotton textiles appeared almost 4,000 years ago at Mohenjo Daro in the Indus River Valley.

Connections

In addition to uncovering artifacts, archaeology explores the links between cultures and eras. The oldest known carpet in the world (opposite, top) lay sealed in ice for almost 25 centuries in the subterranean tomb of a Siberian chieftain. Then, in the late 1940s, Soviet archaeologist Sergei Rudenko led excavations in the Pazyryk Valley of southern Siberia. One expert believes the oldest rug may have been made by nomads. Others claim that the design is Persian. The rug's quality and workmanship—with 1,125,000 knots and an extra weft looped to form a pile—suggest a centuries-long history of contacts between people expert in rug weaving. In an ancient Greek household, much of a woman's time was spent spinning. In her left hand she held a stick—the distaff—that bore a clump of wool or flax. Individual fibers were drawn off and twisted into a continuous strand. The Greeks used a loom on which odd- and

even-numbered warp threads were tied to weights hung behind the loom and alternately brought forward as weaving progressed. Similar warp-weighted looms were employed in northern Europe. On a Norwegian tapestry "calendar," a Viking horseman illustrates the month of May. In central Sweden, a Viking grave yielded a silver-embroidered silk cuff. The silk could have come from as far away as Byzantium. Great trading empires followed the spread of Islam across Europe, Asia, and Africa. Muslims—who invaded Spain in 711—perhaps taught the Spanish to make silk. Found in Spain, a piece of silk with gold and silver thread shows Chinese influence in its design of cockatoos and lions. It may have been woven in Central Asia, Persia, or even in Italy, but declares its Islamic source in the borders of angular Arabic script. Another piece of Islamic-Spanish silk displays the intricate, interlaced geometric patterns also characteristic of Islamic architectural detail.

Tapestry, Norway, ca A.D. 1200

Silk and silver cuff,
Sweden, 10th century A.D.

Cotton openwork shirt, southwest U.S., ca A.D. 1300

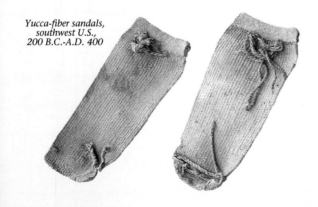

Yucca-fiber sandals, southwest U.S., 200 B.C.-A.D. 400

Indian artisans were among the first to master the various methods of dyeing. They knew the use of mordants—metallic salts that fix a dye by combining with it to form an insoluble compound. They used the root of the herb madder to obtain shades of red or pink, lilac, or black, depending on the mordant it was combined with. From oak gall they prepared black dye. From the indigo plant they obtained deep blue.

Other cultures, too, produced notable dyes. Archaeologist Sir Leonard Woolley found evidence of red textiles some 4,000 years old at Ur. Phoenicians made a "royal purple" derived from a sea snail.

Indian fabrics earned great renown. In addition to developing elaborate dyeing techniques, craftsmen perfected the art of printing fabrics with wooden blocks. Around 300 B.C., a Greek envoy who visited the court of an Indian emperor described the finely woven flowered muslins that people wore, and the robes embroidered in gold that he saw on the nobility. In producing brocades of silk, silver, and gold, Indian weavers relied heavily on silk from China.

Although silk making originated in China, legend surrounds its beginning. Tales say that, as long ago as the 27th century B.C., an emperor's wife discovered that she could unwind a long thread from the cocoon of a moth that lived in mulberry trees. With carbon dating, archaeologists have confirmed the relative antiquity of sericulture, if not the legends. Red silk threads, ribbons, and woven cloth 5,000 years old have been found.

In some ways, silk textiles became political instruments. In China, the court established factories to weave silk for ceremonial use and as gifts to foreign powers. At times, death by torture awaited any persons who revealed the secrets of sericulture. Envoys carried silks and other treasures to Persia and Mesopotamia.

Japan placed no less emphasis on the language of silks. "The garment was the person" wrote Lady Murasaki Shikibu in *The Tale of Genji*. This early 11th-century novel emphasized propriety in dress: the correct layering of colors of several kimonos worn at once, the apt selection of pattern and design in courtly apparel.

The Japanese were expert dyers, employing, among other techniques, a fine tie-dyeing called *kanoko-zome*, after *kanoko*, or fawn—supposedly because the emperor, who admired the muted shading of a fawn's coat, ordered his dyers to produce the pattern in silk.

Archaeologists have been able to study Egypt's textile history through a trove of documents, artwork, tools, and surviving fabrics, all preserved by the dry climate. Men cultivated the flax and prepared the bast fibers, while, through the early dynasties, women did the spinning and weaving. By about 1550 B.C., the horizontal loom had given way to the vertical loom.

Most fine linen was bleached to meet the Egyptian preference for the whitest, "cleanest" cloth possible. Enormous quantities of linen were needed for bedding, for clothing—loincloths, kilts, shirts—and for the wrapping of mummies.

Wool, not much used in Egypt, was important to people living in colder climates. A burial mound on the Jutland peninsula in northern

Feather-covered headband Paracas, Peru, ca 450-175 B.C.

Europe has yielded a tunic and skirt of wool from about 1400 B.C.

People in the Americas have long produced sophisticated woven goods. One early piece of evidence lay shrouded by a 10-foot layer of peat in a central Florida pond, where hunter-gatherers who lived from 7,000 to 8,000 years ago buried their dead. They wrapped the bodies in grass mats and tightly woven fabric, perhaps blankets or ponchos, of plant fibers.

In Peru, where cotton also was important, wool has been the chief fiber and fabric of daily life and of ritual for more than 3,000 years. During the Inca era, the state encouraged llama herding and maintained textile storehouses in urban centers. Peas-

Wool mummy bundle, Paracas, Peru, A.D. 400-800

Stylized painted textile, Peru, A.D. 1100-1200

The New World

In the Americas, textiles ranged from the sophisticated, mystically patterned fabrics of Peru to the straightforward simplicity of the twisted yucca fiber that made Anasazi sandals. Square at the toe, rounded at the heel, they fastened by means of loops and a connecting string tied around the ankle. The Anasazi grew and spun cotton, which they wove on looms or fashioned into openwork shirts. In Peru, the textiles produced by legions of unknown artists have been fundamental to cultural identity for some 4,000 years. This model of weavers at work illustrates the back-strap, or belt, loom. Peruvian workers probably used back-strap looms as long ago as 1800 B.C. Warp threads were attached at one end to a bar strapped to the weaver's body and, at the opposite end, to a fixed bar. The weaver controlled the warp tension by leaning forward or backward. Bells, beads, and feathers sometimes adorned woven textiles.

When archaeologists opened desert graves at Paracas, a coastal settlement, among the multitudes of textiles wrapping mummies they found this animal-faced headband of wool from alpaca, guanaco, or vicuña covered with feathers of tropical birds. Another Paracas fabric, part of a mummy bundle, is an embroidered portrait, perhaps of a high-ranking personage. The snakes he holds link him to the forces of nature and ritual. Other Peruvian textiles show stylized animals and anthropomorphic figures. Some bear fish—an important part of the diet of coastal Peruvians.

Fabric, probably alpaca wool, Peru, pre-15th century A.D.

ants were obliged to weave cloth for the king as a tax.

In the Andes, even among the peasantry, textiles bore ceremonial roles at every stage of life. Weaned infants were presented gifts that included cloth.

Puberty and marriage were occasions for the ritual making and wearing of new clothes. In religious ceremonies, the Inca burned sacrificial offerings of cloth and llamas. At death, in common with cultures worldwide, textiles were called upon to play their role. Mummies huddled in quantities of fabric layers. The shrine of a deceased woman held, along with a clump of cotton, her spindle—the universal instrument of creation and continuity.

Wool model of weavers, Peru, pre-15th century A.D.

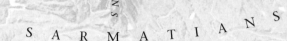

Tolstaya
Mogila •   • Solokha

• Kostromskaya

CARPATHIAN MOUNTAINS

MEDITERRANEAN SEA

BLACK SEA

CAUCASUS MOUNTAINS

CASPIAN SEA

URAL MOUNTAINS

SCYTHIANS

SARMATIANS

CIMMERIANS

PERSIA

KHWARAZM

Amu Dar'ya

HINDU KUSH

PAMIRS

Tillya
Tepe •
• Balkh

BACTRIA

Central and North Asia

2000 B.C. to A.D. 1400

Bounded by desert and mountain to the south and by taiga or dense forest to the north, the steppes of Central and North Asia once stretched like a sea of grass some 3,500 miles from the Carpathians to the Amur River region. It was an ideal environment for the native horse that ranged the region, and for the mounted nomadic lifestyle that developed there.

From horse bones in ancient middens of Neolithic farmers dating to about 4000 B.C. in what is now Ukraine, archaeologists have discovered the first known use of domesticated horses—for meat, milk, and hides. About that time also, as has been determined from bit marks worn into prehistoric horses' teeth, people began to ride horses.

By about 900 B.C., the region's tribal peoples had become skilled horsemen. For them, the horse clearly held a primary place, both socially—signaling power—and culturally—as evinced by sacrifice and burial of favorite, elaborately adorned mounts with the deceased.

Over the centuries, a succession of mounted nomads—Scythians, Sarmatians, Hsiungnu, Yueh-chi, Kushan, Huns, and Mongols among them—streamed across the steppes. Herding huge numbers of sheep, cattle, and horses, they alternately traded with or terrorized the local populace. Sometimes they settled down, or, as in the case of the Mongols, they conquered and ruled.

Most of them were constantly on the move, on horseback or by wagon, and they left few physical records,

except for their tombs. Because these groups came into contact with one another—through conquest, intermarriage, and the exchange of technical skills—they seem to have shared a common lifestyle. Ethnic roots blur and cultures blend.

Only the chance discovery of a burial site or writings of a contemporary observer from the outside world—or perhaps observation of the lifestyles of more recent Kazakh and Mongolian herdsmen—have shed light on their rugged, individualistic way of life. The creative energy that other cultures have devoted to building temples or palaces was expended by the ancient nomads on portable objects for life on the move. Their heritage rested in the adornment they bestowed on their tent-homes, their horses, and themselves.

B E R I A

Amur

Pazyryk ◆

ALTAI MOUNTAINS

TIAN SHAN

G O L S

Khanbaliq ◆

KOREA

J A P A Z

Yellow

PLATEAU OF
TIBET

CHINA

Yangtze

HIMALAYA

INDIA

PACIFIC

OCEAN

● Ancient and modern town site

◆ Archaeological site only

0   600 mi
0   800 km

INDIAN

OCEAN

Scythians

7th to 1st century B.C.

Gold stag,
width 12.5 in

Like a nightmare, the Scythians swept across the steppes of Central Asia north of the Black Sea and into Crimea. In about the seventh century B.C., these fearsome nomadic warriors drove people known as Cimmerians from the area. Among the earliest skilled horsemen, the Scythians, as the Greeks called them, trailed immense herds of sheep, cattle, and horses. In random raids, they plundered settlements and extorted money for safe passage of goods. In more peaceful times they traded grain, furs, and cattle for wine, fine crafts, and metalwork, especially that made by Greeks.

For three centuries the Scythians held sway over much of present-day Ukraine and prospered, developing a taste for luxury. In the third century B.C., they lost most of their steppeland to another nomadic group, the Sarmatians, who came from the east. In the following two centuries, the Scythians succumbed to the Sarmatians and merged cultures with them.

Like other nomads, the Scythians left few permanent traces, except for their kurgans, impressive burial mounds, some rising several stories above timber-roofed sepulchers. In some regions, especially near the Black Sea, kurgans numbered in the hundreds, fueling legend and speculation for centuries. No one is certain exactly who the Scythians were. They left no written record, but their presence is noted in Assyrian documents and on monuments. Their language was probably Iranian-based. They may have been a confederation of several nomadic tribes.

In the fifth century B.C., the historian Herodotus marveled at their ability to remain unassailable and "one and all of them, to shoot from horseback." Some, however, were not nomadic, but semisettled cultivators of grain, which they sold. Herodotus called a particularly prosperous, powerful group near the Black Sea, with elaborate burial customs, the Royal Scythians.

Herodotus cataloged numerous Scythian customs. That they drank outrageously and took wine undiluted shocked the temperate Greek, accustomed to watered wine. The nomads also imbibed the blood of the first man they killed in battle, collected scalps of enemies as trophies, and drank from the skulls of their most detested foes. They blinded slaves to prevent them from stealing the cream they churned. A concubine, servants, and horses were sacrificed and buried, together with much wealth, alongside a dead chief. To attend one Scythian ruler in death, 50 fine horses were slain and 50 youths strangled.

The historian admired their prowess in war, however, noting in particular their adroit handling of superior Persian forces under Darius I, who at the time threatened the Greeks. Though many of his anecdotes seemed far-fetched, Herodotus's descriptions remained for centuries the basic source of information about the Scythians.

Now archaeological studies are proving the ancient historian often reasonably accurate. At Kostromskaya, for instance, where the gold stag above was unearthed, 13 servants and 22 slaughtered horses had joined the chieftain in death. At another kurgan in the Caucasus, remains of 360 horses were found.

Modern awareness of this rich nomadic heritage begins in the early 18th century, as gold artifacts started showing up, pilfered by grave robbers from kurgans in Siberia. Peter the Great of Russia took interest in fine examples presented to him and decreed that all such treasure be turned over to the crown. In the 19th century, scholars began to probe the mounds in a serious way. Though many sites were already vandalized and archaeological evidence destroyed, remarkable finds still surfaced. In 1913, for instance, the gold comb at top right came out of a side grave at the previously ransacked Solokha kurgan. In 1971, the elaborate gold pectoral at right was found in a side grave at Tolstaya Mogila. Thieves had ignored this part of the burial chamber beneath the huge mound where a high-ranking family had been laid to rest.

Research and digging at various sites continue today, revealing more about the symbolic significance of the Scythians' complex burial rites and the social structure required to create such rich monuments to the dead.

Storied Gold of Scythia

Panoply of life parades around a gold pectoral. The magnificent neckpiece, found in Tolstaya Mogila, in present-day Ukraine, measures a foot across and weighs two and a half pounds. Though likely created by a Greek goldsmith commissioned by a prosperous Scythian, the fourth-century B.C. ornament offers a vivid picture of Scythian life. Forty-four animals in all, domesticated and wild, and four men adorn the piece. Two men team up to stitch a sheepskin shirt, their quivers at the ready in case of enemy attack. Another man milks a ewe. In the outer band, fantastical griffins tear into horses, and a panther and a lion share a stag. The gold pectoral illustrates in extraordinary detail the Scythian preoccupation with animals, mythic and real, upon which their nomadic life depended.

In a much older piece, a magnificent rack of antlers caps a stag that once embellished a shield found at Kostromskaya, in the Caucasus. Dating from the late seventh century, the simpler, stylized stag expresses a shamanistic energy and power missing in the later, ornate Greek style. A mounted warrior and two other nomads on foot engage in fierce combat atop a gold comb. The five-inch-high, Greek-crafted ornament probably adorned a king's long hair. Scythian men and women both wore earrings such as this fourth-century pair, decorated with little birds. Their taste for such luxuries may have softened Scythians to the hardships of nomadic life. Hundreds of Scythian burial mounds dotted the steppes before much of this ancient grassland region fell to the plow. Those that remain gradually yield evidence about this intriguing nomadic people.

Gold comb, 5 in

Gold earrings

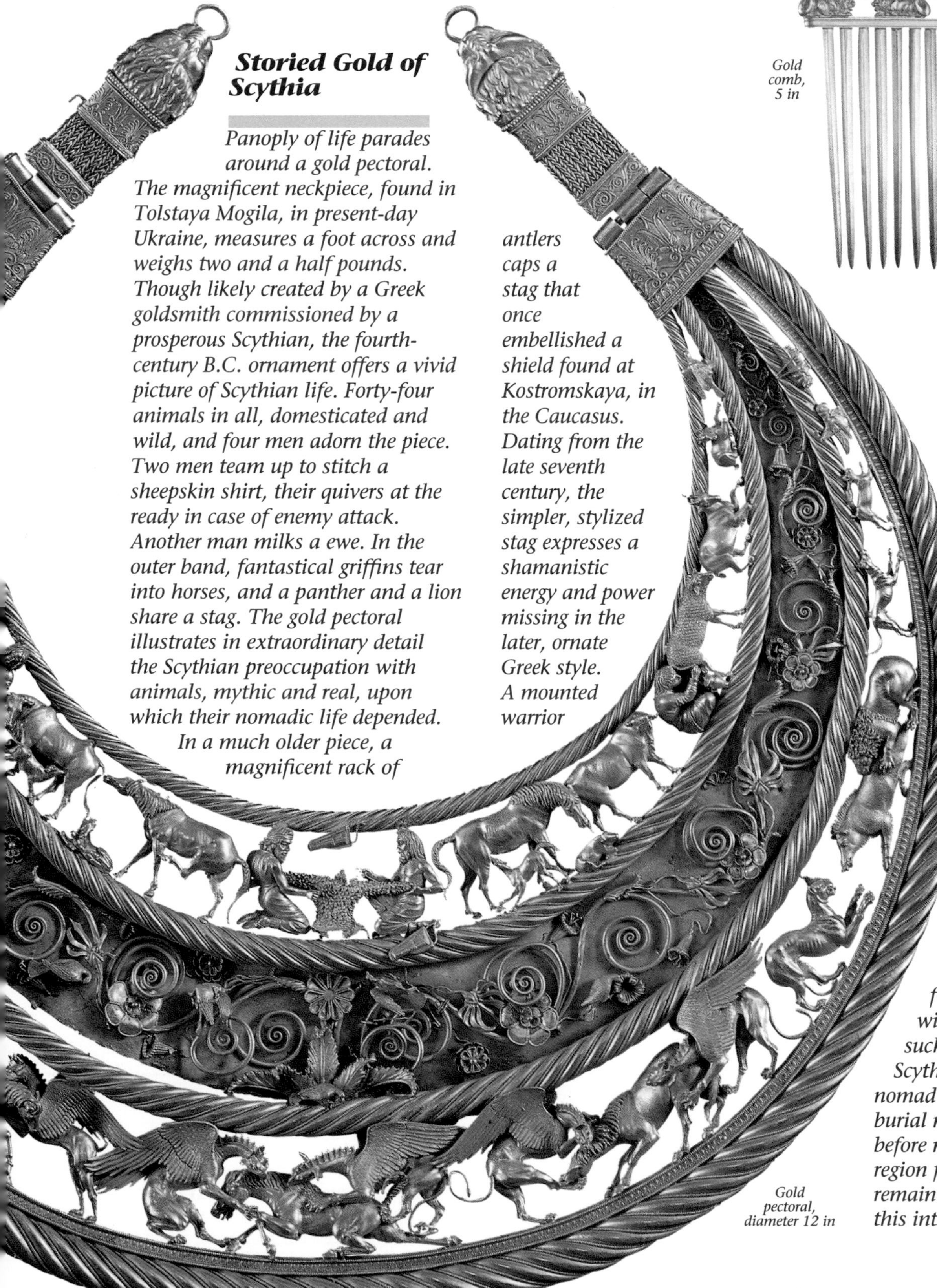

Gold pectoral, diameter 12 in

Pazyryk

5th to 3rd century B.C.

Human greed and a fluke of nature combined fortuitously for archaeologists in the Altai Mountains of southern Siberia. Like the Scythians, nomadic tribes at Pazyryk constructed elaborate burial mounds, but they piled stones atop their kurgans. Working here in the 1920s, then again in the 1940s, archaeologists made a startling discovery. Many of the kurgans had been frozen since shortly after they were built in the fifth century B.C. Grave robbers had penetrated the cairns early on, making it easier for water to flow in. Eventually ice layers had formed inside the burial chambers. By dissipating summer's heat, the cairns atop the kurgans prevented melting. Almost intact, within log-framed burial chambers, were mummies of the ancient nomads, along with fragile clothing and other accoutrements. Precious metals had been looted long before. But a unique array of wood carvings, leather, felt, and Chinese silk goods, as well as a wool carpet older than any previously found, had survived. Buried also were fine horses, fully caparisoned, with elaborate headdresses.

The tribes at Pazyryk had no written language, and no one really knows who they were. Some scholars think that they spoke a Turkic language and that their nomadism may have been vertical, from steppe to mountain meadow, rather than across the vast grasslands. Some burial objects indicate clear ties with China and Persia—through trade, plunder, or, perhaps, intermarriage. Many scholars now prefer to categorize the people of Pazyryk simply as Altai tribesmen.

In 1993, scientists opened an undisturbed tomb to reveal yet another mummified body—that of a high-born young woman, remarkably preserved in a block of ice. Tattoos of mythical monsters marked her skin. A tall, elaborate felt headdress capped her dark hair. In the burial chamber, remains of a ceremonial meal of mutton and horsemeat had survived. Horses, sacrificed at her death, still had stomachs full of their last meal of grasses.

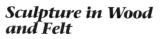

Sculpture in Wood and Felt

A rainbow of color emerges at Pazyryk, an archaeological site unlike many where only metal or stone is found. Thanks to ice that filled burial barrows, richly colored textiles, furs, wood, and leather objects, which normally decay, survived for nearly 2,500 years. A graceful felt swan, a typical Chinese motif,

Wooden griffin head and stag, 10.6 in

Felt swan, 13.8 in

adorned the canopy of a carriage that came out of one kurgan. Possibly a wedding gift, the vehicle may have accompanied a Chinese princess given in marriage to a Pazyryk chieftain. The Chinese used such nuptials to cement treaties of "peace and kinship" with warlike nomadic tribesmen. On a superb carved wooden standard, a griffin slays a stag. The oft-repeated theme of mortal combat between predator and prey continues on a felt saddle cover, where an eagle-griffin attacks an ibex. Out of the recently opened kurgan (opposite) came the almost perfectly preserved remains of a high-ranking woman. Felt carpeted the coffin in her log-framed burial chamber, which was furnished with low tables and other household goods, much as the deceased lady's earthly dwelling must have been. To gain access, archaeologists removed a pyramid of dirt and stones about nine feet high that capped the barrow.

Felt saddle cover

Kushan

100 B.C. to A.D. 100

Collapsible crown

Since ancient times, the Bactrian Plain, along the Amu Dar'ya River in what is now Afghanistan, has been a crossroads of cultures and goods. It is a desert region, relieved occasionally by fertile oases. Many different groups of people have moved through here, each leaving its mark. Rising in the mid-third century B.C., a century after the death of Alexander the Great, the Greco-Bactrian kingdom held sway here for about a hundred years. As in many Hellenistic outposts, Greek colonists infused the region with their culture and artistry. In about 130 B.C., the kingdom declined as the nomadic Kushan, pushed westward out of China by Huns, united with Scythian nomads and laid siege. At first the invaders destroyed much of what they found. Then they, too, settled into urban ways and expanded over a large territory. Like their predecessors, the Kushan prospered as merchants, trading with the caravans that followed the Silk Road between Europe and China and the north–south routes out of India. Objects from China, Rome, and Siberia reveal Bactria's importance in trade. Later, the Kushan seem to have expanded southward into India, becoming absorbed into the Hindu society of the subcontinent.

Very little is known about the Kushan or Bactria during this early period from about 100 B.C. to A.D. 100—which scholars have named

Aphrodite pendant

206

the Dark Period. In 1978, however, Viktor Ivanovich Sarianidi and the team of Russian and Afghan archaeologists he co-directed focused on a site known by locals as Tillya Tepe, or "golden hill," near the ancient Bactrian capital of Balkh.

The team probed the crumbling ruins of a templelike edifice. Suddenly a small golden disk gleamed in the dirt. It was the first of a trove of more than 20,000 items—consisting mostly of gold and precious stones. The archaeologists had stumbled upon what may have been the family cemetery of the rulers of a Kushan princedom. A rich array of bracelets, necklaces, diadems, rings, anklets, and toilet articles of varying styles was unearthed.

By carefully charting the position of hundreds of gold disks that once adorned the now decayed garments worn by the dead, the archaeologists were able to determine much about the style of clothing and burial rites of these people. Sarianidi surmised that the graves had been rendered deliberately inconspicuous in order to camouflage the importance of the deceased and the wealth of treasure buried with them. These aristocrats, he thinks, may even have been interred secretly at night.

By the time the research team departed in 1979, forced out by Afghanistan's civil war, six of the eight graves at the site had yielded a dazzling legacy. The last two graves, however, remained unexplored. Soon after, treasures suspiciously like those found at Tillya Tepe began to show up in the shops of the Afghan capital, Kabul.

Treasure of Tillya Tepe

Still wearing her crown, a haunting visage emerges from the dust at Tillya Tepe. In the sixth grave they opened, the archaeologists discovered the remains of a young woman (opposite), perhaps a princess, arrayed in the gold spangles that had embellished her now decayed garments. The palmette-decorated crown—collapsible for easy transport—well suited a nomadic princess. After lying hidden for nearly two millennia, this golden legacy came to light in 1978. Cultural lines became fuzzy in ancient Bactria as Greek artistry met that of the steppes, India, and the Far East. Wings on a chubby Grecian Aphrodite derive from Bactrian tradition. Her caste mark comes from India. Stretched out at full length, carnelian-eyed antelope—in the typical contorted style of Scythian and Siberian animal art—spanned the wrist of a matriarch in Grave

Two. The braided gold belt cinched the burial tunic of a warrior-prince, the only male unearthed. Each of the nine medallions in the belt shows a goddess astride a fierce lion. Out of the warrior's grave also emerged a finely executed ibex. It probably came off a Greco-Bactrian diadem, perhaps booty seized by the Kushan as they invaded. A turquoise-studded shoe buckle, found beside the warrior's foot, portrays Oriental figures in a Chinese-style chariot drawn by griffins. The treasures Russian archaeologist Viktor Ivanovich Sarianidi and his team unearthed at Tillya Tepe await further study in Kabul.

Turquoise-studded shoe buckle

Ibex ornament

Antelope bracelets

Warrior's belt

Mongols

A.D. 1100 to 1400

"The Accursed of God," the Muslims called the ferocious Mongols who swept across Asia into Europe in the 13th century A.D. In reality a loose confederation of tribes on the Mongolian steppes, these nomads shared a lifestyle with other pastoral peoples. From behind their Great Wall, the Chinese had long managed to keep the warlike Mongols divided and restrained. But unification came under the ruthless and skillful Genghis Khan. Within a century Mongol control extended from Korea to Hungary.

In about 1160, Temujin, later known as Genghis Khan—Universal Ruler—was born into an aristocratic nomadic family. After a brutal childhood, the ambitious young leader forged alliances among fellow tribesmen to carry him toward what was considered his divine destiny— the conquest of the world. To friends supremely loyal, Genghis was merciless to anyone who stood in his way—not shrinking even from murdering his half-brother. His reaction to defiant behavior was ferocious, as Shah Muhammad of Khwarazm—in the area of present-day Afghanistan—learned after spurning the khan's peace offering and executing his emissary. Mongol warriors overran his kingdom, slaughtering hundreds of thousands of people and ravaging cities.

After the death of Genghis Khan in 1227, his empire was divided into four khanates, led by a string of sons and grandsons who continued his expansionism. The Mongols conquered China later in

Genghis Khan

Kublai Khan

the 13th century and ruled as the Yuan dynasty. Factional infighting and, perhaps, the Black Death brought about their decline.

Archaeology reveals little about these warriors. One reason for this may be that, unlike many nomads, the Mongols built no tombs, exposing their dead instead on the steppes. Tradition holds, however, that Genghis was buried on a mountain in Mongolia. The search to locate his tomb continues.

Strangely enough, for a culture without writing, the written record is substantial. Genghis Khan respected writing and enlisted the literate Uyghurs to transcribe Mongolian into their own script. The Mongolian code of law appeared in that script, as well as an account of Genghis Khan's life. Narratives by a string of travelers include Marco Polo's description of his 17-year stay at the court of Kublai Khan in China.

Bronze seal and impression

Techniques of Warfare

At one with his galloping mount, a Mongol hunter (below) takes steady aim at his quarry. Such hunting was practice for mounted warfare. For hunting or fighting from horseback, stirrups, such as these iron ones, offered a stability unknown to earlier nomads. A silver-inlaid helmet provided protection. In the 13th century, Genghis Khan's forces conquered much of Asia and part of Europe. Genghis Khan proudly retained his nomadic lifestyle, but his grandson Kublai Khan relished the luxuries of the Chinese capital at Khanbaliq (now Beijing). Under Kublai Khan, expansionism continued. A bronze seal, recognizable to illiterate soldiers, announced the bearer as the commander of up to a thousand troops.

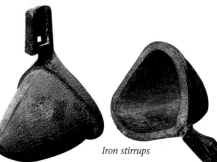

Iron stirrups

Helmet with silver inlay

ASIA

PACIFIC

M I C R O N E S I A

Caroline Islands

Nan Madol
Pohnpei ◆

M E L A N E S I A

Bismarck
Archipelago

NEW GUINEA

Solomon
Islands

Cape York

Efate ●

Fiji
Islands

AUSTRALIA

Nullarbor Plain

Darling

Lake
Mungo ◆

Murray

Snowy
Mts.

Mt. Camel ◆

NEW

ZEALAND

North
Island

Wairau
Bar ◆

Tasmania

South
Island

● Ancient and modern town site

◆ Archaeological site only

0	800 mi

0	1200 km

Hawaiian Islands

OCEAN

POLYNESIA

Samoa
Islands

Raiatea

Society Islands

Tonga
Islands

Easter I.

Pacific Islands

50,000 B.C. to A.D. 1800

The Pacific Ocean covers a third of the globe—70 million square miles—and its myriad islands lie like glittering stars in an endless sky, scattered randomly across its enormous breadth. Geographers divide the islands into three groups: Micronesia—in the western Pacific, lying generally north of the Equator; Melanesia—islands northeast of Australia, between the Equator and the Tropic of Capricorn, including New Guinea; and Polynesia, a triangle of islands defined by Hawaii, New Zealand, and Easter Island. The Pacific's largest island—Australia—is a continent unto itself.

The islands range from tiny coral atolls that ring blue lagoons to forest-clad volcanic mountains soaring into the clouds. Climatically, they run the gamut from tropical through subtropical and temperate to near subantarctic.

European explorers in the 16th century found them peopled by diverse but apparently related cultures. Most of the indigenous languages of the Pacific belong to the same family, Austronesian, which originated thousands of years ago in Southeast Asia or Melanesia.

Prehistoric islanders' mythologies were rich with complex religions and numerous gods and spirits. The people fished teeming seas for food, or grew taro, bananas, breadfruit, and coconuts. Pigs, dogs, and fowl were domesticated. The islanders lived in dispersed households or in villages; their social organization ranged from small-scale and egalitarian to stratified societies with hereditary chiefs.

Art could be ephemeral—singing, dancing, body painting—or permanent and elaborate. Much art was associated with ritual and religion. The stone temples of some islands and the giant stone statues of others, such as Easter Island and the Marquesas, indicate highly developed stoneworking skills. Many functional goods, such as canoes, war clubs, and fishhooks, were elegantly crafted and decorated.

Oceania was one of the last regions on earth to be settled. Its original colonists came from Asia, brave seafarers peopling a new world. The earliest came some 50,000 years ago and moved into Australia, then part of a larger continent called Sahul that included Tasmania and New Guinea.

Archaeologists trace a later group eastward, after about 1500 B.C., through a trail of distinctive pottery called Lapita ware. The Lapita culture spread throughout Melanesia as far as Fiji and reached western Polynesia by 1000 B.C.

Evidence of the Lapita people—largely their pottery, which consists of cooking pots, beakers, and bowls—has been found from New Guinea eastward to Samoa. Much of it bears geometric designs that were produced by stamping the unfired clay with a toothed implement.

Skilled sailors and navigators, the Lapita people subsisted largely by fishing along the coasts of the islands on which they lived. Their culture faded early in the first millennium A.D., and pottery making there died out. Except in New Guinea, metallurgy was unknown in the region until the arrival of Europeans.

Because prehistoric lifestyles often continued until recent times in Oceania, there is ample material from which to re-create the past.

Australia

40,000 B.C. to A.D. 1800

Some 40,000 years ago, the peopling of Australia was well under way. Migrants first reached the continent from the north, and the stone tools and other artifacts found by archaeologists at various sites indicate that bands of hunter-gatherers soon found their way to the farthest corner.

They adapted well to the land and developed the longest continuous cultural history in the world. They never used metals or pottery, never developed the bow and arrow or the wheel, and never raised crops or livestock. Yet their culture was rich in myth, religion, art, and ceremony. They had far-flung trading networks and a democratic system of justice and decision making.

At Lake Mungo, a dried lake bed in southeastern Australia, archaeologists have found cremation burials—which implies a burial ritual—and food remains that include freshwater mollusks, fish, and small marsupials dating back 30,000 years.

Most early settlements were on the coasts and along river valleys. But changing climate led to higher sea levels beginning about 10,000 years ago, and the earliest coastal settlements now lie underwater. Of necessity, archaeologists have relied heavily on interior sites.

By 5,000 years ago, cremation and burial were common; new types of stone tools had been developed; and the dingo, a relative of the pariah dog of India, had been introduced from the mainland of southeast Asia. Walls of caves and rock-shelters were covered with art.

By 3,000 years ago, long-distance trade networks facilitated the movement of raw materials. In fertile areas, such as the swamps of Victoria, the people settled down in stone houses and created villages of up to 700 people. Ceremonial gatherings at painted rock-shelters or bora grounds—areas used in rituals—attracted crowds; people gathered from afar to celebrate the harvest of certain foods—the cycad nut, for instance, which needs careful preparation to render it nonpoisonous, or a kind of moth found only at certain times in the Snowy Mountains.

Ancestor or creator being

Emu tracks, hands, arms, and boomerangs

Aboriginal Rock Art

Bone fragments emerge from the sands of an Aboriginal hearth (opposite) perhaps 25,000 years old, built beside now dry Lake Mungo in New South Wales. For millennia, Aboriginal artists used rocks as a medium for depicting their people, their myths, and the creatures they knew. On Cape York, giant wallaroos hop across the wall of a shelter. A male ancestor or creator being nearly 14 feet long reaches skyward in New South Wales. Hair or feathers sprout from his head. Stenciling produced striking art: Artists mixed pigments in their mouths, then sprayed them around an object held against a rock. Stylized emu tracks were made with tips of boomerangs.

The Aborigines produced an extraordinary body of art. Some of the earliest known was scratched on the walls of a cave on Nullarbor Plain more than 20,000 years ago. Thousands of other rock art sites exist throughout the continent—many recent, but many others prehistoric.

The different styles of Aboriginal art reflect the diversity of the culture. Some rock artists engraved the outlines of figures; others "pecked" their engravings into the stone. Some artists painted figures, either mythical or realistic, animal or human. Intriguing X-ray art revealed the skeletons and internal organs of creatures, as well as their external features. Stencil art—in which various objects were stenciled with red, yellow, or black pigments—is found in much of Australia.

Aboriginal art was never done purely as art, but figured in religious life or accompanied rituals. Art was a manifestation of spiritual beliefs to the Aborigines, linking them with their mythical Dreamtime.

Great Spirit Ancestors

At some sacred sites, Aborigines believed, ancestors from the Dreamtime came to rest and transformed themselves into images on rocks. As if on guard, malevolent Quinkan spirits raise outstretched arms in a rock-shelter on Cape York. Ancestral beings known as Wandjina have stripes hanging from their shoulders that represent rainfall. Over the years, people have retouched these paintings. Rainbow Serpent, who created rivers, mountains, and people on its mythical journey down from the north coast, slithers across a rock face in central Australia. Inverted U shapes represent unborn babies.

Quinkan spirits
Rainbow Serpent

Ancestral Wandjina from the Dreamtime

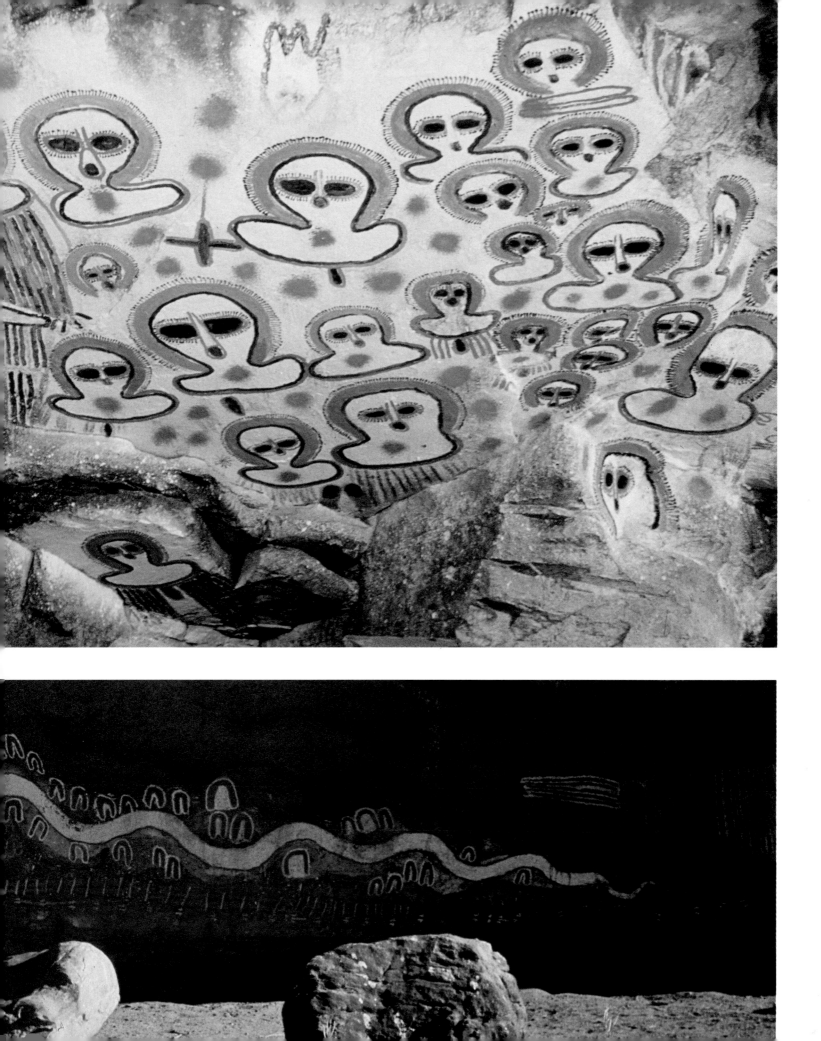

Peopling the Pacific

40,000 B.C. to A.D. 1000

Australian Aborigines call it the Dreamtime, their age of creation, when ancestral humans and animals traveled the world, creating the land and all living things. The peopling of Australia began more than 40,000 years ago. Colonists reached the Bismarck Archipelago and the Solomon Islands in Melanesia by 30,000 years ago, and settlement was well under way.

Another wave of voyaging and colonization began around 3,500 years ago. These colonists' canoes were large, seaworthy cargo ships, filled with both fresh foods and preserved—dried bananas and breadfruit, sugarcane, dried fish, flour—and gourds of fresh water. Livestock, seedlings, and rootstocks were also aboard. Probably the canoes carried small biological families. Thus outfitted—and blessed by their gods—they could travel as much as 500 miles in 5 days.

Their navigators evidently saw the Pacific Ocean as a highway. Knowledge of winds, stars, and currents grew with experience;

Grave of followers of Roy Mata, Retoka

Shell necklace

Micronesian navigator's stick chart

Raiatea, Society Islands, French Polynesia

Navigation Aids

Small targets in a big ocean, the atolls and coral-rimmed islands of the Pacific lured colonists for millennia. With stick charts— whose shells indicated islands and sticks the prevailing currents— and blessed by sea gods such as Tangaroa of the Polynesians, brave and curious navigators eventually found virtually all the thousands of islands in the Pacific. Archaeologists trace their progress from island to island with artifacts such as Lapita-style pottery and evolving fishhooks.

Polynesian sea god, 44 in

distant islands could sometimes be spotted by the overhanging cloud cover or by tracking the flights of birds. Still, to set off in search of islands they did not know existed required a great leap of faith and boundless self-confidence.

By 1000 B.C. colonists had reached Samoa, where they developed the culture we know as Polynesian. By A.D. 300 they were in the Marquesas; during the next few centuries, they settled the Society Islands, Easter Island, the Hawaiian Islands, and New Zealand.

The first colonists had voyaged east, against the prevailing winds. Though this made sailing maneuvers more difficult, it was generally safer, because it facilitated a return to the home island if no new lands were discovered. Archaeologist Geoffrey Irwin wrote, "Some theories of Pacific colonisation prefer many explorers to die at sea, but there is nothing to show Pacific explorers were unconcerned about their lives."

There were voyages of discovery as well as colonization. These would avoid risking women and children, plants and animals, on every voyage. Explorers might return with tales of newly discovered islands. As navigational skills improved, the collective memory of the geography of the Pacific increased. This necessitated a system for passing down navigational information from generation to generation. The Micronesians developed ingenious stick charts, which showed islands and currents.

To learn more about early island-ers, archaeologists also study their oral traditions. One myth led to the small island of Retoka off the coast of Efate. There, in 1967, archaeologists unearthed a mass burial (opposite) dating from about A.D. 1265. Thirty-nine subjects, including eleven aristocratic couples, had died at the same time as their chief. The men probably were drugged, the women strangled or buried alive. Fine shell ornaments decorated their bodies.

Lapita pottery sherd, 2.8 in

Fishhooks

Nan Madol

A.D. 100 to 1600

Few Pacific island peoples were more unusual or created more monumental and striking architecture than the Pohnpeians, who settled an island in eastern Micronesia. They chose an unlikely spot as their ceremonial center—a shallow reef area of about 200 acres just offshore. There they created 92 man-made islets by stacking large basalt "logs" into retaining walls and filling in the massive structures with tons of coral rubble. One translation of the name Nan Madol, "the place of spaces," may be a reference to the many channels that thread between the islets.

The site of Nan Madol was occupied as early as the first century A.D., and people had begun constructing islets by enlarging sandbars by around 500. Construction reached a peak some 500 years later, with the unification of Pohnpei under a sovereign of the Saudeleur dynasty and continued through the 16th century.

The Saudeleur and some 1,000 nobles, priests, and attendants lived on the artificial islands, accepting tribute and food—yams, taro, and breadfruit—from the 25,000 ordinary citizens living on Pohnpei itself.

Outer walls of Nan Douwas

Basalt "logs" and main burial chamber, Nan Douwas

Offshore City for the Elite

Stacked in header-and-stretcher style, basalt "logs" form the imposing walls of Nan Douwas, best preserved of the structures of Nan Madol. The man-made political and religious center lies just off the shore of the island of Pohnpei in Micronesia. Inside Nan Douwas are stones quarried on the main island, from a type of lava that cooled slowly and broke naturally into prisms. Laboriously transported by workers to the site, they tumble and sprawl as they are loosened by time. Mortar and pestle typify stone tools found throughout the Pacific.

Mortar and pestle

Stone platforms supported wood structures such as meeting places and the dwellings of priests, the royal family, and the nobility. House sizes reflected differences in rank.

One of the central mysteries of Nan Madol has to do with its construction: How did workers maneuver heavy stones from quarries on the main island to the site? Some of the basalt columns are nearly 20 feet long and weigh 6 tons; boulders as heavy as 50 tons were also brought to the site somehow, without sinking the rafts that carried them.

More mystery surrounds the purpose of the elaborate and difficult construction in the first place. Certainly the offshore site reinforced the distance between rulers and ruled. Evidently religion also played a role. The site itself had divine associations, and the large number of burials that recent excavations have uncovered suggests that life at Nan Madol was filled with ceremony and ritual.

Sacred eels swam in artificial pools and either accepted or rejected offerings of sacrificial turtle entrails, thereby pardoning or condemning the people for their transgressions.

By the time Europeans found Nan Madol in the 19th century, it was abandoned and overgrown. According to legend, a leader named Isokelekel and his 333 warriors overthrew the dynasty around 1600 and created a system of district chiefs that is still in place on the island today.

Easter Island

A.D. 400 to 1800

Easter Island is the Pacific's most remote inhabited island, lying 1,130 miles east of Pitcairn Island and 2,300 miles west of Chile. It was also one of the last islands to be settled in the vast reaches of that ocean. But by the year 400, settlers had arrived—probably from east-central Polynesia. The Rapa Nui—the name today's residents give themselves and their island—constructed one of the world's most intriguing civilizations.

European contact began in 1722, when Dutch explorers sighted the island on Easter Sunday and gave it the name by which it is generally known. The Spanish, the French, and British Capt. James Cook also visited. Because the island lacks running streams, drinking water is

Ancestral guardian, 12 in

in short supply, so none of the European visitors stayed more than a few days. They left scholars little information about the island.

European contact was calamitous for the few thousand islanders. In 1862, before the culture could be properly studied, a thousand islanders were taken by slavers to work in Peru. Not until about 900 of them had died and some of the world's governments had protested were the survivors repatriated. On the return voyage, 85 died and the rest arrived home carrying with them the deadly seeds of their further destruction—smallpox and tuberculosis. By 1877, only about 110 people remained alive on the island.

With the culture's collective memory virtually destroyed, the stage was set for decades of theorizing, speculation, and downright fantasizing by people trying to explain this most mystifying of societies.

For when the Dutch landed, they were met by the fierce gazes of hundreds of giant stone statues called *moai,* erected on stone platforms called *ahu.* The statues were as tall as 33 feet and weighed as much as 89 tons. Some wore 10-ton red scoria topknots. Using only stone tools, the islanders had carved the giant figures from the crater of an extinct volcano, then somehow maneuvered them to ahu all over the island. The platform

for the earliest statue yields a radiocarbon date of A.D. 713. Hundreds of statues, in various stages of construction, remain at the volcano.

The islanders were hard on the environment of their island. Trees were felled, partly to provide sleds for moving the statues and partly through slash-and-burn agriculture. Environmental degradation may have caused food shortages and hastened the decline of the culture.

Author Thor Heyerdahl, of *Kon-Tiki* fame, conducted archaeological research on the island in the 1950s. He theorized that the culture was founded by immigrants from South America. The toppled statues resulted from warfare with Polynesians who arrived much later. Archaeologists discount Heyerdahl's origin theory. But they do have evidence for a period of social upheaval and warfare, beginning about 1600.

By the 19th century, Easter Island's society had collapsed; people lived in small, terrified groups in caves, fighting among themselves, toppling and destroying one another's moai. There are even tales of desperate cannibalism. Ironically, the ancient, traditional Polynesian means of escape was not available to them: The large trees from which they might have constructed canoes to carry them to new lives on other islands had all been destroyed.

Eye made of coral and red scoria

Guardians of a Mysterious Heritage

Blank-faced stone statues called moai *(opposite), meant to honor ancestors, rise from the Easter Island hillside of their genesis—an extinct volcano named Rano Raraku. Some 400 figures remain here, unfinished when warfare and the disintegration of the island's enigmatic society caused workmen to abandon them. They were generally assumed to be purposely blind until discoveries in the late*

1970s by archaeologist Sergio Rapu— himself an Easter Islander—changed the way they are viewed. At a site on the north coast of the island, Rapu dug up what was clearly an eye—a central disk of volcanic red scoria set in an almond-shaped piece of white coral. The whole construction fit perfectly into the eye socket of a nearby statue. Some statues, reerected since then, have had their eyes restored. A wood-and-bark-cloth figure, its tattooed face fitted with similar eyes, served a family as an ancestral guardian.

Serpentine amulet, 2.8 in

New Zealand

A.D. 1000 to 1800

An island nation larger than the rest of Polynesia combined, New Zealand was the last of the major islands to be settled. By about A.D. 1000, the Polynesian ancestors of today's Maori

On the North Island, sites have been found largely along the coasts near the mouths of rivers. Mount Camel, a 3.7-acre site on the island's northern tip, yielded much detailed information on life in Archaic times: Earth ovens and evidence of food preparation were found here. Artifacts included bone ornaments and fishhooks. Some 21,000 bones—of fish, dolphin, seal, rat, dog, and moa—were cataloged.

Like most Polynesian settlers, the

Sacred Carvings

Carving was an invention of the gods, according to Maori legend. A mythical hero named Rua, rescuing his kidnapped son from the sea god Tangaroa, found the god's richly adorned house and brought back carvings for his own home. Thus sculpturing has been considered a semi-sacred pastime. An elegant carving—probably used to decorate a house or gateway—was found in a drained lake in 1920 and is perhaps 600 to 800 years old. Even older— possibly from A.D. 1000—is a serpentine amulet depicting the torso and limbs of a dancing figure. The whale-tooth pendant, its chevrons representing human arms and legs, has two back-to-back figures at the left, their arms upraised. A grimacing wooden figure, to be inserted into the ground or placed in a niche, held the bones of a deceased Maori; the figure's fierce expression was meant to frighten off meddlers. A wooden memorial post represents Uenuku, war god of the Waikato tribes. The jade pendant is a stylized human; such figures were passed down as heirlooms, as was the patu—a chief's nephrite war club.

House carving, 7.4 ft

were ashore. Linguistically, they developed several distinct but similar dialects; economically, however, regions differed widely. Warm, temperate coastal areas of the North Island developed agriculture. In the colder, southern half of the North Island and on the South Island, farming generally was not successful.

Archaeologists divide Maori prehistory into two phases: the Archaic, which lasted until about 1350 on the North Island and until about 1650 on the South Island, and the Classic.

On the South Island during the Archaic period, the population spread rapidly, moving seasonally from place to place. The Wairau Bar site on the northeast coast yielded the finest collection of archaeological grave goods recovered in New Zealand: fishhooks, stone adzes, harpoons, and necklaces made of bones and shark teeth. Giant moas— now extinct birds that were a reliable source of food for the Maori— were plentiful in the Wairau Bar area.

early Maori dramatically altered the environment of the islands, clearing forests and killing off perhaps 20 species of flying birds and 13 or more species of moa. Erosion followed the clearing of forests.

Rock art of the Maori is similar to that of other parts of Polynesia. Nearly all the rock art sites are found on the South Island and date from the Archaic phase. The best examples are drawings on the walls of rock-shelters in the limestone regions of Canterbury and Otago. Birds, dogs, people, and mythical creatures called *taniwha* are depicted.

Classic Maori art included curvilinear elements unique among Polynesian styles. Some archaeologists have suggested that the development of this distinctive style might have been a conscious validation of a new social order. But recent analysis favors a more gradual evolution.

Trade, which began during the Archaic period, was extensive, with long-distance exchanges of stones

Whale-tooth pendant, 5.8 in

Wooden bone box, 25 in

Memorial post, 8.7 ft

needed for toolmaking; these included greenstone (nephrite), argillite, and silcrete.

The Classic Maori phase was closely tied to sweet potato cultivation. The plant, though difficult to grow, was very important to the Maori economy. Much of the North Island's soil had to be aerated by adding sand and gravel before the plant would thrive.

Sweet potatoes cannot survive if the temperature falls below 40°F, so arrangements had to be made to store the tubers in frost-free subterranean storage pits if they were to survive the winter. Today these pits provide valuable clues to archaeologists studying the Maori.

Where the climate permitted, agriculture was a settling influence, and by 1500 a fairly homogeneous culture had spread across the North Island. Tools and utensils became more sophisticated; whale-tooth ornaments, popular in Archaic times, were replaced by pendants; and new types of weapons appeared.

During Classic times, the Maori built fortifications called *pa* throughout New Zealand, though most of the 5,500 found so far were in the northern part of the North Island. Pa served as defensive works and, where local conditions were suitable, some may have been occupied year-round. Most had large storage pits for preserving sweet potatoes.

There were three basic types of pa—those with terraces but no ditches; those built atop ridges and promontories with ditches and banks protecting them; and those with ring-ditches around them. Terraced

pa often were built on the slopes of extinct volcanoes; some had storage pits, houses, and palisades along their edges. Most common were promontory and ridge pa, ideally located to scan the rugged New Zealand terrain.

In 1769 one such pa was visited by Capt. James Cook and sketched by an artist aboard his ship. It was built on a narrow promontory overlooking Mercury Bay. Its landward side was protected by a steep bank and two ditches. Palisades protected raised platforms from which defenders could hurl stones and spears at attackers. Within the pa's defenses lay a large village. Many of the houses were built on artificial terraces, and some of the land was planted with crops of sweet potatoes.

On the South Island, the population of Maori gradually declined as resources diminished. On the North Island, on the other hand, the ability to cultivate crops led to the warlike yet artistic culture that European settlers encountered when they arrived in the 18th century.

Jade pendant, 5.5 in

Nephrite war club, 14 in

The Americas

North America

12,500 B.C. to A.D. 1500

We don't know why humans first came to the Americas, or even when, but we do know how: They crossed from Asia to Alaska over a broad, low-lying land bridge now known as Beringia. Their arrival was linked inextricably to that of ice. Throughout the Pleistocene epoch, vast ice sheets up to a mile thick periodically blanketed much of North America, locking up huge amounts of water and dropping the world's oceans by 300 feet or more. At such times, the bulk of today's shallow Bering Sea was dry land. Yet while the greatest glaciations reached as far south as Illinois, some of the continent's northernmost reaches—including most of Alaska—remained ice free. Thus Beringia provided a relatively iceless corridor between two of the harshest regions on earth: Siberia and Arctic America.

For at least the past 600 centuries, Beringia has resurfaced every 10,000 to 15,000 years, each time providing a prolonged window of opportunity for plants, animals, and people to migrate back and forth. The fossil record shows that, in Pleistocene times, Asia and America shared the same menagerie of mammoths, mastodons, long-horned bison, and other large herbivores, all of which died out in America. Such animals were prime game for human hunters on both sides of Beringia.

Indeed, the first North Americans may have arrived in pursuit of these migratory creatures. They also may have been driven by the pressures of Asia's expanding human populations. Or they may simply have responded to the basic human urge to explore the unknown. Whatever the reason, human migrations from Asia almost certainly occurred more than once.

They began relatively late, however; only the remains of *Homo sapiens sapiens* have been found in North America. And while such humans initially may have entered the New World many thousands of years ago, no archaeological sites have been reliably dated to more than about 12,500 years ago. Yet these humans seem to have spread rapidly, peopling virtually every niche of two continents from tip to tip and adapting to environments that range from Arctic tundra to tropical rain forest.

Archaeological evidence and anatomical similarities with Asian peoples suggest that today's Eskimos and Athapaskans are descended not from Arctic North America's first immigrants but from its most recent ones, who came only 5,000 or 6,000 years ago. Earlier arrivals had moved south into different areas, giving rise to the wealth of diverse Native American cultures that greeted the likes of Columbus and Magellan.

In the Great Plains, these descendants of Asian hunters remained hunters and gatherers. In the Eastern Woodlands, they developed the trading centers of the mound builders. Pueblo cultures would dominate the American Southwest, and some desert groups, such as the Hohokam, were perhaps in touch with the Mesoamerican cultures farther south.

PRECEDING PAGES: Stark, squarish dwellings of adobe rise above a curve-walled kiva—ceremonial room— at Cliff Palace, a Mesa Verde pueblo abandoned around A.D. 1300.

PACIFIC OCEAN

● Ancient and modern town site

◆ Archaeological site only

0   600 r

0   800 km

ASIA

BERING SEA

CHUKCHI SEA

Point Hope

Bering Strait

Diomede Islands

Point Barrow

NORTH SLOPE

ALASKA

Yukon

ELLESMERE ISLAND

GREENLAND

BAFFIN ISLAND

LABRADOR

ROCKY MOUNTAINS

Ozette
Olympic Peninsula

Lake Superior

Yellowstone

Missouri

Mississippi

SIERRA NEVADA

Lovelock Cave

Hogup Cave

Humboldt Sink

GREAT BASIN

Colorado

ANASAZI

HOPEWELL

ADENA

Adena

Appalachian Mountains

Cahokia

Serpent Mound

Kayenta   Mesa Verde

Ohio   Hopewell

Canyon de Chelly   Chaco Canyon

Santa Fe

Phoenix   Grasshopper

Gila   Salt

Snaketown   HOHOKAM

Casa Grande

Pottery Mound

MOGOLLON

Gila Cliff Dwellings

Hueco Tanks

Casas Grandes

Mimbres River

Spiro

MISSISSIPPIAN

Etowah

Moundville

Key Marco

227

Nomads of the North

4000 B.C. to A.D. 1500

They chose a remote land of fleeting summers and permanently frozen ground, of sparse vegetation and endless sweeps of stony, ice-encrusted terrain. Here they thrived for scores of centuries as they roamed the far north from Siberia's frigid Chukchi Sea across Alaska's North Slope, through Canada's Yukon and northern archipelago, to the eastern shores of Greenland. A notoriously fierce and brutal region, it has been even harsher during times of glacial advance.

Yet it also has been rich in animal life, both of land and sea, and the Asian societies that took this region for their own were hunters, first and foremost. Who were they? While archaeologists have named numerous different tool traditions in the Arctic, they are quick to add that the archaeological potential has hardly been tapped. Speculation, they admit, vastly exceeds the data so far recovered.

From about 9000 to 6000 B.C., Arctic North America was occupied by various Stone Age cultures—generally termed Paleo-Arctic—that originated in Siberia. By 4000 B.C., as the North Pacific Ocean stabilized near what would be its current level and extent, human exploitation of coastal resources increased. About

Core and miniature chert blades, Ellesmere Island, av 1.75 in

2,000 years later, a new, highly distinctive tool kit appeared in these coastal areas: the Arctic Small Tool tradition, marked by needlelike stone flakes. The same people who mastered this technology also introduced the bow and arrow to the continent, a major advantage over the spear in terms of harvesting the region's vast aggregations of caribou and birds.

The Arctic Small Tool tradition disappeared from the Bering Sea and other parts of Alaska by 1500 or 1000 B.C., to be replaced by the Norton tradition, which used similar weaponry but added other innovations from Asia, such as oil lamps, pottery, and decorative arts. While Norton peoples continued to rely on land-based animals, they increasingly turned also to marine creatures. Toggle harpoons of various sizes indicate that they successfully harvested whales as well as seals, probably year-round. By about 200 B.C., kayaks and umiaks appeared in some Norton cultures of the Bering Sea, further underlining a growing reliance upon—and mastery of—ocean resources.

Norton peoples also were artists, elaborately adorning harpoons and other objects. Ultimately, their maritime culture gave rise to the Thule tradition that dominated Arctic regions and directly preceded modern Eskimo societies.

Thule peoples were ingenious gadgeteers, using polished slate rather than flaked stone, as well as bone, antler, and ivory, to create weapons and tools that include a wide range of harpoon parts, fish spears, snow and meat knives, scrapers for blubber and hides, awls, needles, mattocks and other devices, all of which ensured their long-term survival in a challenging realm.

Spreading rapidly throughout the Arctic, Thule family groups wintered in large, semisubterranean houses of sod, stone, and whalebone; summers were spent in portable skin tents. Blubber provided not only food but also light and heat. In addition, they experimented with iron tools—fashioned both from terrestrial sources and from meteorites—as well as native copper ones, long before contact with Europeans. The arrival of Vikings in Greenland and eastern Canada sparked increased Thule use of—and trade in—iron implements across the vast Arctic.

Thule snow goggles

Thule Norseman figurine, 1 in

Ipiutak burial mask, Point Hope, Alaska

Dorset ritual image, arctic hare, 1.75 in

An Arctic Chronology

Once high points on the lowland plain of Beringia, the Diomede Islands (above), shared by the United States and Russia, underscore Asia's geographic proximity to North America. Eskimo cultures flourished on both sides of this former land bridge for centuries. Their predecessors include people of the Arctic Small Tool tradition, whose signature artifacts are narrow stone "microblades" an inch or two long, struck from roundish cores of chert, then carefully chipped into sharp-edged scrapers and knives. By 600 B.C., similar traditions in the eastern Arctic gave rise to a culture known as Dorset, named for a site on Baffin Island and exemplified by realistic, small-scale carvings such as this arctic hare, etched with skeletal markings. Between A.D. 800 and 1000, the Dorset people abruptly vanished and were replaced by the Thule, the direct ancestors of modern Eskimos. Thule people were great hunters, inventing and refining designs for toggle harpoons and other ingenious weaponry that would revolutionize Arctic life as they focused on harvesting the sea's bounty. Snow goggles of walrus ivory protected eyes from the intense glare of polar ice. A diminutive ivory effigy suggests the hooded image of a Norseman. Vikings visited Thule settlements in Greenland and northeastern Canada as early as the tenth century A.D. In the western Arctic, Ipiutak peoples—an offshoot of the Norton tradition—lavished art on various implements and ritualistic items, such as this square, fitted ivory burial "mask," found at a site over a thousand years old. Art sustained Thule and more modern Eskimo cultures as well: Grouped with an Inupiat Eskimo harpoon point and a bone-and-wood pick, this tiny ivory face may have been a bola weight—used to snag birds—that also served its owner as a charm.

Inupiat pick, Point Barrow, Alaska

Inupiat charm, Point Barrow, Alaska

Inupiat harpoon head, Point Barrow, Alaska

229

Ozette

500 to 1500 A.D.

Bone-and-wood fishhooks

Pompeii of the Pacific Northwest, the Makah Indian village of Ozette was buried some 500 years ago by mud slides that—while catastrophic to the inhabitants—preserved their material culture almost perfectly. The mud sealed human remains as well as tens of thousands of highly perishable artifacts, preventing decay and permitting archaeologists a rare glimpse of an ancient lifestyle along America's northwest coast.

Skilled artisans, the Makah relied on the region's dense, temperate rain forests for their raw materials. Cedar was especially prized, not only for Makah longhouses and seagoing canoes but also for storage chests, watertight cooking containers, and various implements. Cedar bark, shredded and woven, served in basketry, matting, and clothing. Forests offered sustenance as well, for they sheltered elk and other deer, birds, beaver, and the plentiful berries that made up almost the entire vegetative portion of the Makah diet.

Most food, however, came not from the land but from the sea. Great whales were of prime importance to these thoroughly maritime people, and Ozette's position—poised at the very edge of the Pacific, on a tip of the Olympic Peninsula—made it the most important Makah village for hunting such prey. Whalers were the ruling elite of Makah society, comprising its hereditary chieftains.

Gray whales appeared every spring, migrating along the coast to feed a few miles offshore. Humpbacks and sperm whales also frequented this region. At such times, Ozette's whaling teams stealthily paddled their 36-foot-long cedar canoes out to the behemoths, harpooning them with points edged in sharpened mussel shells and attaching sealskin floats to slow and buoy up the fleeing animals. Successful hunters immediately sewed shut the mouth of each carcass to prevent seawater from entering and sinking it, then towed it ashore for butchering. Meat from a single kill could feed the whole village for weeks; oil rendered from the blubber was an important foodstuff and trade item.

Petroglyphs

Fur seals, sea lions, porpoises, and other marine mammals flocked seasonally to the waters off Ozette, and they too were taken. So were myriad species of ocean fish—from rock cod to giant halibut—often from rich kelp beds offshore. Salmon traps efficiently harvested yet another seasonal and regional bounty, while tidal areas furnished plentiful supplies of sea urchins, clams, mussels, and other shellfish. By all archaeological evidence, the Makah people fully exploited the many resources of their homeland, one of the richest marine environments on earth.

They also practiced slavery, using captives taken in raids and their offspring to help in labor-intensive activities such as gathering firewood, harvesting timber, and cleaning and drying fish.

At the Sea's Edge

Human faces and a killer whale, etched centuries ago on a seaside boulder near Ozette, attest to the sea's importance among the Makah. Large, curved fishhooks of steam-bent wood were baited for thousand-pound halibut; smaller, double-barbed versions hooked lingcod and sea bass. A whimsical wooden effigy bowl bears traces of oil and human hair—after its 500-year-long burial. Makah carvers created a wealth of items both ritual and practical. Bird heads grace the whalebone handle of a war club (right), while more than 700 sea-otter teeth stud a ceremonial whale fin worked in cedar.

Wood effigy bowl, 3.7 in

231

Desert Dwellers

2000 B.C. to A.D. 1450

In 1924, archaeologists M. R. Harrington and Llewellyn L. Loud made a remarkable discovery while excavating Lovelock Cave in western Nevada. In a pit in the cave's floor, cleverly hidden by rush matting and basket fragments, was a cache of 2,000-year-old duck decoys, exquisitely fashioned of tule reeds from the marshes of Humboldt Sink. Remarkably lifelike, the world's oldest surviving duck decoys even bore feathers. Some were recognizable as male and female canvasbacks.

Other finds at Lovelock paint a picture of human use stretching back 4,500 years. Baskets, bags made of tule, fiber nets, ropes, wooden fishhooks, twig snares, bone awls, ornaments, and stone tools have been uncovered. Many of the perishable items were preserved only because of the cave's dryness. To archaeologists, the decoys and other items suggest that Great Basin hunter-gatherers were ingenious in exploiting the scant resources of their arid environment.

Second only to the Arctic as the most inhospitable environment for humankind in North America, the Great Basin lies between two mountain chains that trend north and south: the Rockies on the east and the Sierra Nevada on the west. Both chains rob the region of moisture from incoming clouds.

The scant resources of this desert region supported only small populations of prehistoric peoples who were often sparsely spread over wide areas. Except for rare communities occupying rich bottomlands along rivers, peoples of the desert region moved frequently to take advantage of seasonal food resources. Survival demanded a high degree of flexibility and mobility in this hostile and unforgiving environment.

The people of the Great Basin remained hunters and gatherers until historical times. Many of their artifacts have been found in caves,

Canvasback duck decoy, Lovelock Cave

Willow winnowing basket

Great Basin and Hohokam Cultures

Ancient hunter-gatherers in the Great Basin region of Nevada and Utah depended on resourcefulness and a large arsenal of tools to wage their struggle for survival in the desert. Hunters created elaborate duck decoys to exploit spring and fall waterfowl migrations. Carefully fashioned out of tule reeds and feathers, painted with black and reddish-brown pigments, and stitched, the decoys lured ducks into marshes where hidden hunters caught them by hand or spear. Other implements, remarkably preserved in dry caves, include winnowing baskets.

Made from twined willow strips, these baskets could have been used for harvesting foods such as piñon nuts, a Great Basin staple. The people parched the nuts in baskets by mixing them with hot embers and then tossing the mix into the air. A decorative clay incense burner from the Hohokam site of Snaketown resembles a mountain sheep. Part of a funeral offering from A.D. 1000, it suggests social stratifications of the kind that emerge only in a sedentary,

Clay incense burner, 7 in

Horned lizard stone palette, length 6 in

though archaeologists believe the caves represent just one stop on a system of seasonal migrations.

In western Utah's Hogup Cave, deposits from human activity reach 14 feet in depth. Full of baskets, fishhooks, bones, seeds, and numerous implements, the refuse heap has helped archaeologists flesh out a picture of life in the Great Basin. Experts can even tell the contents of actual meals eaten long ago by analyzing desiccated human waste.

With simple tools—a wooden digging stick and a small grinding stone—the people of the Great Basin could process a wide array of seeds, plants, and tubers. Grass seeds were gathered by shaking them from stalks into baskets; berries were collected by women with chest-mounted baskets; and piñon nuts were carefully harvested. Small rodents, hares, and rabbits were caught frequently; larger animals, such as deer, bison, antelope, and sheep, were less commonly killed.

In the Southwest, the people also lived as hunter-gatherers until about A.D. 300. Their environment, relatively richer in resources and nearer to civilizations in Mexico, spawned a much wider range of subsistence

strategies than in the Great Basin. Revolutionary imports from Mexico—agriculture, pot-making, and irrigation techniques—emerged and were adapted locally. Archaeologists still debate the degree of indigenous development of these skills.

Around A.D. 300, in the Gila and Salt River valleys of southern Arizona, the Hohokam people emerged. Archaeologists are not certain whether they arose from local societies that developed Mesoamerican ideas, or whether people from Mesoamerica migrated northward. Perhaps both happened.

At first, groups of 25 or more people lived in small towns of pit houses, using canal systems to irrigate fields of maize. At a large site called Snaketown, the inhabitants diverted water three miles from the Gila River to their fields. Hard-pressed in their arid environment, Hohokam farmers probably raised crops twice each year, tied to the spring snowmelt and the late summer rains that swelled the rivers. Some canals ran as far as ten miles. Main canals were six to ten feet wide, and smaller channels

branched from them. Eventually the Hohokam built hundreds of miles of canals, using pointed sticks and flat, rectangular stones to carve them out of the desert.

From the sands that consumed Snaketown, archaeologists dug pottery, stone bowls, exquisitely etched shells, and turquoise

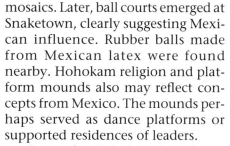

Acid-etched shells, width 4 in

mosaics. Later, ball courts emerged at Snaketown, clearly suggesting Mexican influence. Rubber balls made from Mexican latex were found nearby. Hohokam religion and platform mounds also may reflect concepts from Mexico. The mounds perhaps served as dance platforms or supported residences of leaders.

Later, the Hohokam built large, aboveground houses, such as

agricultural society. Favorable climatic conditions, engineering ingenuity, and trade with the more advanced societies of Mesoamerica helped propel the Hohokam from living in small nomadic bands to settling in large communities. Archaeological digs at Snaketown have revealed other symbols of emerging cultural sophistication, such as a carved stone palette in the shape of a horned lizard. The Hohokam people used these palettes to hold pigments with which they painted their bodies for games and religious ceremonies.

Sacaton red-on-buff effigy vessel, 6 in

Archaeologists carefully reconstructed this pot-bellied pottery vessel from many fragments smashed more than 950 years ago in a funeral ritual. Its red-on-buff design is characteristic of Hohokam ceramic style and reflects some Mesoamerican influence, common in the culture. Unique to the Hohokam are acid-etched shells with various motifs, such as this image of a horned lizard on a large cardium shell. Artisans created these works by coating the shell with pitch in the shape of an animal or other design. Then the shell was soaked in a weak acid solution, probably fermented juice from the fruit of the saguaro cactus. The acid ate away the unprotected parts of the shell, leaving the raised design.

four-story Casa Grande south of Phoenix, which is constructed of caliche—hard desert earth mixed with water. Casa Grande probably served as the hub of a complex society consisting of many towns spread across the desert.

Climate changes and incursions by newcomers—Athapaskan speakers known as Apache—contributed to the decline of the Hohokam culture by A.D. 1450. The area became home to the descendants of the Hohokam, the Pima Indians. To the Pima, the name "Hohokam" translates as "those that have vanished."

Another culture evolved to the east in the Mogollon Mountains of eastern Arizona and southwestern New Mexico. From about A.D. 300, the Mogollon people lived in circular pit houses with conical roofs built into the high ground of ridges and bluffs. They may have been the first Southwesterners to learn the art of pottery making, a skill probably acquired from people farther south.

Although among the region's first agriculturalists, the Mogollon never developed such sophisticated techniques as the Hohokam or the Anasazi—though they did terrace hillsides, as well as halt erosion by diverting runoff with stones.

They were also the first people of the Southwest to cultivate corn. They harvested wood for implements and building, and got much of their food—nuts, seeds, fruits, berries—from plants. They wove reeds into baskets, sandals, and mats. They chipped stone for small tools and also for shallow, troughlike grinders for seeds and corn. They even filled reeds with wild tobacco and smoked the world's first cigarettes.

Under Anasazi influence, they eventually built multiroom houses, and each community contained a round ceremonial building, known as a kiva, where meetings were held.

One settlement, Grasshopper Pueblo in Arizona, contained some 500 rooms arranged around plazas.

At the multistoried buildings of Casas Grandes, in northern Mexico, archaeologists discovered buildings holding stores of copper, turquoise, iron crystals, paint pigments, and tons of marine mollusk shells. In the center of the complex a large marketplace suggested a strong commercial traffic. Turkeys and colorful macaws were bred for trade, and dogs were domesticated.

The Mogollon are best known for their masterful pottery, such as the style that developed in the Mimbres area of southwestern New Mexico. Unfortunately, the beauty of the Mogollon pottery has attracted pot hunters, who have not only stolen much of the pottery but also destroyed archaeological evidence that scientists need.

Due to changing climate and the rise of the Anasazi culture to the north, into which they gradually merged, the Mogollon had largely disappeared by A.D. 1150, though pockets of them survived in northern Mexico until the 15th century.

Mimbres fisherman pot

Mimbres pot, feather design

Mogollon

Elegant simplicity marks Mogollon pots, with fisherman and feather designs, from the Mimbres Valley of southwestern New Mexico. Borrowed from the Anasazi, this distinctive black-on-white style emerged between A.D. 1000 and 1150. Intended as grave goods, many Mimbres pottery pieces contain a kill-hole, a perforation in the vessel that enabled the spirit of

Mogollon pictograph

Ceramic effigy vessel, 7.3 in

the artwork to escape and join the soul of the dead owner. Other Anasazi influences on the Mogollon included the building of cliffside, square-roomed pueblos, such as those found in New Mexico's Gila National Forest (above). This 42-room, 5-cave complex housed Mogollon families from 1280 to 1300, according to dendrochronology, or tree-ring dating. During the 13th and 14th centuries, many of the Mogollon moved south to the Casas Grandes region of northern Mexico. A ceramic effigy vessel suggests the extent of Mesoamerican influence on Mogollon art at this site. Strangely expressionless, a Mogollon face stares from a rock wall at Hueco Tanks State Park near El Paso, Texas.

Anasazi

A.D. 900 to 1300

In the high, harsh San Juan Basin of northwestern New Mexico, deep yellow-and-gold sandstone cliffs enclose a 22-mile-long gorge. Clinging to its rugged, windswept walls are the ruins of nine immense pueblos, structures that once rose as high as five stories and held hundreds of rooms.

Chaco Canyon served as the center of a remarkable flowering of the Anasazi—often translated as "the Ancient Ones." Between A.D. 900 and 1300, the Anasazi made advances in engineering, architecture, trade, and social organization that would result in the highest cultural development and the most concentrated move toward urbanism in the ancient Southwest.

Chaco Canyon served as the hub of a vast homeland that encompassed some 40,000 square miles. A network of almost 500 miles of roads connected nearly 100 outlying settlements. Ramps and steps carried the roads over steep obstacles.

The pueblos themselves—known by names such as Pueblo Bonito and Chetro Ketl—suggest the existence of a well-organized workforce. They average 216 rooms, many with high ceilings. The numerous rooms could have supported a population of some 5,000. Walls show great artistry and were constructed solidly with cored masonry. Great round kivas—or ceremonial rooms—were built with dressed pine logs brought from 30 miles away. Everywhere are signs of the ingenuity and adaptability the Anasazi needed to deal with the harsh realities of desert life: long winters, poor soil, little water. They built diversion dams and canals to capture rare but torrential rains and diverted the water into gardens of corn, beans, and squash.

Archaeologists theorize that Chaco Canyon served as the center of a large trading network. The discovery of more than 60,000 turquoise fragments and many ritual turquoise ornaments suggest that Chaco Canyon played a large role in the processing of turquoise into finished ornaments. Chacoans may have controlled turquoise sources near present-day Santa Fe, New Mexico. Other items found in the Chaco Canyon network support its importance as a trade and ceremonial center: macaw skeletons and feathers, cylindrical vases, wooden effigies, copper bells, clay incense burners, and items of shell, wood, and basketry intricately inlaid with turquoise and other decorative materials.

The earliest signs of Anasazi culture emerged in the Four Corners region—where Utah, Colorado, New Mexico, and Arizona meet. Archaeologists describe these early people as Basketmakers, for their distinctive wicker containers. Between A.D. 500 and 700, the Anasazi developed pottery, borrowing from the styles of the Mogollon and Hohokam peoples. They also began building multilevel structures—their famous pueblos.

At the Mesa Verde site in southwestern Colorado, the progression of their housing is clearly visible—from pit houses to aboveground structures. At first, the pit houses were shallow and crude, though the ground proved an effective insulator against cold winters

Black-on-white mug, Chaco Canyon

Tularosa black-on-white jar

Anasazi Artifacts

The Southwest's most complex prehistoric culture took shape at the Anasazi sites of Canyon de Chelly in Arizona (opposite), Mesa Verde, and Chaco Canyon. Jet-and-turquoise inlaid items, such as this bone scraper, served as valuable trading commodities. Its owner probably enjoyed a high status. Black-on-white pottery, a style evident in a mug from Chaco Canyon and a Tularosa jar, is perhaps the Anasazi's most striking creative legacy. By A.D. 1350, when this wooden effigy figure was created, Southwest civilization represented a blending of many cultures, though Anasazi styles were predominant.

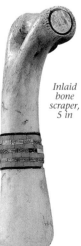

Inlaid bone scraper, 5 in

Wooden effigy figure, 25 in

and hot summers. Gradually, the pit grew deeper and the smoke hole became the entrance to a completely underground dwelling. The old entrance became a ventilation shaft to help direct smoke out through the ceiling. A small hole, known as a *sipapu,* lay near the hearth pit. It symbolized the hole that ancient Anasazi ancestors used to enter this world.

Archaeologists surmise that, by A.D. 700, increasing population and a more sedentary lifestyle based on growing maize and squash forced the Anasazi to build large adobe storage rooms above ground. Eventually these farmers built rooms abutting each other, which helped keep them cool in summer and warm in winter. These were the first Indian pueblos. The final building adaptation at Mesa Verde occurred about A.D. 1150, when the Anasazi constructed easily protected pueblos underneath the overhang of the mesa's cliffs.

By A.D. 1200, the Anasazi had left Chaco Canyon, and all major pueblos were abandoned by around 1300. The reasons remain unclear, although they may include a prolonged drought, raids by northern nomadic Indians, or a breakdown in the socioeconomic system.

Dancers and Flowers

Sandstone ruins of 800-room Pueblo Bonito in New Mexico's Chaco Canyon (opposite) hint at the grandeur the Anasazi achieved at their zenith. All of Chaco Canyon's pueblos contain numerous round rooms, known as kivas, places for religious rites and other ceremonies. Often kivas were decorated with paintings, such as the 15th-century mural of a dancing woman (upper) at Pottery Mound. This collection of wooden sunflowers and a bird (left) was buried in a clay jar deep in a cliff pueblo near Kayenta, Arizona, early in the 13th century. The dry climate preserved them.

Builders of the Eastern Mounds

1000 B.C. to A.D. 1500

Built by different cultures at different times, thousands of American Indian mounds sprinkle the East. Most of those constructed between 1000 B.C. and A.D. 700 contained tombs.

Organized cemeteries emerged as early as 4000 B.C., often on riverside ridges. By the time of Christ, they had evolved into burial mounds, artificial hills that not only honored departed souls but also helped define ancestral territories. They would grow increasingly elaborate over succeeding centuries, becoming easily recognizable monuments. Their builders were the distant descendants of the Paleo-Indians.

The waning of the Pleistocene and its glaciers had witnessed rapid die-offs of mammoths and other

megafauna and also sweeping environmental changes. The Indians of the Eastern Woodlands survived by exploiting a broad range of smaller prey: deer, bear, turkey, opossum, squirrel, and other forest creatures, as well as riverine turtles, fish, and shellfish. In addition, they harvested various edible nuts in the expanding deciduous forests: hickory, acorns, chestnuts, pecans, walnuts, and oth-

ers. Their stone projectile points evolved into a huge array of new designs. Exchange networks blossomed, resulting in wide dispersal of many raw and finished materials. Trade, rather than warfare, ruled.

Societies gradually grew larger and more sedentary. People still hunted and gathered, but wandered less. Pottery revolutionized both the storage and the preparation of food.

Ohio's Great Serpent Mound

Writhing more than a thousand feet through wooded countryside near the Ohio River, this snake-shaped earthwork may have functioned as a sacred effigy. It contains no burials or artifacts and so remains difficult to date. Experts variously attribute it to Adena or Hopewell cultures.

Crude agriculture—squashes and gourds—took root.

As neighboring communities better defined their lands and inter-relationships with each other, they prospered. Trade brought not only new items but also prestige and social stratification. The Adena culture that spread through the central Ohio Valley from about 600 to 100 B.C. progressed from simple burial sites to increasingly complex mounds. Larger and larger burial chambers held richer and richer collections of grave goods—not just personal weapons, tools, and ornaments of the deceased but also "status goods" such as sheet mica from North Carolina, marine shells, Ohio pipestone, and Lake Superior copper. Trade was basic to Adena life, more than ever before in North America. So was decoration: Zoomorphic designs adorned stone tablets perhaps used for grinding red ocher, while ceremonial pipes took on human and animal shapes.

Adena gave rise to the even more complex Hopewell culture, centered not only in the Ohio River Valley but also along the upper Mississippi, in present-

Mica bird claw, 11 in

Copper serpent head, length 20 in

day Illinois. Both areas generated important religious, political, and economic activities. Hopewell—also known as Middle Woodland—lasted from about 200 B.C. until A.D. 400. It exhibited even more flamboyant ceremonial trappings than its predecessor, even more spectacular earthworks, and even more far-flung and complex trade networks. As with Adena, both raw and finished goods were exchanged—but over a much larger region, one that stretched from the Rocky Mountains to the Atlantic coast, from Florida to southern Manitoba. Materials included exotic and apparently highly coveted substances: copper and silver from the Great Lakes, Florida seashells and alligator teeth, galena from Illinois and Missouri, North Dakota chalcedony, and obsidian from as far afield as Yellowstone.

The Hopewell culture was not a uniform civilization like the Maya; rather it was a general style that overlay scores of locally different groups and communities. It blossomed throughout the Midwest and into the

East, especially along major rivers—resource-rich areas that spawned numerous villages and hamlets. Such communities were separate but inter-dependent, possibly led by "Big Men": aggressive leaders who secured their political and economic powers through kinship networks and traditional gift exchanges. Successful trading enabled them to accumulate wealth and increase the prestige of themselves, their loyal followers, and their villages.

Another mark of the Hopewell tradition was a dramatic increase in the cultivation of native plants, such as sunflower and goosefoot. Success-

Mica human profile, 6 in

Hopewell Culture

Named for an Ohio farm, Hopewell was less a single culture and more a complex of traits linking groups that remained socially and linguistically distinct. Its hallmarks included complex and extensive trade networks, enormous mound constructions, flamboyant burial customs, and a great diversity of finished

Mica hand, 10 in

products, wrought from exotic raw materials such as mica, copper, marine shells, and obsidian. Hopewell dominated much of eastern North America, building on earlier Adena accomplishments to attain new artistic heights. Gleaming, larger-than-life renderings of a raptor's foot and a human hand were cut from sheets of natural mica, far too fragile for any utilitarian use. Both probably were burial gifts, their significance lost in time. So it is for the highly stylized snake's head, made of native copper that first had been hammered flat, then laced with cutouts. Bird and

serpent imagery dominated 2,000 years of Eastern Woodlands prehistory. Hopewell craftsmen varied their creations from the lifelike to the highly stylized, from functional to purely decorative. A whimsical human head of mica still grins after centuries of burial. Effigy pipes of clay or Ohio pipestone, carved in various animal shapes, also were commonly interred in the mounds. Two finely sculptured examples, both in stone, include a spoonbill duck atop a fish, and a toad. The recumbent trumpeter swan, painstakingly fashioned from a turtle carapace, served as a comb and

242

ful farming of such crops on the East's fertile floodplains contributed to more secure lifestyles, and food surpluses, and may have led to population booms.

Hopewell burial mounds often were spectacular affairs, both in size and design. Many were located on ridges along river valleys. Some were hundreds of feet long and thirty feet high; smaller ones often clustered together on sites that spanned many acres. They were built laboriously by hand, one basketful of earth at a time. Some were so massive that certain 19th-century observers considered them forts built by some "lost civilization."

In fact, the mounds were funerary monuments to important people. Elite individuals were either cremated or buried, their remains often entombed in log-lined crypts sunk beneath the surface, then covered with earth. Later burials enlarged and raised the mounds. Also interred—but not always with the bodies—were rich caches of grave goods that often included personal accoutrements, such as copper earspools and breastplates, thousands of freshwater pearls, weapons, and signs of

Spoonbill duck pipe, 4 in

Toad pipe, 4.1 in

office.

Some sites contained finely detailed ceramic figurines of humans, or ceremonial stone pipes sculptured in a wide variety of animal shapes. Tools and caches of exotic raw materials occurred in others, sparking some experts to infer that the deceased were especially talented artisans.

While relatively little is known of day-to-day life in Hopewell times, the widespread building of complex and massive funerary structures suggests religious underpinnings, perhaps an elite priesthood class, and an increasingly stratified society.

About A.D. 400, Hopewell trade networks and traditions of art and

cooperation all began to break down. Regional differences strengthened; mound building ceased. Archaeologists can only speculate why, but apparently much was happening at that time. Bow-and-arrow weaponry had just made its way to the Eastern Woodlands, replacing less efficient spears and atlatls. Did this technological revolution spur the decimation of game—or increase warfare—in turn undermining the stability of sedentary human societies?

Climatological evidence indicates that temperatures turned colder as well, just about the time that Hopewell began its decline. How did this trend affect the nuts and other crops, both wild and cultivated, upon which Hopewellian peoples depended? Did widespread failures of game or crops cause human communities to abandon past traditions of trade and cooperation in favor of raiding their neighbors' storehouses?

Or perhaps agriculture's success contributed to Hopewell's demise. Large food surpluses might have weakened trade net-

undoubtedly was a burial gift. An elaborate spearpoint of obsidian reflects not only the artisan's skill and technology but also the effectiveness of Hopewell trade networks: Obsidian of this sort came from distant quarries in

the Rocky Mountains. Sometime after A.D. 400, Hopewell networks collapsed and mound building halted, for reasons still unclear to archaeologists. A three-hundred-year hiatus followed before the rise of what

would be one of North America's climax aboriginal cultures: the Mississippian tradition that began about A.D. 700 and lasted into historic times.

Obsidian spearpoint, Hopewell

Turtle-shell comb, length 7.2 in

243

works by removing the incentives for long-distance exchange. Hierarchies based on trade would become less important. Yet another possibility is that intensified horticulture created a false sense of security. Plentiful harvests encouraged larger populations that, in times of drought or other hardship, suffered major collapse.

Whatever caused Hopewell's undoing, human cooperation and coordination would blossom anew in the Mississippian tradition that evolved throughout various tributaries of the Mississippi River and the southern Appalachians, from about A.D. 700 into historic times.

It was a golden age, one of prehistoric North America's most brilliant achievements, a complex patchwork of chiefdoms large and small. Its name refers to the river valley where it reached its ultimate complexity, but in fact it occurred across much of the Southeast. Like Adena and Hopewell, the Mississippian was a riverine culture with communities hewing to the floodplains of numerous and varied tributaries, where fertile and easily cultivable soil abounded, as did diverse game and water animals. A

Southern Cult clay pot, 7 in

conquistador Hernando de Soto, who recorded the looting of such communal granaries by his own men.

As in Hopewell times, trade networks flourished, linking hundreds of relatively autonomous communities not only to one another but also to major regional centers at Cahokia (Illinois), Moundville (Alabama), Etowah (Georgia), and Spiro (Oklahoma). All four were large, sophisticated complexes. The largest, Cahokia, lay just south of the confluence of the Illinois, Missouri, and Mississippi Rivers, occupying at its zenith an area of more than five square miles and harboring perhaps 30,000 people. Cahokia's inhabitants erected more than a hundred earthen mounds, including the terraced, flat-topped pyramid Monks Mound, which rises 100 feet and covers 16 acres. It is North America's largest such site, more than twice the size of any other mound. Like many other major monuments of the period, it was built in stages. Archaeological evidence suggests that Mississippian cultures practiced some human sacrifice and trophy taking. This, as well as the terraced pyramids, plazas, maize-and-beans agriculture, and some artistic motifs, hints at distant links to Mesoamerican influence.

Wood feline effigy, Key Marco, 6 in

major difference, however, was increasingly sophisticated agriculture, the cultivation of maize and, later, beans. Lands had to be cleared and tended regularly. Though climate fluctuations, disease, and weed blooms periodically threatened crop harvests, Mississippian communities often were able to accumulate considerable stockpiles of food. We know this in part from

Despite what archaeologists have learned about the mounds, they still evoke wonder. National Geographic Staff Archaeologist George E. Stuart first dug professionally at Etowah. He remembers an earlier childhood walk, when he happened upon a mound. "Never will I forget my sense of awe at the mound's sheer mass, or my intense curiosity about its origin and purpose," he later wrote.

Cedar mask with shell inlays, 11.5 in

Mississippian Climax

Major shrine of the Southern Cult, Alabama's Moundville thrived as one of four major political and ceremonial centers during North America's Mississippian period. Excavation of its 20-odd mounds has yielded more than 3,000 graves, richly accoutered with various burial goods. Mississippian artifacts often display exceptional artistry. The kneeling, humanlike feline figure recalls a theme favored by ancient Egyptians; a cedar deer mask bears inlays of shell. Pottery also flourished, both as containers and as art. A clay head's closed eyes and stitched mouth imply that at least some members of this society practiced head-hunting. Evocative designs of rattlesnakes and men dance across a conch shell, their meaning lost. An effigy pipe depicts a warrior beheading his victim.

Stone effigy pipe, height 10 in

Conch shell, length 12 in

Ceramic effigy figures from Copan, 7th century A.D., average height 2 ft

The Potter's Art

Large bison, finely shaped in soft clay, were discovered in 1912 deep in a cave in the French Pyrenees. Still intact after 14,000 years, they were a rare find; normally such prehistoric clay artistry would have long since succumbed to weather. Humans have probably been molding clay—one of the most malleable and widely available materials in the world—since the earliest times. At first they used it to make ritual objects, as was probably the case with the bison, and later for practical purposes. The first clay items were laid in the sun to dry.

The era of ceramics, however, could begin only after the discovery that high heat—such as the red heat from a hot fire—renders clay hard enough to be impervious to water. Theories vary as to how that discovery came about. At what prehistoric hearth did someone first observe that the clay lining of a firepit had been transformed into a crude vessel? Or find that a ceramic bowl remained after a basket waterproofed with clay went up in flames? Mystery also veils the first worshiper to offer a sculptured clay fertility figure or deity to the fire—later to find in the ashes a baked-clay treasure.

Ceramic human or animal figures might serve both spiritual and functional purposes. Form and function join in the elaborate, two-foot-high Classic Maya effigies at left. The clay figures, representing past Maya rulers, capped lids of incense burners used in a burial ritual at Copan. Archaeologists reassembled them after they had been found smashed, perhaps in a symbolic "killing"

First Pottery

Voluptuous "Venus" probably served as a fertility symbol. The world's oldest known ceramic piece, the 26,000-year-old, 4.3-inch figurine surfaced in Eastern Europe. Few such figures have survived. Scholars surmise they were intended to explode when they were being fired—that they were made to be destroyed for ritual or divination purposes. Archaeologists look to Japan's Jomon people for the earliest ceramic culture, beginning about 11,000 B.C. The cord motif, or jomon, incised or impressed on these handsome, hand-built vessels gives the culture its name. This group of pots dates from about the third

"Venus," Dolní Věstonice, 24,000 B.C.

Jomon pots, 3rd millennium B.C.

millennium B.C. Sometimes the Jomon people placed ceramic figurines, broken into pieces, in such pots. In the fifth millennium B.C., during the Ubaid period at Eridu in present-day Iraq, baked-clay figurines accompanied a deceased person to the grave, either as attendants, or perhaps as substitutes for human sacrifices. Pellets on this figure may represent decorative scarification. By about 4000 B.C., in the Indus River Valley, potters were shaping vessels such as

these three on the potter's wheel. Long-horned cattle locked together on one pot and horns painted on another may attest to domestication of livestock and the owner's prosperity. Egyptians also utilized the wheel, as a limestone statuette of a potter, dating from about 2500 to 2200 B.C., demonstrates. Egyptians made an important contribution to ceramics in glazes, such as that used on the Egyptian faience figurine of the goddess Isis with infant Horus. Copper produced the turquoise blue—a royal color. Bristling oars propel a barge around an Egyptian pot made

before an important tomb was sealed.

Pottery evolved generally—though not always—along with a sedentary lifestyle. The fragility of ceramic artifacts and their weight made them impractical for people on the move, such as hunter-gatherers or nomads. As societies grew more complex and people settled down, the need increased for ways to store water, food, and other commodities.

For a long time, archaeologists regarded the Middle East as the region where pottery first developed, in about the seventh millennium B.C. More recent discoveries in Japan, China, and Africa have pushed back the appearance of a true ceramic culture several millennia. People known as the Jomon, from the

about 3300 B.C. Such decorations on ceramics present detailed information about the cultures that created them. Elsewhere in the Middle East, ceramics also flowered. Through trade and conquest, styles spread and evolved. On the island of Crete, the exuberant painted decorations of the Minoans reached a high level of spontaneity and sophistication, as exhibited in the bold geometric designs on a beaked jug dating from about 1800 B.C. This particular style is called Kamares, for the cave near Phaistos where such pots were discovered. Minoans also favored themes

Japanese word for "cord motif"—the cordlike decoration impressed onto their pottery—were making ceramics as early as 11,000 B.C. Over the next 10,000 years, a highly decorated, sophisticated, hand-built pottery evolved. The Jomon also produced ceramic cult figurines, which were used in fertility rites to exhort bountiful yields from sea and forest, or broken to absorb symbolically human pain and misfortune.

The basic procedure of preparing clay, shaping it, and applying heat evolved early and along similar lines in many parts of the world. Refinements in clay types and colors, firing, and glazing came more gradually. Many of these processes have altered little since prehistoric times.

Ubaid baked-clay figurine, Eridu, 5th millennium B.C.

Indus Valley pots, ca 4000 B.C.

linked to the sea—motifs that later influenced the Mycenaeans. This 15.7-inch-tall Mycenaean two-handled jar, made about 1350 B.C., resembles Minoan models in its shape and its octopus motif, but lacks the lively spontaneity of Minoan handiwork. Its large size made it suitable as a container for dry commodities. Replicas of earthenware storage jars, massed in a cave-cellar in Israel, also are testament to the importance of pottery for storage and for shipping goods along ancient trade routes. The originals, which date from about 250 B.C., probably held olive oil or wine.

For shaping clay, a number of techniques developed. To hand build, potters had several options: They could simply pinch the clay into the desired form; roll it into slabs for further shaping; or stack coils one on top of the other and smooth them together. Craftsmen also pressed clay into or around molds or shaped it over a form with a paddle.

The potter's wheel probably evolved from a disk on top of a fixed pivot, which was used to maneuver a pot as it was shaped. This developed into a simple turntable—or tournette—powered by hand, as demonstrated by the Egyptian statuette below. Used in China, Egypt, Mesopotamia, and several other areas by the fourth millennium B.C., the tournette greatly speeded up the process. A stone pottery wheel, dating from about 2200 B.C., has turned up at Ur and another from about the same era in Israel.

Turning fast, the true potter's wheel balanced its centrifugal force against pressure from the potter's hands to shape the clay. This method permitted the crafting of thinner-walled, more graceful vessels. Potters could quickly produce quantities of virtually identical pots that could be traded far and wide. The potter's wheel never developed in the pre-Columbian New World.

Various methods for firing also emerged around the world. At first, pots were placed in open fires, a method still used in many places for earthenwares, which do not require temperatures above 1472° to 1652°F.

The world's earliest known kilns,

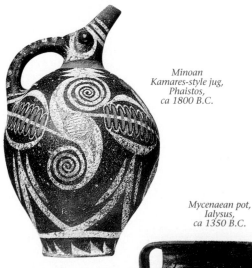

Minoan Kamares-style jug, Phaistos, ca 1800 B.C.

Mycenaean pot, Ialysus, ca 1350 B.C.

dating from 28,000 to 22,000 B.C., fired ceramics that were ritually shattered inside them. Beginning in about the seventh millennium, kilns were in use in the Middle East and China. By experimenting with different configurations, craftsmen developed kilns that could attain controlled temperatures above 1832°F. Along with efficient kilns came centers where large quantities of pottery could be fired.

A wide variety of decorated

Gerzean pot, Egypt, ca 3300 B.C.

Potter with turntable, Giza, Egypt, ca 2500-2200 B.C.

Egyptian faience figurine, Thebes, Egypt, ca 600 B.C.

Beaker,
Laa an der Thaya,
2nd millennium B.C.

pottery emerged in the Middle East, China, and Southeast Asia. Archaeologists often use these to identify the rise of different cultures and to show how they influenced one another. At a site in Iraq called Tell Halaf, from the late fifth millennium B.C., "Halafian" potters apparently had modified their kilns so that the pots were separated from the flame and smoke, which tend to darken pottery; thus the Halafians protected the clarity of their notably fine painted designs.

Before true glazes were invented, potters sometimes burnished the clay or used slip—a thin layer of fine clay—before firing, to make the surface less porous. Alternatively, a solution of bark or leaves was applied to the pot while it was still hot. The Halafians also mixed beads of soap-

stone with azurite and malachite and heated the mixture, probably in an attempt to create a lapis lazuli-like substance. It formed a simple glass of a brilliant ultramarine color. This may have marked the beginnings of glassmaking and of glazes. By about 2000 B.C., true glazes were being utilized in Mesopotamia. A recipe for glaze on a clay tablet dating from about 1700 B.C. notes that the addition of lead would make glaze adhere to clay—a method that produced the decorative tiles on the gates and walls of ancient Babylon.

In an odd twist, pottery, which is so fragile that it usually requires a semisettled society to develop, has proved indispensable to archaeologists because of that very propensity to shatter. Once broken into sherds,

ceramic objects are among the most indestructible of human artifacts. Archaeologists have traced types of pottery and styles of decoration in various parts of the world to deduce local routes of migration or trade. By studying ceramic objects and fragments, scholars can often determine the progression of technological change in a particular culture and tell much about the social order.

In the late 19th century, in reaction to the chaos he observed in the handling of artifacts at digs in Egypt, British surveyor William M. Flinders Petrie formulated a system of sequence dating important to archaeologists to this day. In excavating ancient burials, he established a definite stylistic evolution in the shape and decoration of the pottery he unearthed. By linking those styles to ones of known age at another site, he could work out a timetable. Later,

Attic red-figure kylix,
ca 470 B.C.

Fine Pottery

"Come Athena, and extend your hand over the kiln, and may the cups darken well, and may the vases be well baked, may they obtain a fair price," goes an ancient Greek hymn for potters. The mass production and export of ceramic wares formed an important element in the economy of ancient Greece. The pottery also opens a window on everyday life in these times. In a charmingly intimate scene on an Attic red-figure kylix, two women fold away their clothing. A black clay slip covers the drinking cup, which dates from about 470 B.C., leaving the red clay exposed for the noted Athenian painter

Douris to render his finely drawn figures. On earlier Greek pottery, artists usually painted black on red. Ceramic crafts have followed different courses around the world. During the third millennium B.C., across western and central Europe, potters produced red-brown, bell-shaped pottery vessels, or beakers, from which archaeologists derived the name Beaker People. Found today in burials, the beaker was a status symbol and probably held a drink for the deceased's final journey. This particular vessel came out of a burial site in Austria. Ceramics apparently developed in Africa, as early as the ninth millennium B.C., in fishing communities along lakes in the north-central part of the continent. A later, incised vessel made in Kush in sub-Saharan Africa, this lidded pot is a hand-built, utilitarian piece, typical of traditional African

Earthenware vessel,
Kush,
ca 1st-3rd century A.D.

through his system of cross dating, he discovered trade links between Egypt and other places around the Mediterranean. British archaeologist Arthur Evans, using Petrie's technique on pottery found at the palace at Knossos on Crete, identified a civilization that he named Minoan.

Archaeologists classify Europe's Beaker People, too, by their principal artifact—a distinctive, bell-shaped ceramic vessel called a beaker found frequently in graves of the wealthy. By studying similarities and variations in the decorations and shapes of this pottery, scholars can trace movements and cultural connections across Europe.

Even the contents of a ceramic vessel can prove informative to archaeologists. Traces of chocolate found in a Maya pot, for instance, helped confirm the glyph for cacao painted on the pot.

Modern technology now assists archaeologists in determining the age of clay objects. When fired at more than 930°F, clay releases all its thermal energy in the form of light

Ceramic figure, Tang dynasty, China, 7th-8th century A.D.

Celadon vessels, China

medium to a degree that became the envy of the world. With flamboyant ferocity, a tomb guardian, or lokopala, *performs his duties. The seventh-to-eighth-century A.D. earthenware figure exhibits the brilliant "three-color" glaze attained by the Chinese during the Tang dynasty. A small celadon-glazed figurine of an immortal does double duty as a water dropper. Marine monsters form handles for a vase, also celadon glazed. Iron oxide produced the prized soft green tint, developed in about the fourth century A.D. The two pieces were salvaged from a 14th-century Chinese merchant vessel probably en route to sell the wares in Japan. Chinese stonewares and porcelains were exported far and wide. In the 1970s, underwater archaeologists explored murky Yellow Sea waters off Korea to retrieve more than 12,000 artifacts. Hundreds of different ceramic pieces from the ship have added much to knowledge of Chinese artistry in clay.*

pottery. *A stylized terra-cotta horseman came from a tumulus near the ancient city of Jenne-jeno, in modern-day Mali. The statuette dates from around A.D. 1400 and probably served some ritual or cult purpose. Though China was not the first region to develop ceramics, the Chinese invented porcelain and complex glazing techniques, refining the*

Terra-cotta figure, Jenne/Mopti, Mali, ca A.D. 1400

or thermoluminescence. The clay then begins storing energy once more. By heating sherds and measuring the intensity of energy in the form of light released, scientists can determine how much radioactivity the clay has absorbed since its original firing. Researchers can then deduce how much time has passed since it was made.

Ceramics can provide other kinds of information for archaeologists. Scenes of everyday life and sacred rituals that appear on pottery offer striking insights into the ancient past. Simple line drawings of oar-powered Nile barges on Egyptian pots, for instance, reveal much about how ancient boats were constructed and propelled. Toy wagons, made out of terra-cotta around 2500 B.C. by Harappans in what is now Pakistan, provide some of the earliest known models of wheeled vehicles. Another wheeled pottery animal toy, made much later in Mexico,

Bahía figurine, Ecuador, ca 500 B.C.- A.D. 100

Maya polychrome vase, ca A.D. 600-800

is the only precontact example of wheel use in the New World. Also in Mexico, miniature village scenes rendered in clay portray aspects of ceremonial and everyday life.

In Greece, pottery painting reached high levels of sophistication, as finely drawn figures on the famous black- or red-figure wares show. These ceramics reveal much about life, rituals, and mythological lore. At times the potter and the painter signed their work, aiding scholars greatly in establishing chronologies.

Ceramics clearly had a major eco-

Maya ceramic sculpture, Jaina, ca A.D. 700-900

New World Pottery

Remarkable face—probably of a noble—peers up from a large clay jar made about A.D. 400 by a Moche potter. Master sculptors in clay, Moche artists created vivid likenesses of individuals in their communities, which flourished from about A.D. 100 to 800 along Peru's coast. New World potters developed a rich and diverse tradition of artistry in clay. In a figurine made by Ecuador's Bahía culture, a woman presents her child—probably as a sacrificial offering. A sacred ball game and glyphs painted on a Late Classic Period Maya

polychrome vase evoke a legend recorded in the Popul Vuh. Scholars continue to unravel the complex symbolism that appears in Maya art. A sculpture of a couple, found on the island of Jaina off Yucatan's west coast, may portray the sun and the moon—married to each other in Maya tradition. Two dogs romp in a ceramic figurine sculptured by potters of the Colima culture, which flourished along Mexico's west coast between 250 B.C. and A.D. 450. Scientists think that the incised lines on the figurine represent wrinkles on bare skin, showing that the dogs lack a regular coat of hair; this confirms reports by early Spanish chroniclers of a breed of hairless dogs in the New

Moche pot, Peru, ca A.D. 400

nomic as well as artistic role in ancient Greece. A quarter of Athens, known as the Kerameikos, was devoted to potters and their workshops. Here were produced quantities of standardized ceramics for domestic use and export as far afield as the Black Sea and North Africa.

In China, ceramics also became a large-scale endeavor. The earliest known pottery discovered there dates to the ninth millennium B.C. By 5000 B.C., the Chinese were hand building and painting the pottery of the Yangshao culture. Complex kilns were developed that reached temperatures higher than 1450°F. Utilizing fine white kaolin clays to make delicate, translucent porcelains, the Chinese fired ceramics even higher—above 2200°F.

The Chinese developed numerous glazing techniques, including the highly prized gray-green celadon and three-color glazes. Their export trade flourished as they modified colors of glazes and designs to please various markets. Their porcelains and stonewares have been found all over the globe and have inspired imitation by potters of many cultures, par-

Hohokam pot fragment, ca A.D. 1050-1200

Sikyatki-style polychrome jar, ca A.D. 1400-1625

Walnut-style black-on-white jar, ca A.D. 1100-1125

Tularosa-style ladle, ca A.D. 1100-1250

ticularly those of the Islamic world.

Judging from fragments of very early pottery found on the north coast of Colombia, the first ceramics in the Americas appeared in about the fourth millennium B.C. New World potters never achieved the high technology exhibited elsewhere by the use of the potter's wheel, true glazes, or high-firing kilns. But in their ceramics, shaped by hand from coils and slabs or made in molds and lavishly adorned, these artisans have left a rich and varied legacy. Decorations range from the geometric

designs of the North American Anasazi, full of symbolism, to the expressive portrait pots of the South American Moche. Meticulously executed polychrome paintings on Maya pots have provided details about their ceremonial life and helped to elucidate the complex Maya mythology, calendar, and language, as well as the chronologies of their ruling dynasties. Beyond their aesthetic appeal, such artifacts have provided unique insights to archaeologists, as have ceramic traditions around the world.

World. Aztec ceramic artisans used a mold, found at Tenochtitlan, to produce a fertility goddess. In the desert Southwest of North America, other types of ceramic artistry emerged. The distorted face above once formed the rim of a Hohokam effigy

jar from central Arizona. Bringing the pottery tradition north from Mexico into Arizona around A.D. 200, Hohokam potters shaped their vessels with wooden paddles over stone anvils and fired them in mesquite wood fires. Scholars use pottery types as a kind of "index fossil" to trace the development of individual cultures. Beginning around A.D. 600, Anasazi potters were producing distinctive designs. This bold, black-on-white pot was painted in the 12th century A.D. Anasazi work foreshadows the clay artistry of modern Pueblo peoples, who are their descendants. A butterfly-design, Sikyatki-style polychrome jar from Anasazi times shows clear ties to work produced by Hopi potters today.

Aztec ceramic figure and mold, Templo Mayor, Tenochtitlan

Ceramic dogs, Colima, Mexico, ca 250 B.C.-A.D. 450

GRAN
CHICHIMECA

GULF OF MEXICO

TOLTEC
Tula
Valley of Mexico
Teotihuacan
Lake Texcoco
MICHOACAN
Texcoco
Tlacopan
Tenochtitlan
Cacaxtla
Malinalco
Cholula
Chalcatzingo
La Mojarra
Tuxtla Mts.
Laguna de los Cerros
La Venta
Oaxaca
Monte Albán
San Lorenzo
El Manatí
Palenque
Yaxchilan
Kaminaljuyu
Quirigua
Copan
Dos Pilas
Tayasal
Lake Peten Itza
Tikal
Nakbe
El Mirador
Cuello
Usumacinta
Ulúa
Yucatan Peninsula
PUUC
Jaina
Chichen Itza
Bay of Campeche
A Z T E C
O L M E C
M A Y A

PACIFIC   OCEAN

● Ancient and modern town site

◆ Archaeological site only

0   300 mi

0   400 km

Mesoamerica

7000 B.C. to A.D. 1697

Defined as a region of shared traditions in Mexico and Central America, Mesoamerica at its largest extent stretches from north-central Mexico to Costa Rica. Its heartland lies between the parched zone of the Gran Chichimeca in the north and the Río Ulúa far to the southeast.

Archaeologists of the five modern nations of Mexico, Belize, Guatemala, Honduras, and El Salvador—and many foreigners as well—have studied its past in this century, but thousands upon thousands of unexcavated sites await attention.

Ecological diversity is extreme here. Highlands and lowlands differ sharply within short distances: chilly above 6,000 feet, temperate above 3,000, tropical to sea level. Perils include frost and drought and hurricanes, volcanic eruptions and earthquakes. Bounties include minerals and stone, coniferous and tropical forests, and marine resources—but no native animals suitable for domestication, except for the dog and the turkey. Humans relied entirely on their own labor from the time of their arrival until the Spanish conquests began in the 16th century A.D.

Bands of hunter-gatherers had entered the region by filtering down from earlier arrivals across the Bering Strait. Their descendants were settling into farming villages between 7000 and 1500 B.C. Around 3000 B.C., corncobs appeared in their rubbish—one cob measuring less than an inch—as people grew and crossbred the crop that became the great staple food, even a deity in its own right. As the Preclassic Period developed between 2000 B.C. and A.D. 250—a time of cultural elaboration—other deities would take on new and powerful characteristics.

High civilizations had their origins in this period, and the ritual calendars probably took form. Oldest is the sacred almanac of 260 days, about the term of a human pregnancy, with 13 numbers and 20 days combining to identify each day and, often, to name a newborn. Drawn symbols—known as glyphs—for these day names came into use: 8 Deer, 13 Serpent, 6 Monkey. The Zapotec of Monte Albán, in the Valley of Oaxaca, were carving their complex symbols as early as 700 B.C. The practice spread—with local modifications—as useful innovations usually did in Mesoamerica, despite distance and linguistic barriers.

Modern scholarship has defined three language families in the region. However, linguistic and cultural boundaries did not coincide tidily. Archaeologists still puzzle over the relationship of, for instance, the Olmec to the Maya, or the Toltec to the Aztec. Continuing archaeological investigations or fresh analyses of known sites may yet shed some light.

Excavation continues, deep in tropical rain forests or in downtown Mexico City. Glamorous discoveries still occur: a lost city, a vividly painted cave, an unlooted burial. Yet perhaps the most significant work of recent decades has been the long slog of field surveys, settlement-pattern studies, and the documentation of modest household remains. These reveal ancient societies in authentic human complexity; they let the subjects of these realms join their sovereigns and their goddesses and gods as treasures of modern knowledge.

CARIBBEAN SEA

Olmec

1200 to 400 B.C.

Recognition of a compelling art style, and ignorance of its makers, led to the label "Olmec." The name of a historic group in the 16th century A.D., it became linked to the mysterious finds made in the 1930s—shortly before Matthew W. Stirling and Alfonso Caso demonstrated that these ancient artists predated the Classic Maya. Despite its inappropriateness, the label has stuck.

Simple village societies were flourishing when the archaeological Olmec built their unprecedented center at San Lorenzo, by a sizable river on the swampy coastal plain south of the Bay of Campeche. Michael D. Coe and Richard A. Diehl, who dug here in the late 1960s, saw the location as crucial to the evolution of a complex society. Abundant crops from the best riverside land would give certain families—and their heirs—wealth, status, and power over their neighbors. With such a legacy, an able man could become a true ruler whose authority would be respected. Ten huge stone heads are thought to portray rulers of San Lorenzo.

Coe estimates 1,000 people as residents, with more living in the vicinity. He reckons that several hundred strong men could drag a 20-ton stone from its source in the Tuxtla Mountains to a river, raft it home, and place it for carving. At least 60 major sculptures were set up here, but they were minor tasks as against the creation of the center itself—an artificially leveled landscape using hundreds of thousands of cubic feet of fill, moved by the basketload. About 950 B.C., in obscure circumstances, statues were mutilated and buried. The site was abandoned.

About 50 miles away, at La Venta, another community assumed dominance for several centuries. Its feats included the construction of

Sculptured Images

Mirrored against an agricultural landscape near the Tuxtla Mountains, a six-inch nephrite figurine called the Tuxtla Statuette (right) shows a shaman wearing a duck mask. Glyphs incised on head and body record a date equivalent to A.D. 162. They helped in the recent decipherment of a stela from La Mojarra as the annals of a king named Harvest Mountain Lord; it was written in the same script. Of unknown but earlier date are two Olmec treasures: a fine greenstone ax with a left footprint, about a modern size 7; and the celebrated basalt figure called "Wrestler"— perhaps a ballplayer taking part in a game of sacred character.

Basalt "Wrestler," 26 in

Greenstone ax

immense mosaic pavements in the form of masks—which were formally buried immediately after their completion. Its artists carved superb jades from material obtained from distant sources. They ground iron ores into concave mirrors, possibly worn by priests and used in divination. Perhaps La Venta had traders who imported exotic goods and exported finished wares.

Nearby sites and distant ones bear the Olmec stamp, notably Chalcatzingo in the central highlands—apparently a frontier outpost and hub for a trading network. Never bigger than a village, Chalcatzingo boasted about 30 monuments carved in Olmec style. One stela shows a standing woman, the earliest such figure known in Mesoamerica.

Were the Olmec centers really cities? More digs may clarify their character. Were Olmec realms chiefdoms, organized by kinship, or had they become authentic states, with officials and a system for enforcing laws? Specialists argue the point. Did the Olmec conquer an empire? Probably not, although they may have formed alliances to defeat enemies.

Did the Olmec create the first civilization of Mesoamerica? Many people think so. Their magnificent sculpture represents the first monumental art and the earliest indication of a unified art style in Mesoamerica. The ambitious scale of their public works suggests the existence of centralized authority and considerable organizational skills.

The sites of the steamy Olmec heartland had received relatively little attention within the past quarter of a century. Then, new excavations in the 1980s and 1990s at La Venta and San Lorenzo unearthed household remains and the workshops of

Monument 1, San Lorenzo

sculptors and other artisans. At a site at El Manatí, miraculously preserved wooden sculptures have been found.

Research in the Tuxtla Mountains, a resource zone of clays and cinnabar and salt, may supply new clues to the much debated question of Olmec origins. And excavation almost anywhere in Mesoamerica may enrich the treasury of Olmec art: Stone Olmec masks of exquisite quality have been found among the heirlooms of the Aztec at Tenochtitlan, the last of the great Mesoamerican cities, and in the remains of the first, the metropolis called Teotihuacan.

Stone statuettes, La Venta

Ceramic figurines

Olmec Enigmas

Still unexcavated, the major heartland site of Laguna de Los Cerros (left) displays the formal plan of a ceremonial center. Walls and mounds and plaza lie masked by green pasturage. Two other major sites have supplied a framework for the Olmec story: San Lorenzo flourished from 1200 to 900 B.C., La Venta from 800 to 400 B.C. Both featured huge landscaping projects and imposing sculpture. Largest of the colossal heads from San Lorenzo, the multiton basalt called Monument 1 stands nine feet high. It comes from a series of ten, generally accepted as portraits of dynastic rulers, warriors all. Immense effort went into moving, carving, and eventually mutilating such major sculptures. Bashing and drilling these

images may have been done to control spiritual power at the ruler's death. Other fine works were buried intact. Among these: the famous group from La Venta, with 15 statuettes in precious serpentine or jade around one in rough reddish stone, framed by highly polished celts. A trait typical of Olmec art is the long face with downturned mouth, seen here on hollow ceramic figurines; fangs and a cleft forehead give other heads the "were-jaguar" look that may reflect an origin myth. Small artifacts in these styles appear far and wide in Mesoamerica in Olmec times. Major sculptures, including colossal heads, dignify several sites on the Pacific coast. Do these finds indicate an Olmec presence? Or trade? Or copying by local artists? Archaeologists do not know the answers yet.

Teotihuacan

200 B.C. to A.D. 750

First metropolis of the New World, this deserted city goes by an Aztec name meaning "Place of the Gods." Even as a ruin it seemed to the Aztec beyond human scale.

Intensive archaeological investigation of Teotihuacan, beginning early this century, culminated in 1973 in a detailed map of the great city. Current excavations under the direction of Mexico's National Institute of Anthropology and History continue to reveal the city's secrets.

Settlement came late and rose rapidly: from about 2,000 inhabitants at 200 B.C. to 60,000 at A.D. 100. Most of the people of the Valley of Mexico had moved—or been moved—into the city before the Pyramid of the Sun was erected between A.D. 150 and 225. A planned grid of streets and an orderly array of some 2,000 apartment compounds served a population of 125,000 by A.D. 600. Craft specialists had distinct neighborhoods, as did foreign residents.

Perhaps 10,000 square miles came under the control of the Teotihuacanos. They may have held Kaminaljuyu, far southeast in the Maya highlands; they had links with Tikal and Copan. They controlled trade and wealth, if not an empire. Murals show an anonymous male elite, with ornaments like those of gods, standing in profile to honor their deities.

If there were statues of rulers, the monuments vanished in the devastation that wrecked the ceremonial area between A.D. 650 and 750. Temples and palaces burned; apartment compounds generally were spared. It now seems that the city may have lasted past 750, but its distant contacts had been broken earlier. Two of its deities, the Rain God and the

Carved stone disk

Feathered Serpent, remained prominent, but its reigning supernatural, now called the Great Goddess, did not appear in later art. Half-abstract murals depict her in a fertile paradise, or bestowing gifts. Her image has not been found at other sites, nor in Teotihuacan's successor states. Like her city, she was unique.

Aspects of Power

Hallmarks of Teotihuacan include slab-footed tripod vases, cylindrical in form; a few still bear a painted stucco coating with images such as this head of a feathered jaguar (right). Buildings devoted to religion and government—overlapping spheres in Mesoamerica—display walls that alternate a sloping base (talud) and a vertical framed panel (tablero); examples flank the stairways (below) at Teotihuacan. Stabilized and restored, such structures line the ceremonial avenue that the Aztec named Street of the Dead. To the left rises the enormous mound called Pyramid of the Sun, 230 feet high; a four-lobed cave below it probably attracted pilgrims long before the growth of the city, Mesoamerica's largest by far around A.D. 600. Surviving murals and newly discovered burials hint at a cult of war and sacrifice. A stone disk suggests later Aztec motifs, notably the skull with a pleated paper crown that portrays a Lord of the Dead.

Tripod vase, 4 in

Maya

1200 B.C. to A.D. 1697

More than four million Maya people are alive today, recognized heirs of an imposing civilization and renowned for their cultural tenacity. Ancient Maya achievements include superb art and architecture, a highly developed style of hieroglyphic writing and of mathematics, and a precision in tracking time day by day over centuries and eons.

Currently, archaeology's earliest firm date for the Maya is 1200 B.C., given by radiocarbon for the site of Cuello, in Belize. Here Norman Hammond's teams have traced a village through 1,500 years. Its early residents had plastered patio floors with firepits for cooking and a haphazard placing of graves. Postholes suggest comfortable houses like those still built today, with walls of poles that admit breezes and high thatched roofs that shed the rain. Then formality appears. After centuries of minor reworking, Cuello changed radically. Its courtyard was paved to make a ceremonial

Ceramic censer, 14.5 in

Temples of Tikal

Cleared and restored, Tikal's Great Plaza (right) reveals the grandeur of one of the largest Maya cities. Temple I rises at right, built about A.D. 700 by the ruler Ah Cacao for his funerary monument. His grave held riches, including jades. A burial, probably from A.D. 426, yielded this two-part ceramic censer; it portrays an aged god sitting on a stool of human bones and holding a severed head.

Classic Maya

Sculpture in various materials shows the majesty of Maya rulers and the mastery of their artists. A portrait in stucco lay beneath the sumptuous sarcophagus of Pacal the Great, lord of Palenque from A.D. 615 until 683, when he died at the venerable age of 80. In 1952, archaeologist Alberto Ruz discovered his tomb below the Temple of the Inscriptions, named for its hieroglyphic texts. Flamboyant silhouettes, patiently chipped in flint or chert, carry the label "eccentrics" because of their unusual shapes. This one was found wrapped in blue fabric, shreds of which still cling to it. Some flints defy identification; others may depict profiles of kings or gods and perhaps served as ceremonial staffs. Jade, most precious of substances in Mesoamerica, was difficult to carve. The jade statuette set in a Spondylus shell comes from recent excavations at Copan, in Honduras. Fine-grained limestone let the artists of Yaxchilan record minute details of features and fabric. On lintel 24 of structure 23 (opposite), by sculptor Macaw Chac, Shield Jaguar holds a torch while the royal lady Xoc draws a cord of thorns through her tongue to offer blood to the gods. Insignia from Teotihuacan—her tasseled headdress, his pointed cape—had long since become standard as Maya regalia. Rituals ending units of time held special importance for the Maya. This rite of self-sacrifice marked a momentous event: the 28th anniversary of Shield Jaguar's accession and the 80th of his father's—four sacred katuns, or 20-year periods. The day of the ritual: 5 Eb 15 Mac by the Calendar Round;

9.13.17.15.12 by the Long Count, the Classic Maya reckoning from a date in the mythical past; October 28, A.D. 709 in modern terms. Sculptors indicated such numbers by combinations of a dot (for one) and a bar (for five) and a shell or other symbols (for zero), or by images of gods personifying days. With the collapse of Classic Maya states, the Long Count fell out of use; but it gives precision to archaeology in the Maya area and, indirectly, to research elsewhere in Mesoamerica.

Eccentric flint, Copan, 12.9 in

Jade figure in shell, Copan

Stucco head of Pacal, Palenque, 16.9 in

platform—and into it was laid a mass burial: two men at the center; by each a bundled mass of mutilated bones from nine other men—victims of sacrifice, like the young men buried in multiples of nine at the Temple of Quetzalcoatl in Teotihuacan. The grave goods for Cuello's honored pair included bones carved with the woven-mat design called *pop,* symbol of rulership in later times and places. The generations of equality were ending, and the characteristics of a complex society were taking shape.

In similar fashion, dramatic changes appear at other sites in Late Formative, or Late Preclassic, times. By convention, the Classic Period runs from A.D. 250 to 900, but many of its aspects are now seen to have begun earlier. While Cuello's villagers refined their small terraced pyramid—actually three, one superimposed on another—work gangs at Nakbe, El Mirador, Tikal, and other places constructed gigantic pyramids, some more than 230 feet high. Many of these early cities had declined by A.D. 100, but Tikal continued to flourish.

The famed ruins of Tikal lie on an ancient and important trade route. Today a visiting expert points out a sedate *talud-tablero* structure and remarks, "There's the Teotihuacan embassy—or office of the high commissioner for trade." Fine ceramics, green obsidian, and portraits of rulers underline a connection between Tikal and Teotihuacan that is not yet fully understood.

Other relationships, however, are becoming clear to an enthusiastic set of epigraphists. Since 1958, the decipherment of Maya writing has moved faster and faster. Heinrich Berlin recognized "emblem glyphs" for places; Tatiana Proskouriakoff showed that dates in inscriptions fit human life spans; and personal names were identified. Yuri Knorozov of the Soviet Union argued for phonetic patterns in the hiero-

glyphic script. Now, specialists say, more than half the Classic inscriptions have been read, and a sketch of political history is in print.

At times it reads oddly. Some researchers use austere tags such as "Ruler A." Others assign names by the look of the glyphs, such as Bird Jaguar. Yet others spell out the phonetics, as for Pacal, Lord of Palenque. The events, however, are often basic

(birth, marriage, death) or happy (accession or formal seating on the ruler's reed mat, and capture of an enemy). At face value, Maya texts are aptly called "winner's history."

Archaeology can supply a corrective element, as at Copan, the southernmost major site and scene of major projects since 1975. Here the famous "mat stela" was erected in 695 to honor new ruler 18 Rabbit,

Lintel 24, structure 23, Yaxchilan

Mural, Cacaxtla

Late Classic plate, diameter 12.5 in

who disdained the lord of nearby, smaller Quirigua. American archaeologist William L. Fash and epigraphist David S. Stuart explain what happened next.

Quirigua's inscriptions refer five times to the date 9.15.6.14.6 6 Cimi 4 Tzec (May 3, 738), when its ruler, Cauac Sky, captured 18 Rabbit—an astonishing upset. A glyph called the "ax event" implies that the prisoner was beheaded. After that Cauac Sky started to enlarge and beautify his city.

Copan's new ruler responded to his predecessor's defeat by installing the celebrated Hieroglyphic Stairway, recently read as a record of glorious victories of old. Moreover, he married a noble lady of Palenque—a triumph for prestige—and her son became the 16th king, Yax Pac.

In his time the best land had long been settled; new fields were spreading up infertile hillsides. Commoners were weakened by malnutrition and disease, while men of elite lineage were portrayed in ceremonies recorded elsewhere only for

kings—possibly a sign of a top-heavy social structure with dangerous rivalries among the elite. About 822 a sculptor was carving a monument for Copan's royal heir, Caretaker of Flint, but he never finished it. The dynasty disappeared from the archaeological record, but the people of the surrounding valley carried on for some years much as before.

Such was the much debated Classic collapse at one site. Specialists have stopped looking for simple explanations of why the Maya abandoned Classic cities. Depletion of natural resources undoubtedly played a part—a pole-and-thatch house requires about 50 young trees, and a family of five about 3,000 pounds of corn a year. Recently identified techniques of intensive farming—terracing on hillsides, draining of "raised fields" in wet lowlands—gave greater yields than slash-and-burn methods, but apparently that was not enough.

In the Maya highlands, life followed a slightly different course. But here, as in the lowlands, small states built their temples and palaces and ball courts for the sacred game, a hallmark of Mesoamerican civilization. The key text for the myth that underlies the game is the *Popul Vuh*, creation epic of the Quiche Maya.

Influences from the Valley of

Mexico seem to have been strong in the highlands all along. Details of how these people affected the northern Maya lowlands, however, is presently under investigation.

North of the Puuc region, the Yucatan Peninsula flattens into limestone country where water runs underground and sinkholes called cenotes attract settlement. The most famous is Chichen Itza (Mouth of the Well of the Itza), a site cleared and partly restored in the 1920s and '30s. Current excavations by Mexican archaeologists continue to shed light on this celebrated center.

Did it become powerful under the Putun Maya? These were Chontal speakers from the Gulf coast whose culture had a strong central Mexican flavor. Was it overrun by invading Toltec? Answers will come as evidence continues to accumulate and be analyzed.

Postclassic texts use a Short Count dating by katuns, 20-year periods labeled by the name of the final day. Any single katun will recur after approximately 256 solar years, and in Maya belief it will bring its proper train of events: 8 Ahau, for instance, is a katun of profound change.

Some of the ruling Itza, driven out of Chichen by local rivals around 1200, founded a new city, Tayasal, on Lake Peten Itza, far to the south. They resisted the conquering Spaniards until 1697. In that year, the last free Mesoamerican kingdom fell to its impatient attackers as Katun 8 Ahau drew near.

Blended Traditions

At Chichen Itza in northern Yucatan (opposite), rattlesnake columns once supported the roof of the Temple of the Warriors. It and other buildings in the style called Toltec may—or may not—betoken the presence of invaders from the Mexican highlands; archaeologists argue the point today. The stiffly

posed figure, called chac mool *by a 19th-century explorer, holds a receptacle for offerings. Counterparts have been found at Tula and in Tlaloc's shrine at the Templo Mayor, in Mexico City. Murals at Cacaxtla, a fortress in central Mexico, imply Maya artistry in a mixture of styles. The male dancer above, wearing a scorpion's tail, holds up a half-star*

symbol associated with warfare and the planet Venus—known to the Maya as xux ek, *or "wasp star." Such half-star glyphs mark a red painted band in a chamber excavated at Teotihuacan, perhaps once used in rites of human sacrifice. The plate at top depicts a woman kneading dough on her stone metate, which was used for grinding corn with a stone called a* mano.

Toltec

A.D. 400 to 1200

"Tales of ancient splendor cluster about them," wrote a scholar in 1917, "but there is a woeful lack of definite information...." Since 1940 archaeology has added a treasury of data to the lore of the Toltec, but puzzles remain.

A village before A.D. 400, Tollan, now called Tula, the key site of the Toltec, lay near the northern limit of arable land but close to lime deposits and not far from Pachuca, the source of Teotihuacan's green obsidian. After that city's fall, Tula attracted new settlers of varied ethnicity; in its prime it held more than 30,000 people. Tollan, or Place of Reeds, implied residents as numerous as rushes.

Their houses, single-story but multiroom, stood in small groups; each cluster had a modest shrine in its central courtyard. These dwellings suited the climate—thick walls of adobe brick, mortared with mud, kept the interiors cool by day and warm by night. Here and there, stone veneer or cut-stone trim suggested a status above the ordinary.

Apparently, Chichimec warriors from the northwest had secured power here: Tula's sculpture, stiff and crude by Classic Period standards, has war and victory, sacrifice, and elite status for its themes. Coyotes and jaguars, priests or rulers, parade in single file; eagles grip human hearts in their beaks.

Ceramic figurines show males in armor, females with fancy hairdos. Animal effigies with axle holes suggest wheeled toys; and the so-called Palacio Quemado has the patterns for three different board games incised in its plaster floors.

Tula's wealth evidently came in part from the far northwest, the source of turquoise and other much prized minerals. Traders probably dealt in copper items—knowledge of metalworking was spreading from Michoacan and other western areas—but no vestige of metal has been reported from Tula itself. The city had an extensive economic sphere; its political domain was small in comparison. A rival to the southeast may have been Cholula, where current excavations are beginning to provide new data.

Regrettably, there is no definite information about the connection between Tula and Chichen Itza, the celebrated site in northern Yucatan. Legends—and 20th-century scholars who have cited them as evidence—imply a Toltec conquest of Chichen; more and more archaeologists doubt that this ever took place.

Calamity certainly struck down Tula around 1200 or earlier, in a general time of troubles. Drought was afflicting the Gran Chichimeca; people moved southward; barbarian invaders and established enemies were in conflict.

Legend says that a ruler named Huemac fled south to the Valley of Mexico, where the name Toltec came to imply to local people a heritage of legitimate sovereignty and ideal craftsmanship—the very essence of civilization itself.

Coyote with mother-of-pearl inlay, Tula, 5.5 in

Turquoise mosaic disk, Chichen Itza, diameter 9.5 in

Themes of Warfare

Tula's warrior columns (opposite), each made of four great basalt drums doweled together, have stood atop the reconstructed Temple B since the late 1950s. Their stubby 32-inch counterpart, portrayed in quilted armor, once supported an altar. Although the Aztec later praised Toltec works as "all good, all perfect, all wonderful, all marvelous," what survives at Tula is often mediocre—perhaps because the Aztec carried off relics of value. The turquoise mosaic disk above, found at Chichen Itza, suggests Maya artistry in a medium typical of central Mexico. The little sculpture of a warrior's head in a coyote's jaws, with mother-of-pearl inlay, crowned the lid of a jar of Plumbate ware, a popular glazed pottery imported from the Pacific coast of what is now Guatemala.

Warrior altar support, 32 in

Aztec

A.D. 1200 to 1521

"We shall proceed to establish ourselves, and settle down, and we shall conquer all peoples of the universe; and I tell you in all truth that I will make you lords and kings of all that is in the world...." Thus, according to legend, the tribal god Huitzilopochtli promised glory and dominion to his people, the Aztec or Mexica, whose name lives on in that of the modern nation: Mexico.

These people did in fact build a great if precarious empire. It embraced much of western Mesoamerica before it confronted invaders as ambitious as itself. The victorious Spaniards demolished most of the city of Tenochtitlan, officially replaced native cults with Christianity, and—without meaning to—introduced lethal contagious diseases. Nevertheless, they made the Aztec Empire the best documented of New World realms.

Spanish officials noted points of Aztec administration and law, of land tenure, water rights, and inheritance. Missionaries, eager to identify traces of idolatry, recorded many details of native belief: At a harvest festival, for example, the appearance of a footprint in a bowl of corn dough marked the midnight arrival of the deities. Fray Bernardino de Sahagún, a Franciscan, trained young Indian noblemen to help compile a general history with text in Nahuatl and Spanish: a unique and invaluable ethnographic record.

Some postconquest histories, such as that written by Fernando de Alva Ixtlilxochitl, tell how Tenochtitlan was founded in the year 1 Rabbit. Others say 4 Rabbit, or 2 House, or 1 Flint, a portentous year indeed. (In the 52-year cycles, 1 Flint was cited for the founding and the fall of Tula, the birth of Huitzilopochtli, and comparable events.) Different

Relief of Coyolxauhqui, diameter about 11 ft

Deities and Their Doom

Found by a work crew in 1978, the broken stone disk of the moon goddess Coyolxauhqui (opposite) prompted excavation of the Templo Mayor— Great Temple—in Mexico City. In myth she and 400 brothers killed their mother Coatlicue (She of the Serpent Skirt), shown fatally wounded in the statue below. Twin snakes symbolize blood from her neck. The Sun Stone contains an emblem of the Fifth Sun, or present era, that frames those of four earlier "suns," worlds destroyed by cosmic violence. The Fifth Sun would be destroyed by earthquake. In Aztec belief, only human sacrifice could avert a final, universal calamity.

cities had different year counts, to say nothing of patriotic bias, and their pictorial codices might mislead even the expert. Significantly, to read such books was "to sing the pictures." Thus the Aztec past shades from clear tales of the early 1500s through a murk of war and intrigue into obvious myth. Archaeology adds a vivid counterpoint.

For instance, the goddess Coatlicue became pregnant by a miracle; thinking her dishonored, her daughter Coyolxauhqui and her 400 sons beheaded her. A colossal statue of the dying goddess, found by chance in 1790, so horrified officials that it was concealed until 1823. Born full-grown in her death throes, her son Huitzilopochtli killed and dismembered his sister, hurling her body down a hill called Coatepec (Serpent Mountain). A relief carving of her remains, found by chance in 1978, inspired a momentous project.

The Proyecto Templo Mayor, carried out between 1978 and 1982, escaped the haste and frustrations of salvage archaeology in Mexico City from 1900 (a sewer line) to the 1960s (a subway network). Eduardo Matos Moctezuma directed an exemplary study. His teams uncovered the layers of superimposed masonry that made up a giant twin-shrine complex, "the ritual heart of the Aztec empire," sacred to Huitzilopochtli and to Tlaloc, the ancient goggle-eyed rain god. They documented details of architecture and sculpture as well as 86 offertory caches containing more than 6,000 objects.

Legend says that the Mexica built a shrine to their patron god whenever they paused in their wanderings before and after they entered the Valley of Mexico around A.D. 1200; they were the last of the Chichimec tribes from the north, poor and barbaric. They made themselves unwelcome almost everywhere they went by

*Sculpture of
Coatlicue, 8 ft*

271

Mosaic serpent
pectoral, length 17 in

Diorite
rattlesnake,
21 in

Stone knife
with mosaic hilt,
length 13 in

Andesite jaguar,
7.4 ft

their cruelty and warlike character. In desperation, they took refuge in the shallows of Lake Texcoco and began building up its marshy islands for a settlement. According to tradition, the year was 1325.

Although the lake has been filled in, the high water table kept Matos's team out of the lowermost levels of the Great Temple. The oldest elements examined, crude work with mud-daubed walls, reflect a time when the Mexica were mercenaries for the dominant state nearby, that of the Tepanec. They did have a ruler of their own, Acamapichtli, son of one princess of Toltec lineage and husband of another. The name Culhua-Mexica thereafter

Natural and Supernatural

Creatures of the earth, such as the rattlesnake above, inspired Aztec sculptors to a naturalistic manner, yet supernatural attributes and roles were often present. This superb andesite jaguar has a receptacle in its back for human hearts, ripped from the chests of the victims by a knife such as the one above it. The two-headed serpent, of turquoise mosaic on hollowed wood, was probably worn as a badge of office by a priest or other dignitary. Masks of wood were burned in cremation rites; the use of stone masks is uncertain. The miniature obsidian mask opposite may represent Ixtlilton, a god of drunkenness. A turquoise mask was part of the regalia proper to Quetzalcoatl, or Plumed Serpent, patron of creativity and of priests; his guises included the wind. The skull banded in turquoise evokes his eerie antagonist Tezcatlipoca (Smoking Mirror), overlord of earthly rulers, bringer of good or evil fate at his unknowable sovereign whim.

flaunted a claim to true Toltec descent, a link with the glories of the past and a sign of civilized standing.

Earliest of the undamaged date glyphs at the Templo Mayor is 4 Reed, or 1431, from the reign of Itzcoatl (Obsidian Serpent). With guile worthy of his name, he found allies at Tlacopan, a small polity west of the lake, and Texcoco, a larger one east of it; together, in 1428, they overthrew the Tepanec, and as a triple alliance they would build the Aztec Empire, which never became a single unified state. Itzcoatl gave his city a realm on the mainland and renovated his temple.

Natural calamities threatened the young empire at mid-century: a plague that struck the lake fauna; frosts early and late; drought; and famine that drove people to eat dry husks and vultures' flesh. The date glyph 1 Rabbit, 1454, marks the time of the worst suffering and of mass sacrifices. It also names the first year of a new 52-year cycle: a time of crisis and hope.

Tenochtitlan's ruler from 1440 to 1469 was Motecuhzoma Ilhuicamina (Angry Lord, Archer of the Sky), who extended the Aztec sway to the Gulf coast, to the Mixtec lands in Oaxaca, and beyond. Tribute in unthinkable plenty flowed into his capital, to be shared out in portions of two-fifths each for the stronger allies and one-fifth for Tlacopan: green feathers, greenstone beads, fine blankets and cloaks, red dye, gold dust, and works of art. Captured cult images were not put in the Templo Mayor but in a separate building in the ceremonial area. It was from the Toltec center at Tula that the Mexica took iconography for their chief monument, especially for the shrine of Tlaloc, and they seem to have stripped that city's burned ruins with eager piety.

Perhaps the ashes of the Angry Lord were interred in one of two funerary urns found by Matos's crew

near the great Coyolxauhqui stone. The ruler died in the year 3 House, or 1469, and his son or grandson Axayacatl wore the turquoise diadem. This vigorous man led his hosts to numerous victories—and to one defeat, the worst in Aztec annals. He took 32,000 men westward against the Tarascans of Michoacan, who met them with 50,000; of Tenochtitlan's 20,000 warriors, only 200 returned home.

About 1481, Axayacatl died, of unknown causes. The council that decided the succession chose his younger brother Tizoc. The rituals for a coronation had become occasions of splendor, but orators warned the new sovereign that "Thou wilt not find pleasure on the reed mat…" and rulership is perilous, "for things slip, things slide." And he would implore the favor of Tezcatlipoca, also called The Mocker, The Enemy on Both Sides, The Night Wind—the god who was fickleness personified. "Perhaps thou mistakest me for another," the king would pray in all humility; "perhaps thou seekest another in my stead."

Ironically, a superb monument found in 1791 depicts Tizoc as conqueror, presiding over his warriors and their captives. In fact, he suffered humiliating reverses in the field, and after five years he died—by poison, it was said. His reign shows how quickly a Mesoamerican state could falter under an unsuitable leader. His younger brother Ahuitzotl inherited restless lands; he staged a spectacular coronation as a show of wealth and began a period of waging successful wars.

About 1487, the year 8 Reed, Ahuitzotl celebrated his completion of work on the

Miniature obsidian mask

Turquoise mask, 9.5 in

Inlaid human skull

Great Temple with four days of sacrifices. His subjects and foreign rulers saw 20,000 victims bent over the fatal stone to have their hearts cut out and their bodies hurled down onto Coyolxauhqui's image. So it was remembered. The gods were fed, the fortunes of the realm restored, enemies cowed for a time. According to interpretations of the documentary evidence, the later lords of Tenochtitlan took the ancient practice of human sacrifice to an extent never exceeded in the history of the Aztec Empire.

By 1500, that empire held some 15 million people in at least 38 provinces—and more than 80 percent of the Templo Mayor offerings came from the distant areas. The

Reversal of Fortune: Final Conquest

One of a pair, a life-size ceramic eagle warrior (left) stood guard to the north of the great temple complex at the Temple of the Eagles: Excavators found the statues where Cortés's victorious men may have seen them in August 1521. Trophies sent to Europe included two items of military gear rendered as ceremonial finery. The atlatl, or spear-thrower, added power to a man's arm and length to a projectile's flight; carving and gilding embellish this example. Gold leaf adorns a feathered shield with a disputed emblem: either a coyote or the "water-monster" glyph of the emperor Ahuitzotl. The map of Tenochtitlan, first published with Cortés's letters in 1524, shows the Great Temple "where they sacrifice" at the center of the city, the palace of "Lord Muteezuma" beside it and his residence of leisure on the southwestern shore of Lake Texcoco. Near it floats the banner of the Holy Roman Empire, under Charles V, with its two-headed heraldic eagle.

archaeological sites of the Aztec are spread over that same vast area, with enough to explore for the foreseeable future. Some lie outside the Valley of Mexico, like the town of Malinalco with its rock-cut temple for military governors with eagle and jaguar emblems. Others survive in the crowded homeland of the Valley.

In 1989, Felipe Solís and Richard F. Townsend mapped the temple enclosure and processional way high on Mount Tlaloc, where rulers would make offerings and pray for rain, and Townsend has analyzed the cosmic symbolism of shrines on the ritual hill of Tetzcotzingo.

Here stood the villa of the greatest king of Texcoco, one of the triple alliance states: Nezahualcoyotl (Fasting Coyote), who was quite possibly Mesoamerica's most appealing figure.

Heir to the reed mat at 16, when his father was killed by the Tepanec, he was a pillar of the triple alliance through a reign of 40 years. A formidable warrior, he was also a humane lawgiver, an engineer who designed a dike to protect Tenochtitlan from floods and an aqueduct to supply it with pure water, an architect, a poet, and a philosopher who accepted familiar cults but worshiped a deity no images could represent.

Perhaps thou seekest another in my stead…. If Hernán Cortés had met that skeptical warrior, or the cold-minded Itzcoatl, or the Archer of the Sky, or the ruthless Ahuitzotl, he might well have ended his days under the obsidian knife. But he had the good fortune to meet Motecuh-zoma Xocoyotzin (the Younger), now officially quasi-divine, who gave him time to win allies in Tlaxcala. *Things slip, things slide….*

The last free lord of Tenochtitlan died as a Spanish prisoner. After his death, his city fell on August 13, 1521. "The shields of our warriors were its defense," mourned a survivor, "but they could not save it."

Ixtlilxochitl, himself of the royal line in Texcoco, preserved a poem by the ruler Nezahualcoyotl that reflects as in an obsidian mirror the reality of his day and vicinity:

For this is the inevitable outcome of all powers, empires, and domains; transitory are they and unstable. The time of life is borrowed, in an instant it must be left behind.

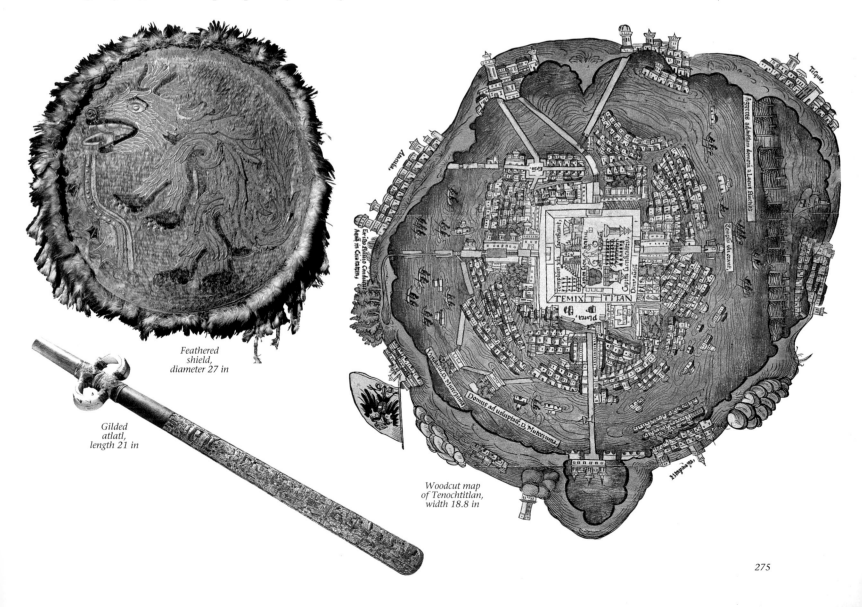

Feathered shield, diameter 27 in

Gilded atlatl, length 21 in

Woodcut map of Tenochtitlan, width 18.8 in

275

South America

3000 B.C. to A.D. 1630

The ancient peoples of South America lived in lands ranging from high mountains to green river valleys and from the largest tropical rain forest on earth to one of the driest deserts. Maize growers, influenced by the cultures of Mesoamerica, settled in the northern part of the rain forest. Fishermen and farmers established villages in the Amazon Basin. Extensive farming communities developed in the Andes. And hunter-gatherers survived in the harsh southern regions of the continent.

In present-day Colombia, the San Agustín people built statues and burial mounds around A.D. 100. About 700 years later, the Tairona people constructed terraced cities on the slopes of the Sierra Nevada de Santa Marta. Tairona craftsmen transformed gold and gold alloys into treasures that attracted Spanish conquerors to their rain forest home.

The central regions of the Andes, which sweep 4,700 miles along the western edge of South America, had a well-established agricultural tradition by the second millennium B.C. The Andean peoples were noted for their political organization, public works, and intensive maize farming. This area was home to South America's greatest pre-Columbian civilizations and has yielded the richest archaeological finds. Textile fragments excavated at Huaca Prieta, a fishing settlement that survived from about 3000 to 1200 B.C., are among the oldest ever found in the Americas. Kotosh, in the north-central highlands, became an important ceremonial center about 2000 B.C. At the same time, the coastal people of El Paraíso were building monumental platforms and pyramids.

Ceremonial centers formed the basis for the first civilizations in South America. These developed without the benefit of writing or wheeled transport. Yet they produced exquisite textiles, painted ceramics, the finest metal technology in the New World, and engineering systems that tamed the Andean landscape.

Brilliant but often short-lived civilizations flourished then faded in the central Andes. From 850 to 200 B.C. the Chavín culture, centered at the temple complex of Chavín de Huántar, united the Andean peoples in a widespread, popular belief. In 1925, archaeologists unearthed hundreds of corpses wrapped in textiles on the Paracas Peninsula, proof of a culture dating to the last centuries B.C. and ancestral to the coastal Nazca people. Farther north, the Moche were fashioning ceramic masterpieces in A.D. 400. In the highlands two commercial and religious complexes—Tiahuanaco and Huari—became centers of empires that dominated the Andean region until about A.D. 1000.

Then the kingdom of Chimor, with its capital at Chan Chan, began to expand. It ruled the desert coast until about A.D. 1470, when Inca from the highlands conquered it and added it to their empire.

South American civilization reached its height in the Inca Empire, an efficient and highly organized political entity administered from the city of Cuzco. The Inca was the last great prehistoric civilization in South America. It fell to Spanish conquerors in 1532, and the culture of the continent changed forever.

CARIBBEAN SEA

ATLANTIC

OCEAN

Buritaca 200

*Sierra Nevada
de Santa Marta*

TAIRONA

Magdalena

San Agustín

SAN AGUSTÍN

Amazon

CHIMU

Sipán
Chepen
Huaca Prieta
Chan Chan
Moche
Cerro Sechín

Cajamarca

MOCHE

Moche River

CHAVÍN

Chavín de Huántar

Kotosh

El Paraíso

Huari

Machu Picchu

Nazca River

Cuzco

Paracas

Nazca

Cahuachi

NAZCA

Lake Titicaca

Tiahuanaco

A N D E S

El Plomo

● Ancient and modern town site

◆ Archaeological site only

0   600 mi

0   800 km

San Agustín

500 B.C. to A.D. 1200

San Agustín, in the forested highlands at the head of the Magdalena River in Colombia, began as a cluster of farming villages and evolved into a ceremonial complex. Scattered over about 190 square miles on both sides of the river are some 40 known archaeological sites containing house platforms, field boundaries, drainage ditches, cemeteries, burial mounds, and enormous stone statues.

Until about A.D. 1200, sculptors shaped the statues with stone hammers and blades. More than 320 figures, most combining features of men and animals, mark cemeteries or guard underground tombs.

Dozens of burial complexes reflect the importance of ceremony at San Agustín. Barrows, such as the mounds at Las Mesitas, may have been places of public worship.

Spaniards who entered this remote rain forest area in the 16th century did not comment on the prehistoric stone statues. In 1758 a Franciscan priest, writing about them in his diary, described them as works of the devil. Vines, trees, and underbrush carpeted the ruins until 1913, when German archaeologist Konrad Preuss began the first systematic survey of the stones of San Agustín.

Statues and Stelae

Talons clutching a writhing snake, a stone eagle more than five feet tall guards a burial mound at Las Mesitas, one of dozens of funeral enclosures at San Agustín. This ceremonial site in Colombia probably dates from the first century A.D. Beyond the sentinel, stelae and masks ring the barrow.

Tairona

A.D. 800 to 1630

Gold funerary mask, Calima

Many experts consider the culture of the Tairona the highest achievement among Colombian aborigines. They lived in small, scattered farming villages until about A.D. 800, when they began moving to valleys on the western and northern slopes of the Sierra Nevada de Santa Marta.

The Tairona built about 200 terraced cities in the forested foothills, raising numerous crops including maize, beans, and cotton. They crafted home sites of hewn stone and terraced and irrigated their fields; stone-paved paths and roads linked residential areas to fields. Each town or city had its own chief. A distinct and highly influential class of priests controlled religious life.

The tallest coastal mountain range in the world, the Sierra Nevada de Santa Marta rises nearly 19,000 feet above sea level near the Caribbean coast. The Tairona never disturbed the delicate balance of the environment they made their home.

They remained relatively isolated, living in peace and prosperity until the arrival of Spanish conquerors in the 16th century.

Greed as well as the desire for conquest drove the Spaniards into the rain forest of the Tairona. In northwestern South America, a legend of a man coated with gold by his subjects—El Dorado—promised riches to the conquistadores. The Colombian tribes were indeed master goldsmiths, crafting delicate and detailed artifacts from the metal panned from local streams—such as the funerary mask of hammered gold above, made by the Calima.

The Tairona resisted the invaders and refused to accept the Christianity they preached. Tairona warriors fought with staves, axes, and poisoned arrows, but by about 1630 the Spaniards had prevailed. They drove the Tairona from their homes, executed their chieftains, and destroyed their crops and cities. The survivors fled to higher elevations; they were the ancestors of the modern Kogi.

Overgrown with greenery and inhabited by parrots, monkeys, and snakes, the largest Tairona city lay hidden for nearly four centuries. By 1975, when a grave robber found it, two feet of soil covered the ruins. Based on its location, archaeologists named the site Buritaca 200. Others call it Ciudad Perdida—the Lost City. A five-day mule trip from the nearest town, it sprawls across a thousand acres of gorges, slopes, and plateaus.

At its peak, Ciudad Perdida had 3,000 inhabitants and was the center of an urban society of some 300,000 people. This was divided into residential neighborhoods, ceremonial centers, and farming communities, reflecting a structured social system. Houses and temples, built of wood and thatched with palm, rotted after the Tairona fled. The remains consist of 300 miles of stone stairways and roads, 260 circular house sites, and reservoirs and drainage ditches.

Spanish chroniclers left historical records about the Tairona people. But their living heritage survives in their Kogi descendants, who still live in the remote rain forest and preserve many Tairona traditions.

Golden Lure

Hand-hewn stone foundations (opposite) at least 400 years old defy thick rain forest in Ciudad Perdida, the "lost city" of the Tairona people, in the Buritaca Valley of northern Colombia. Beginning about A.D. 800, the Tairona built terraced cities in the Sierra Nevada de Santa Marta near the Caribbean coast. In addition to being skilled engineers, architects, and farmers, the Tairona excelled as goldsmiths. Tairona craftsmen poured molten tumbaga, *a hard alloy of gold and copper, into a wax-filled mold to cast a four-inch-high pendant representing a warrior or ruler wearing a plumed headdress. In the 16th century, gold-hungry Spanish conquerors looted many Tairona treasures. Among artifacts found by archaeologists at burial sites were a gold necklace and a clay cup. The gold funerary mask at top was one of several found in a Calima grave in western Colombia.*

Tumbaga warrior pendant

Gold necklace and clay cup, Tairona

Chavín

850 to 200 B.C.

In the second millennium B.C., inhabitants of scattered farming villages in the Andes, in the central region of what is now Peru, began to establish some of the earliest ceremonial centers in South America at places such as Cerro Sechín and Kotosh. These people's descendants would become farmers who raised maize, worked gold, crafted ceramics, wove cloth, and constructed masterworks of masonry with stone tools. Religion dominated their lives. Over the centuries their religious traditions developed into the regional cult known as Chavín.

By 850 B.C. a temple complex at Chavín de Huántar in the Peruvian Andes, about midway between the coastal plain and the tropical forest, was becoming a hub of trade and religion among coastal, mountain, and forest peoples. A prosperous highland community, Chavín de Huántar at its peak covered 105 acres. By around 400 B.C., it had become one of the largest and most important ritual centers in the Americas—the heart of a culture that was the first unifying force in Andean prehistory.

Priests ruled at Chavín de Huántar; they lived on wide terraces surrounding the temple. Constructed over a period of 500 years, the stone temple complex is U-shaped, with a sunken square plaza and circular courtyards. The predominant structure is a 50-foot-high truncated pyramid. The temple sprawls across 12 acres and contains several levels of subterranean passageways and chambers. Canals and conduits carried water through and under it, and galleries, roofed with stone blocks, echoed the sound of rushing water.

At a juncture of galleries in the heart of the temple, a 15-foot-tall monolith known as El Lanzón projects like a knife from the floor into the ceiling. It depicts a deity. With his right arm raised and the left one lowered, he seems to be trying to preserve his balance. Some experts interpret the statue as representing the basic dualism to be found at the heart of Chavín religion.

The Chavín venerated jaguars and other jungle predators as gods. The catlike fangs and claws of the Lanzón carving are typical of their art style, which contains both anthropomorphic and zoomorphic elements. El Lanzón, like most Chavín art, is composed of a combination of straight lines, simple curves, and decorative scrolls.

Larger-than-life sculptured heads that projected from the upper walls at Chavín de Huántar share those characteristics, as do squared stone facings—called ashlars—and other carved features in the temple. Chavín artists, who lacked any metal tools, used only stones, sand, and water to achieve their effects. They were so skilled that later Peruvian cultures never surpassed the quality of Chavín carvings.

About 200 B.C., Chavín culture suddenly went into decline. Experts still do not fully understand the reasons for this abrupt change. They join in the opinion, however, that the Chavín culture was responsible for originating and spreading the first distinctive style of art and architecture in the Americas. These people left a legacy to later Peruvian cultures that endured for centuries.

Ceramic bottle, 12.7 in

Art and Religion

Bathed in light from ceiling openings, a snarling statue with feline fangs and serpentine hair called El Lanzón (opposite) juts from the floor in the heart of a temple complex at Chavín de Huántar, in Peru. The ceremonial center dates from about 850 B.C., when the art style and religious practices of the Chavín culture began to spread throughout the central Andes. Stonemasons fastened massive sculptured heads (right) into the upper walls of the main temple. A gold and silver spoon bearing a figure blowing a conch shell attests to the skill of Chavín metalworkers. The priests who ruled at Chavín de Huántar probably used it to dip the hallucinogenic snuff they used in rituals. A ceramic bottle nearly 13 inches high depicts a theme common in Chavín art—a small feline head terminating in a feathered serpent.

Sculptured stone head, 2 ft

Gold and silver snuff spoon, 4.4 in

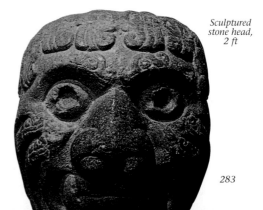

Nazca

200 B.C. to A.D. 700

Textile fringe with flowers and birds, length 13.7 in

Along a stretch of desert in southern Peru, the Nazca people settled in adjoining river valleys and established an isolated civilization, beginning about 200 B.C. The Nazca built homes of tied canes plastered with mud. They traded, fished, hunted, and raised a wide assortment of fruits and vegetables on the dry coastal plain. At its height, Nazca influence reached north and south more than 200 miles and stretched east from the coast to the highlands.

From the first, their harsh environment molded Nazca culture. The very existence of the Nazca people—farmers in an area where it seldom rains—revolved around water. They worshiped it and the mountains from which streams flowed. Those religious beliefs united their civilization and shaped their art.

To tap water from rivers that ran underground part of the year, the Nazca constructed aqueducts that carried groundwater into reservoirs and irrigation canals. They built little else. A stepped pyramid 60 feet tall, the Great Temple of their ceremonial center at Cahuachi is one of the few Nazca structures that remain.

On the desert below their hillside villages, the Nazca created their most famous legacy, a series of figures engraved in the dry earth. Most of these markings, or geoglyphs—called the Nazca Lines—are etched on the pampa between the Nazca and Ingenio Rivers. They may have been an integral part of Nazca mountain and water worship. Some of the patterns are derived from nature—gigantic figures of animals such as hummingbirds, whales, and spiders. Most of the geoglyphs, some 300 of them, are huge geometrical figures—spirals, rectangles, trapezoids, and concentric ray systems. All were created the same way—by stripping a top layer of stones to bare lighter soil below it, then banking the dark gravel against the exposed ditch.

The Nazca Lines still puzzle archaeologists. Did they mark ritual pathways and connect sacred sites? Did they represent constellations or mark water drainage? Were they part of an immense astronomical calendar that signaled the onset of the rainy season? Experts disagree.

Many patterns evident in their earthworks are repeated in brightly colored Nazca pottery and textiles. Birds, lizards, whales, and other animals are common themes, as are fertility symbols that reflect their concern with cultivating their dry land. Nazca warriors decapitated their enemies in battle. Some pots, painted with trophy heads, reveal a growing preoccupation with war in the later years of Nazca culture.

By A.D. 700 the Nazca appear to have fallen under the influence of people from highlands to the east, and their culture began to fade. The arid climate of southern Peru has helped preserve ceramics and textiles at burial sites, the source of most of our knowledge of the Nazca. The desert that ruled their lives also preserved the most spectacular and the most intriguing remains of Nazca culture—their gallery of geoglyphs.

Ceramic whale pot

Ceramic lizard pot

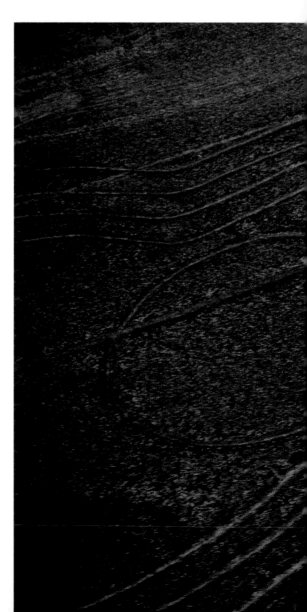

284

Patterns on the Pampa

Spread across dry flatland in southern Peru, a spider etched by Nazca craftsmen two thousand years ago takes shape when seen from the air; the 150-foot-long geoglyph dwarfs human visitors. Although the Nazca erected no great masonry monuments, they carved earthworks across 85 square miles of Peruvian desert near their villages. The markings probably have religious significance. Their pottery also reflects the religious fervor of the Nazca people. A ceramic vessel with a feline theme, a popular Nazca subject, may have served as a drum. Tattoos depicting the sun, rain, and fertility decorate a pottery vase showing a birthing scene; it may represent analogies between human functions and earth cycles. Birds watch lizards race across the surface of a two-spouted pot; they perhaps symbolized animal activity before a rain, a vital concern for the agricultural Nazca society. A polychrome pot in the shape of a whale, a ritual warrior-god figure, may suggest fishing prowess. Flowers and birds link a fabric fringe that may have trimmed a shroud. Scholars relate the boldly designed animal motifs that mark Nazca crafts to the geoglyphs they engraved across the desert.

Ceramic birthing scene vessel

Ceramic feline vessel

Moche

A.D. 100 to 800

Gold beads

The Moche flourished in a series of valleys on the west coast of Peru from A.D. 100 until about 600. They were agriculturalists who channeled rivers into an elaborate system of canals, harnessing Andean runoff to irrigate a hundred thousand acres of arid land. In a nearly rainless climate they grew abundant crops—among them corn,

Gilded copper bell

Gilded copper beads

Ear ornament

beans, squash, and peanuts. They raised llamas and guinea pigs for food, and they fished the ocean in reed boats.

At its height about A.D. 400, the Moche kingdom stretched 370 miles along the Andean coast. Like the Nazca, the Moche maintained a trade network that reached far beyond their frontiers. Roads that 900 years later became part of the Inca highway system threaded their realm. The need for land may have spurred the Moche to conquer neighboring valleys, and militaristic motifs are common in their pottery. Since the Moche had no writing, it is through their elaborate ceramics that we know about their life. They were master potters and metalsmiths.

A diverse and highly organized economy afforded time for leisure and supported Moche artists and artisans. Moche society was complex and must have had a strict hierarchy of power and authority.

The Moche believed in an afterlife. Even the poor and the middle class received

ritual burials, their hands gripping sacred objects. The elite were buried with members of the court, and since the Moche believed possessions served an essential function in the afterlife, many of their worldly goods were buried with them.

Throughout their domain the Moche constructed hundreds of truncated pyramids and adobe brick platforms that still stand. They served as religious enclaves and administrative centers, and tombs are associated with them. When a ruler died, the Moche carved out a burial chamber for him. Peruvians call the ancient adobe pyramids *huacas*. The Huaca del Sol—Pyramid of the Sun— is among the largest man-made structures in South America. It rises 135 feet and covers 12.5 acres in the Moche River Valley. Several hundred yards away looms the Huaca de la Luna—Pyramid of the Moon. Because of their location, they are called the Pyramids of Moche—the name also given to the Moche culture.

At the Huaca de la Luna, German archaeologist Max Uhle excavated 31 graves, beginning in 1899, and made the first contribution to our knowledge of the Moche. However, *huaqueros*, or grave robbers, had preceded him. The pyramids were riddled with

Goldsmiths

Treasure-filled tomb of a warrior-priest (opposite), discovered in 1987 near the Peruvian village of Sipán, offered new insights into the Moche culture. The Moche diverted rivers to farm the coastal desert. By A.D. 400 they had developed one of the most

remarkable civilizations in the ancient Americas. The Moche warrior-priest of Sipán—the Lord of Sipán—wore necklaces of peanut-shaped gold beads that prove the expert craftsmanship of Moche metalsmiths. The Moche gilded objects so skillfully that they looked like solid gold. Another find from the tomb, a gilded copper bell, depicts a god brandishing a knife in one hand and a head in the other. He

portrays the "decapitator," a theme common in Moche art. Gilded copper beads in the shape of feline heads bare teeth of inlaid shell. A figure on a gold and turquoise ear ornament, perhaps the finest example of pre-Columbian jewelry ever found, wears a movable nosepiece and headdress and holds a war club similar to those found with a skeleton near the royal corpse.

tunnels. The looting of ancient graves began with the Spanish conquerors and continues to this day. In the decades of excavation since Uhle's digs, archaeologists only rarely have found an unplundered Moche tomb.

Since 1987, Peruvian archaeologist Walter Alva has excavated several tombs in the Moche pyramid near the village of Sipán. These burials are proving to be the richest in the New World. The tomb of the Lord of Sipán, the first burial Alva excavated, dates from A.D. 300. From a headdress of solid gold to pure silver sandals, the Lord was layered with treasure. An older tomb, dating from A.D. 100, held even richer finds. These discoveries suggest that the elite of Moche society were much more affluent than was imagined before. Incredible wealth was concentrated in the hands of a few members of the nobility. We read the history of the Moche chiefly from art and artifacts found in the graves of the wealthy. Of the lower classes we still know little.

Moche civilization began to decline about A.D. 600. Natural disasters—earthquakes, droughts, or periodic torrential rains—may have contributed to the fall of the Moche kingdom; perhaps outsiders invaded. By A.D. 800, the civilization had disappeared. The most visible remains of the Moche are the adobe pyramids in coastal Peru, but the most memorable are the gold artifacts and richly decorated pottery that display artistry and technical skill unsurpassed by later South American civilizations.

Gilded copper mask

Ceramic "decapitator" figure

Coastal Lifestyle

Scaling a mountain peak, the ruins of Cerro Chepen, a Moche fortress (right), command a view of the Pacific Ocean. The complex, perhaps the main station in a chain of lookout posts in the mountains of Peru's north coast, contains the ruins of what may have been a palace and other buildings, with hundreds of rooms that could house a garrison of about 5,000. Never excavated, the site intrigues the few archaeologists who have visited it. The Moche recorded their lives in their modeled and molded ceramics and finely wrought objects of gold and silver. A "decapitator" holding a severed human head and a tumi, *or ceremonial knife, is the subject of a Moche pot. A gilded copper mask with eyes and mouth of shell and stone gleams after a cleaning; it reflects the success of Moche metalworkers at plating. Patches of gold clinging to a corroded copper insect suggest that it, too, was once gilded.*

Copper insect

Chimu

A.D. 800 to 1470

Largest adobe city in history, Chan Chan, near the coast of northern Peru, served for almost 700 years as the capital of Chimor, the territory of the people known as the Chimu. Beginning about A.D. 800, the Chimu forged an empire that stretched more than 600 miles—the largest on the Andean desert coast before the Inca. Like their Nazca and Moche predecessors, the Chimu built extensive irrigation systems, tapping Andean rivers to water their valley fields. One canal snaked through 50 miles of sand dunes to carry water to Chan Chan.

Nearly every valley in Chimor had at least one urban center, but Chan Chan, the seat of Chimu power, was the largest and most prestigious of the cities. Between 9 and 11 living compounds, each surrounded by trellislike adobe walls, formed the city's core. Each one housed a Chimu ruler, his family, and servants and contained a reception area, dwellings, cistern, pyramid, and temple. According to Chimu legend, two stars created the nobility, and two the common people. Only nobles could own riches such as gold and silver. Rulers were regarded as divine. Each god-king constructed his own compound and was buried there with much of his wealth and as many female subjects as he needed to tend him in the afterlife.

Chimu society was rigidly structured. The walls that divided the palace enclosures kept the nobility segregated from the rest of the population. Religion centered around powerful supernatural forces. The god-kings were the lawmakers, and their rule was harsh. Thieves were executed, shrine defilers buried alive, and adulterers flung from cliffs.

The Chimu nobility was small. The common people of Chan Chan lived in tiny apartments near the

Feline ritual vessel, 15.5 in

royal compounds. Archaeologists estimate that as many as 30,000 people lived in these barrios, which covered about 250 acres. They were craftsmen who molded pottery, wove textiles, carved intricate wooden figures, and shaped metal—especially gold—into works of art.

Although politics and economics tied the inhabitants of Chimor together, they subsisted in a scattering of isolated communities. About 1470, Inca from the southeast conquered Chimor, plundering Chan Chan and its treasures, and borrowing Chimu customs for incorporation into their own Andean empire.

City of Divine Kings

Latticework adobe walls thread royal compounds in Chan Chan, Peru (below, left), largest pre-Columbian city in South America and the

Detail of relief, Chan Chan

capital of the Chimor Empire. Chimu craftsmen used molds to press decorative reliefs into the walls. Each compound housed a Chimu king and his entourage; at his death, it became his tomb. At the rear of every enclosure stood a huge adobe platform containing the corpse of a Chimu chieftain, riches to sustain him in the afterlife, and females sacrificed to serve him there. Chimu craftsmen excelled in working metal, especially the abundant gold of their rich kingdom. A plaque of hammered gold probably represents the sun, a Chimu deity. A carved wood jaguar, inlaid with whale teeth and mother-of-pearl, supports a ceremonial gourd bowl.

Gold sun plaque, 16 in

Inca

A.D. 1200 to 1532

Rainless coastal desert, 22,000-foot mountain peaks, and steamy tropical rain forest—all were parts of an empire forged by the Inca of the Peruvian highlands. Folklore of the Inca people northwest of Lake Titicaca traced their noble ancestry back to about A.D. 1200. By 1500, through conquest and efficient administration, the Inca had created an empire that spanned at least 2,500 miles—the largest in pre-Hispanic America.

The word "Inca" originally described the emperor, and the name was later applied to the whole Inca people. Inca rulers claimed descent from the sun. Like Moche nobility, they were divine, and their word was law.

The city of Cuzco was the base of Inca power. At first it was a small agricultural state, but in 1438 the ruler Pachacuti embarked on a conquest that would transform the Inca world. Pachacuti pushed the empire north to Ecuador; his son and successor, Topa Inca, conquered the Chimu and added lands south as far as Chile. The capital, Cuzco, was the center of political administration for an empire with a population of some 6 million people from 100 different ethnic groups. The Inca language, Quechua, was used in government and helped link the diverse population.

The Inca called their huge empire Tahuantinsuyu—the Land of the Four Quarters. Residents received their basic needs, but each citizen of the realm was obligated to the state and paid a labor tax called *mita*. On a rotating basis, able-bodied citizens farmed government fields, constructed roads and buildings, or served in the army. An Inca army of perhaps 20,000, one of the best organized and most ruthless forces in the Americas, waged war almost constantly to put down uprisings and extend the empire. Conquered peoples paid tribute and provided labor and wealth for the empire. *Miti-maes*— entire populations of conquered peoples—were transferred from one place to another to keep the peace and maintain a ready labor supply. Censuses tracked every resident of the empire. One-third of all crops belonged to the ruler, one-third went to the gods, and one-third remained for the farmers. In a civilization that lacked writing, officials kept strict accounts on knotted, color-coded strings called quipus.

Many of the taxes went toward constructing and maintaining an elaborate road system. Two major highway networks, one winding along the coast and the other switch-backing through the Andes, united the empire. At least 10,000 miles of roads, reserved for government use, sped llama caravans and travelers on official business throughout the Inca domain.

Cuzco, at the heart of the empire, was the religious as well as the administrative center. Governmental and ceremonial functions revolved around the central plaza of the city. It housed the holiest

Gold alpaca

Silver llama

Children of the Sun

Stone stairs climb terraced slopes (left) at Machu Picchu, mountain citadel of the Inca, whose Andean empire stretched some 2,500 miles. The Inca offered human sacrifices to their gods. Pledged to the sun 500 years ago, a young boy found at the peak of El Plomo in Chile still huddles against the cold that killed him. A gold alpaca and a silver llama show how the Inca prized these animals—as sacrifices, food, pack animals, and a source of wool to be spun into cloth.

Mummy of sacrificed boy, El Plomo

294

Star-
headed
mace

Crafts and Craftsmanship

Jagged ramparts of Sacsahuaman (left), the fortress guarding their capital city of Cuzco, reflect the skill of Inca masons. Using only stone hammers and natural abrasives such as sand and water, Inca craftsmen shaped huge stone boulders so precisely that, although joined without mortar, they interlock with hairline seams. Some of the blocks weigh more than a hundred tons. Inca artisans also excelled in wood carving. A ceremonial goblet, or kero, *made in the shape of a puma's head, is embellished with gold and silver. Painted designs adorn a common Inca weapon, a star-headed mace.*

FOLLOWING PAGES: City in the clouds, Machu Picchu straddles a crag in the Andes, in Peru. Spanish conquerors never found the last Inca refuge, but Hiram Bingham located it in 1911.

of Inca shrines—the Coricancha, or temple of the sun. In addition to the sun, the Inca people revered the creator god—Viracocha—the moon, and the stars.

The Inca civilization, the most spectacular in ancient South America, was also the most short-lived, its peak blooming and fading in less than a century. The two sons of the last great Inca administrator, Huayna Capac, fought over the succession after his death. Diseases introduced into South America by Spanish conquistadores ravaged the native Indian population. Growing numbers of subjects rebelled against the totalitarian regime of the Inca state.

In 1532, Francisco Pizarro and his followers captured the ruling Inca, Atahuallpa, and occupied the Inca town of Cajamarca. Perhaps Spanish guns and horses stunned the Inca warriors. Perhaps they surrendered in shock at the sight of their divine ruler as a hostage in chains. For a month fires blazed high in Cajamarca as the Spanish conquerors melted down 24 tons of silver and gold that had been sent to ransom Atahuallpa. After collecting the ransom, Pizarro executed the Inca. Puppet rulers succeeded him. For 40 years, with raids, skirmishes, and a siege of Cuzco, the Inca people fought to regain their power—but they failed. In a single encounter, Pizarro and his men had virtually destroyed the Inca Empire.

Archaeologists regard the century of Inca domination as the zenith of Andean civilization. Much of that heritage has disappeared. Looters, beginning with the Spanish and continuing today, have obliterated it.

After their defeat at the hands of the Spanish, some Inca retreated to Machu Picchu, a fortified city in the Andes. They survived there undisturbed. The Spanish, who pillaged most Inca sites, never found this mountain stronghold. In 1911, American explorer Hiram Bingham came upon the Inca's last refuge. A monumental stone outpost clinging to a Peruvian peak, it is a fitting memorial to a people who called themselves the Children of the Sun.

Illustrations Credits

Abbreviations: AAAC = Ancient Art & Architecture Collection (Ronald Sheridan's Photo Library); BM = British Museum, London; BPK = Bildarchiv Preußischer Kulturbesitz; DM = Photo Archives, Denver Museum of Natural History; FM = Field Museum of Natural History, Chicago; HF = Museum of the American Indian, Heye Foundation, NY; MFA = Museum of Fine Arts, Boston; ML = Musée du Louvre, Paris; MMA = Metropolitan Museum of Art, NY; MNA = Museo Nacional de Antropología, Mexico City; MSG = Musée des Antiquités Nationales, Saint-Germain-en-Laye, France; NAM = National Archaeological Museum, Athens; NGP = National Geographic Photographer; NGS = National Geographic Staff; SHM = State Hermitage Museum, St. Petersburg; SI = Smithsonian Institution, Washington, DC.

Cover: Nathan Benn.

1, Lee Boltin. 2-3, David Hiser, Photographers/Aspen. 4-5, James L. Stanfield, NGP. 6, James L. Stanfield, NGP.

Introduction: 8-9, Sonia Halliday Photographs/Jane Taylor.

Portfolio: Tools of Archaeology: 10-11, Ira Block. 12, Georg Gerster, Zumikon/Zurich. 13, (tl) Nancy Jenkins/DM; (tr) Rick Wicker/DM; (b) William Riseman Assoc. 14, (l) Walter Alva; (r) Nathan Benn. 15, Bill Ballenberg. 16 & 17, (all) Bill Curtsinger.

Human Origins

In the Beginning: 18-19, Ira Block. 20-21, © Jay H. Matternes. 22, (l) David L. Brill; (r) Richard L. Hay. 23, Gordon W. Gahan. 24, (l to r) artifacts 1 & 2, John Reader, courtesy Mary Leakey Olduvai Research Project; artifacts 3-7, Lee Boltin, Columbia Univ., NY; artifacts 8-10, Victor R. Boswell, Jr., MSG. 24-25, © Jay H. Matternes.

Peopling the Earth: 28, Frank Fournier/Contact Press Images/The Stock Market. 29, (tl) Frank Fournier/Contact Press Images/The Stock Market; (tr) © Alexander Marshack; (bl & bc) Erich Lessing/Art Resource, NY; (br) MSG. 30, (t) Louis S. Glanzman; (cl) Ara Guler/MAGNUM; (b) Warren Morgan. 31, James P. Blair.

The Middle East and Europe

Early Settlements: 32-33, Adam Woolfitt/Woodfin Camp & Assoc. 36, Georg Gerster/Comstock. 37, (l) Nathan Benn, Amman Archaeological Museum; (tr) Nathan Benn; (br) AAAC. 38, (l & c) Nathan Benn, Museum of Anatolian Civilizations, Ankara; (r) Ara Guler/MAGNUM. 39, Nathan Benn.

Portfolio: First Farmers: 40-41, courtesy of the Freer Gallery of Art/SI. 42, (t) Ara Guler, Ankara Archaeological Museum, Turkey; (c) MFA, Joint Expedition of the American School of Indic & Iranian Studies and MFA. 42-43, (t) Robert Caputo/AURORA; (b) Victor R. Boswell, Jr., BM; 43, (r) Joseph J. Scherschel, Egyptian Museum, Cairo; (b) Georg Gerster, Zumikon/Zurich. 44, (l) James L. Stanfield, NGP, Nat'l Archaeological Museum, Sofia, Bulgaria; (bl) Erich Lessing/Art Resource, NY; (r) Gordon W. Gahan. 45, (l) Dirk Bakker, Museo Antropológico del Banco Central, Guayaquil, Ecuador; (cr) Mireille Vautier, Nat'l Museum of Anthropology & Archaeology, Lima, Peru; (br) Enrico Ferorelli.

Cities and Civilizations: 48, Lynn Abercrombie, Iraq Museum, Baghdad. 48-49, Victor R. Boswell, Jr., BM. 49, (t) Georg Gerster/Comstock; (cr) BPK. 50, (l) Sonia Halliday Photographs; (tr) Victor R. Boswell, Jr., Museum of Anatolian Civilizations, Ankara, Turkey; (br) Museum of Archaeology, Ankara. 51, (t) Mehmet Biber; (b, both) C.M. Dixon, Canterbury. 52, (l) Victor R. Boswell, Jr., ML; (c) Victor R. Boswell, Jr.; (r) Robert Harding Picture Library. 53, (l) Erich Lessing/Art Resource, NY; (r) Victor R. Boswell, Jr., BM. 54, (all) Bill Lyons, Iraq Museum. 54-55, Victor R. Boswell, Jr., BM. 55, Scala/Art Resource, NY. 56, (t) Winfield Parks, Puig des Molins Museum, Ibiza; (b) Erich Lessing/Art Resource, NY. 57, (tr) Werner Forman Archive/Baghdad Museum, Iraq; (tl) Winfield Parks, Nat'l Museum, Beirut; (br) Erich Lessing/Art Resource, NY. 58-59, Georg Gerster, Zumikon/Zurich. 60, (tl) Archaeological Museum, Tehran/courtesy American Heritage; (bl) The Granger Collection, NY; (r) Werner Forman Archive. 61, S. Fiore/SUPERSTOCK. 62-63, (t) Victor R. Boswell, Jr.; (b) John G. Ross/Photo Researchers. 63, Lloyd K. Townsend, Jr. 64, (both) F.L. Kenett/George Rainbird Ltd. 65, (l & cr) F.L. Kenett/George Rainbird Ltd.; (br) Lee Boltin for MMA & Fred J. Maroon. 66, (l) Fred J. Maroon/Photo Researchers; (r) Brian Brake/Photo Researchers. 67, Richard T. Nowitz.

Portfolio: Origins of Writing: 68-69, Gianni Tortolli, Aleppo Nat'l Museum, Syria. 70, (tl & tc) Département des Antiquités Orientales, ML; (tr) BPK; (cl) courtesy of the Royal Ontario Museum, Toronto; (bl) The Granger Collection, NY; (bc) Geoffrey Biddle; (br) Ciccione/Rapho, Département des Antiquités Orientales, ML. 71, (tr) Scala/Art Resource, NY; (bl) Jurgen Liepe, BPK; (br) The Granger Collection, NY. 72, (t) Gordon W. Gahan, NAM; (c) O. Louis Mazzatenta, Nat'l Museum of the Villa Giulia, Rome; (bl) MMA; (br) David Hiser. 73, (tl) Victor R. Boswell, Jr.; (tr) Brian Brake/Photo Researchers; (cl) Louis Psihoyos/Matrix; (bl) Jehangir Gazdar/Woodfin Camp & Assoc., Nat'l Museum of India, New Delhi; (bc) Victor R. Boswell, Jr., MMA, on loan from Liaoning Provincial Museum, P.R.C.; (r) Wan-go H.C. Weng, Academia Sinica, Taipei, Taiwan. 74, (tl) Justin Kerr; (tr) George F. Mobley; (l) George E. Stuart, NGS. 75, (l) Otis Imboden, MNA; (tr) Codex Nuttall; (cr) B. Anthony Stewart, MNA; (br) Robert Frerck/Woodfin Camp & Assoc.

The Classical World: 78, (l) Gordon W. Gahan, NAM; (r) Edotike Athenon, S.A., Archaeological Museum, Heraklion, Crete. 78-79, Edotike Athenon, S.A., NAM. 79, (t) Farrell Grehan; (l, both) George Xylouris, Archaeological Museum, Heraklion, Crete. 80, Kevin Fleming. 81, (r & bl) C.M. Dixon, Canterbury; (cl) Gordon W. Gahan, NAM; (cr) Edotike Athenon, S.A., NAM; (br) from "The Palace of Nestor at Pylos in Western Messenia, Vol. II," by Mabel L. Lang, permission of Princeton Univ. Press & Univ. of Cincinnati. 82, (l) Otis Imboden, Archaeological Museum, Heraklion, Crete; (tr) Jack Fields/ Photo Researchers; (br) C.M. Dixon, Canterbury. 83, BM. 84, (both) Victor R. Boswell, Jr., American Numismatic Society. 84-85, Timm Rautert/Visum. 85, (l) The Granger Collection, NY; (r) Terme Museum, Rome. 86-87 Scala/Art Resource, NY, Nat'l Museum, Naples. 87, (tl) ML; (tr) Spyros Tsavdaroglou, Archaeological Museum of Thessaloniki, Greece, permission of Dr. Manolis Andronicos; (b) Werner Forman Archive/BM. 88, (r) O. Louis Mazzatenta, Archaeological Museum, Florence; 88 (l) & 88-89, O. Louis Mazzatenta. 89 (r) O. Louis Mazzatenta, Nat'l Museum of the Villa Giulia; (l) Robert Harding Picture Library. 90, Adam Woolfitt. 90-91, Sonia Halliday Photographs. 92, O. Louis Mazzatenta. 93, (t) O. Louis Mazzatenta, Nat'l Archaeological Museum, Naples; (b) O. Louis Mazzatenta. 94-95, James R. Holland. 95, Robert Estall Photo Library. 96, (t) Blaine Harrington; (b) James L. Stanfield, NGP. 97, Jonathan S. Blair, ML.

Crossroads of Faith: 100, (tl & tr) AAAC; (b) Ira Block, Rockefeller Archaeological Museum, Jerusalem. 101, (tl & b) Erich Lessing/Art Resource, NY; (tr) AAAC. 102, (t) Peter Arnold, Inc./Martha Cooper; (b) John C. Trever. 102-103, James L. Stanfield, NGP. 104, (b) Nicolas Thibaut, Explorer. 104-105, Victor R. Boswell, Jr. & Otis Imboden, Naval Museum, Madrid. 105, (t) Scala/Art Resource, NY; (b) Erich Lessing/Art Resource, NY. 106-107, James L. Stanfield, NGP. 107, Lisa Quinones/BLACK STAR. 108, Lynn Abercrombie. 109, (t) Sonia Halliday Photographs; (l) Thomas J. Abercrombie; (r) Freer Gallery of Art/SI.

Europe: Into the North: 112, (t) William Waterfall/The Stock Market; (l) Adam Woolfitt, courtesy Nat'l Museum, Malta. 113, Bob Krist. 114, (tl) Adam Woolfitt, Nat'l Museum of Antiquities of Scotland, Edinburgh; (tr) Adam Woolfitt; (b) Robert Harding Picture Library. 115, Robert Estall Photo Library. 116, (t) SYGMA; (b) Kenneth Garrett, reconstruction by John Gurche. 117, (all) Kenneth Garrett, Romisch-Germanisches Zentralmuseum, Mainz. 118, (l) James P. Blair, Nationalmuseet, Copenhagen; (tr) Erich Lessing/Art Resource, NY; (b) James P. Blair, BM. 119, (t) Patrick Ward; (r) James P. Blair, Musée Historiques et Archeologique de L'Orleanais; (b) Victor R. Boswell, Jr., MSG. 120, (l) Sisse Brimberg, Nationalmuseet, Copenhagen; (tr) The Granger Collection, NY; (br) Museo Arqueológico Nacional, Madrid. 121, (l) Ira Block, courtesy Silkeborg Museum, Denmark; (r) Erich Lessing/Art Resource, NY; (b) Ira Block, courtesy Moesgard Prehistoric Museum, Arhus, Denmark. 122, (t) Giraudon/Art Resource, NY; (cl) Werner Forman Archive, London; (b) Werner Forman Archive/Nationalmuseet, Copenhagen/Art Resource, NY. 122-123, Robert Harding Picture Library. 124, (l) The Granger Collection, NY; (r, both) Werner Forman Archive/Art Resource, NY. 125, (t, both) Victor R. Boswell, Jr.; (b) Jim Brandenburg.

Sub-Saharan Africa

Ancient Kingdoms: 126-127, Enrico Ferorelli. 130 (t & b) Enrico Ferorelli, MFA; 130-131 Enrico Ferorelli. 132, (t) Robert Caputo/AURORA; (l) Enrico Ferorelli, MFA; (b) Enrico Ferorelli, Sudan Nat'l Museum, Khartoum. 133, Enrico Ferorelli. 134, (t) Werner Forman Archive; (b) Georg Gerster, Zumikon/Zurich. 134-35 & 135, (bl) Robert Caputo/AURORA. 135, (r) Georg Gerster, Zumikon/Zurich. 136, (tl, both) Dirk Bakker, Nat'l Museum, Lagos, Nigeria; (bl) C.M. Dixon, Canterbury; (br) Werner Forman Archive/BM. 137, (l) Dirk Bakker, Nat'l Museum, Lagos, Nigeria; (c & r) Michael Holford, Museum of Mankind, BM. 138, (l) Lee Boltin, MMA, Michael C. Rockefeller Memorial Collection, gift of Nelson A. Rockefeller, 1972; (b) James L. Stanfield, NGP, BM, on exhibit, Nat'l Gallery of Art. 139, Werner Forman Archive/BM. 140, James L. Stanfield, NGP. 141, (t) Bibliothèque Nationale; (bl) Michael & Aubine Kirtley, courtesy Nat'l Museum of Mali & the Institute of Human Sciences; (c & r) Werner Forman Archive/courtesy Entwistle Gallery, London. 142, Georg Gerster, Zumikon/Zurich. 142-43, Liba Taylor/Hutchison Library. 143, James L. Stanfield, NGP.

Portfolio: Metal Ages: 144-145, Leonid Bogdanov & Vladimir Terebenin. 146, (tl) James L. Stanfield, NGP, Nat'l Museum of Varna, Bulgaria; (tr) J.B. Roberts, Iraq Museum, Baghdad; (bl) Werner Forman Archive/Nationalmuseet, Copenhagen/Art Resource, NY; (br) Loren McIntyre, Mujica Gallo Gold Museum, Lima. 147, (l) James L. Stanfield, NGP; (tc) O. Louis Mazzatenta, Archaeological Museum, Florence; (r) Miss L. East, BM. 148, (t) Werner Forman Archive/FM; (tl) B.K. Thapar, courtesy of the Archaeological Survey of India, New Delhi; (bl) Adam Woolfitt, courtesy Ashmolean Museum, Oxford Univ.; (r) Erich Lessing/Art Resource, NY. 149, (l) Univ. Museum, Univ. of Pennsylvania, Philadelphia; (cl) Kunsthistorisches Museum, Vienna; (cr) James L. Stanfield, NGP, & Otis Imboden; (r) MMA, Fletcher Fund, 1942. 150, (l) Steve McCurry/MAGNUM, Iraq Museum, Baghdad; (b) Werner Forman Archive/BM. 150-151, Sisse Brimberg, Nationalmuseet, Copenhagen. 151, (l) James P. Blair, BM; (cr) Erich Lessing/Art Resource, NY; (br) Sisse Brimberg.

Asia and Oceania

The Indian Subcontinent: 152-153, David Austen/Woodfin Camp & Assoc. 156, James P. Blair, courtesy Nat'l Museum, New Delhi. 156-157, James P. Blair. 157, (all) James P. Blair, Nat'l Museum of Pakistan, Karachi; 158, H. Kanus/SUPERSTOCK. 159, (l) Lindsay Hebberd/Woodfin Camp & Assoc.; (c) Alan Eaton/AAAC; (r) James P. Blair. 160, (t) Lindsay Hebberd/Woodfin Camp & Assoc.; (b) C.M. Dixon, Canterbury. 161, (l) Richard A. Cooke III; (r) Adam Woolfitt/Woodfin Camp & Assoc. 162, Robert Frerck/Woodfin Camp & Assoc. 162-163, David Hiser. 163, (t) Robert Frerck/Woodfin Camp & Assoc.

Southeast Asia: 166-167, Roland & Sabrina Michaud/Woodfin Camp & Assoc. 168-169, Wilbur E. Garrett. 169, (both) Victor R. Boswell, Jr., Musée Guimet. 170, (t) Charlyn Zlotnik/Woodfin Camp & Assoc.; (c) Barbara DeWitt/Comstock. 170-171, Luis Villota/The Stock Market. 171, Russell L. Ciochon, Univ. of Iowa. 172, Brian Brake, Nat'l Museum, Ayutthaya, Thailand. 173, (cl) Jeremy Horner/Hutchison Library; (cr) Brian Brake, Nat'l Museum, Kamphaeng Phet, Thailand; (bl) Alon Reininger/The Stock Market; (br) Collection of the Art Gallery of South Australia. 174, Lindsay Hebberd/Woodfin Camp & Assoc. 175, (t) Richard Falco/BLACK STAR; (b) Georg Gerster/Comstock.

East Asia: 178, (tl) Fred Ward/BLACK STAR, Museum Rietberg, Zurich; (tr) Fred Ward/BLACK STAR, Nelson-Atkins Museum of Art, Nelson Fund, Kansas City, Mo.; (bl) Museum of Far Eastern Antiquities, Stockholm; (b) Robert Harding Picture Library. 179, (l) Fred Ward/BLACK STAR, Art Institute of Chicago; (r) Seth Joel; (b) Victor R. Boswell, Jr., MMA on loan from Shaanxi Provincial Museum, P.R.C.; 180, (tl) Victor R. Boswell, Jr.; (tr) courtesy of Audrey Topping; (b) Yang Li Min/H.K. China Tourism Press. 181, (both) O. Louis Mazzatenta. 182, (bl) Robert Harding Assoc./Times Newspapers Ltd.; (tc) Cary Wolinsky/Stock Boston, Sichuan Provincial Museum, P.R.C; (bc) Werner Forman Archive/Idemitsu Museum of Arts, Tokyo; (br) Werner Forman Archive. 183, Fred Ward/BLACK STAR, Hebei Provincial Museum, P.R.C. 184, (l) Lowell Georgia, P.R.C.; (r) Seattle Art Museum. 184-185, Cary Wolinsky/Stock Boston. 186, (tl) James L. Stanfield, NGP; (br) Aldus Archive. 186-187, François Charton/BLACK STAR. 188, (l) The Nat'l Museum of Korea; (r) H. Edward Kim, Kyongju Nat'l Museum. 189, (t) H. Edward Kim; (b) The Nat'l Museum of Korea. 190, (cl) Werner Forman Archive; (r) Japan Society; (bl) Georg Gerster, Zumikon/Zurich. 191, Shogakukan, Horyuji, Nara.

Portfolio: Textile Treasures: 192-193, H.R. Dorig/Hutchison Library. 194, (tl) Werner Forman Archives/Petrie Museum; (tr) China Pictorial; (bl & br) AAAC. 195, (l) Werner Forman Archive/Kita-In, Saitumi; (r) Cary Wolinsky/Stock Boston, Smith Art Museum, Springfield, Mass. 196, (t) Cary Wolinsky/Stock Boston,
SHM; (r) Werner Forman Archive/MFA; (bl) Art Resource, NY/Kunstgewerbemuseum, Berlin. 197, (l) AAAC; (cr) C.M. Dixon, Canterbury; (br) Werner Forman Archive/Univ. Museum of Nat'l Antiquities, Uppsala. 198, (tl) Werner Forman Archives/Arizona State Museum; (r) John Bigelow Taylor, American Museum of Natural History, NY; (bl) Bruce Hucko. 199, (tl & cr) H.R. Dorig/Hutchison Library; (cl) Werner Forman Archive; (br) John Bigelow Taylor, American Museum of Natural History, NY.

Central and North Asia: 202, Lee Boltin, MMA, on loan from SHM. 202-203, Beniaminson/Art Resource, NY. 203, (tr) Lee Boltin, MMA, on loan from SHM; (cr) Luka Mjeda/Art Resource, NY. 204, Charles O'Rear. 205, (tl) C.M. Dixon, Canterbury; (r) Lee Boltin, MMA, on loan from SHM; (bl) Cary Wolinsky/Stock Boston, on loan from SHM, 206 & 207, (all), Leonid Bogdanov & Vladimir Terebenin. 208, (t & cr) Nat'l Palace Museum, Taiwan; (cl) Koji Nakamura; (bl) (imprint) Publications Art. 208-209, Wan-go H.C. Weng, Nat'l Palace Museum, Taiwan. 209, (both) Koji Nakamura, Mongolian Invasion Memorial Museum.

Pacific Islands: 212, David Austen. 213, (t) Carroll Seghers II/The Stock Market; (c) John Cancalosi/Peter Arnold, Inc.; (b) Werner Forman Archive. 214, Ira Block. 214-215, (t) Gordon Donkin/Nat'l Library of Australia, Canberra; (b) H. Dacre Stubbs. 216, (t, both) Professor Jose Garanger, Paris; (c) Walter Meayers Edwards; (b) C.M. Dixon, Canterbury. 216-217, Nicholas DeVore III. 217, (tr) James Siers, Univ. of Auckland/Solomon Islands Museum Collection, New Zealand; (cr) Nicholas DeVore III, courtesy of Bishop Museum. 218 (all) & 218-219, James A. Sugar/BLACK STAR. 220, (l) James P. Blair, Peabody Museum, Harvard Univ.; (r) Gordon W. Gahan. 221, Eduardo Gil/BLACK STAR. 222, Brian Brake, Otago Museum. 222-223 & 223, (tl) Auckland Institute & Museum; (cl) Werner Forman Archive; (bl) Brian Brake, Te Awamutu Historical Society; (r) Fred Ward/BLACK STAR, Collection of Topi family, Ruapake Island, New Zealand; (br) Fred Ward/BLACK STAR, Nat'l Museum, Wellington, New Zealand.

The Americas

North America: 224-225, David Hiser, Photographers/Aspen. 228, (tl) Archaeological Survey of Canada, Nat'l Museums of Canada; (l, tr, & bl) Sisse Brimberg; (br) American Museum of Natural History/A. Anik & J. Beckett. 229, (t) Ira Block; (r, all) Victor R. Boswell, Jr. & Scott Rutherford. 230 Lynn Johnson/BLACK STAR. 231, (both) Lynn Johnson/BLACK STAR, Makah Cultural and Research Center, Neah Bay, Washington. 232, (tl) Victor R. Boswell, Jr., HF; (cl) Victor R. Boswell, Jr., Utah Museum of Natural History, Salt Lake City, (b, both) Helga Tiewes, Arizona State Museum, Univ. of Arizona. 233 (t) Richard A. Cooke III, courtesy of Arizona State Museum, Univ. of Arizona; (b) Jerry Jacka, courtesy of Arizona State
Museum, Univ. of Arizona. 234 (l) Jerry Jacka; (r) Jerry Jacka, courtesy Heard Museum, Phoenix. 234-235, Bruce Hucko. 235, (bl) Jerry Jacka; (br) Jeff Foott. 236, Michael J. Howell/Folio Inc. 237, (l) Art Institute of Chicago; (tr) Dewitt Jones; (cr) Jerry Jacka, courtesy Charles Benton Collection; (br) David Brill/SI. 238, (t) Frank C. Hibben; (b) Hillel Burger/Peabody Museum, Harvard Univ. 239, Bronwyn Cooke. 240-241, Richard A. Cooke III. 242, (t) Ron Testa, FM; (l) Richard A. Cooke III, Ohio Historical Society; (r) Peabody Museum, Harvard Univ.; (b) Werner Forman Archive/FM. 243, (t) Ron Testa, FM; (c) Werner Forman Archive/Ohio State Museum; (r) Werner Forman Archive/Columbus Museum, Ohio; (b) Ohio Historical Society. 244, (t) Werner Forman Archive/HF; (l) Otis Imboden, Nat'l Museum of Natural History, SI; (b) HF. 244-245, Richard A. Cooke III. 245, (tl) HF; (tr) Werner Forman Archive/Art Resource, NY/ HF.

Portfolio: The Potter's Art: 246-247, Kenneth Garrett. 248, (tl) Ira Block, Moravian Museum; (cl) Shimizu Kogeisha, Kyoto Nat'l Museum; (b) Lynn Abercrombie, Iraq Museum, Baghdad; (r) Lee Boltin. 249, (tl) Richard T. Nowitz; (tr) FPG Internat'l Corp.; (cr) The Granger Collection, NY; (bl) MMA, Rogers Fund; (bc) courtesy of Oriental Institute of The Univ. of Chicago; (br) Jurgen Liepe, BPK. 250, (t) Erich Lessing/Naturhistorisches Museum, Vienna, Austria/Art Resource, NY; (l) The Granger Collection, NY; (r) Victor R. Boswell, Jr., Univ. Museum, Univ. of Pennsylvania. 251, (l) Werner Forman Archive/Eskenazi Ltd., London; (c, both) H. Edward Kim; (r) Werner Forman Archive/courtesy of Entwistle Gallery, London. 252, (tl & tr) Justin Kerr; (cl) Mireille Vautier/Woodfin Camp & Assoc.; (b) Nathan Benn. 253, (tl) Jerry Jacka, courtesy of Arizona State Museum, Univ. of Arizona; (tr, cr, & cl) Jerry Jacka; (bl) The Proctor Stafford Collection, Museum purchase with Balch Funds, Los Angeles County Museum of Art; (br) Michel Zabe/DM.

Mesoamerica: 256, (t) Kenneth Garrett; (b) Kenneth Garrett, MNA. 256-257, Kenneth Garrett, SI, photographed at Dumbarton Oaks. 258-259, Kenneth Garrett. 259, (tl) Kenneth Garrett, Museum of Anthropology, Xalapa; (c) Kenneth Garrett, MNA; (r) Kenneth Garrett. 260-261, S. Vidler/SUPERSTOCK. 261, (t) Mark Godfrey; (r) Dumbarton Oaks Research Library & Collections, Washington, D.C. 262, Otis Imboden, Museo Nacional de Arqueologia y Etnologia de Guatemala. 262-263, Kevin Schafer/Peter Arnold, Inc. 264, (l) MNA; (c) & (r) Kenneth Garrett. 265, Justin Kerr. 266, (l) Raphael Donis, Nat'l Institute of Anthropology & History; courtesy of Citibank N.A., Mexico; (t) Nicholas M. Hellmuth, Foundation for Latin American Anthropological Research. 267, Steve Krongard/The Image Bank. 268, David Hiser, Photographers/Aspen. 269, (t) B. Anthony Stewart, NMA; (c) Werner Forman Archive; (b) Mark Godfrey, MNA. 270, David Hiser. 271, (t) Robert Frerck/Woodfin Camp & Assoc.; (r) Victor R. Boswell, Jr.,
Museum für Völkerkunde, Vienna. 272, (t & cr) Victor R. Boswell, Jr., BM; (l) Victor R. Boswell, Jr.; (b) Kenneth Garrett/FPG Internat'l Corp. 273, (t) Werner Forman Archive/Museum für Völkerkunde, Basel; (c) Victor R. Boswell, Jr., Museo Preistorico et Etnografico Luigi Pigorini, Rome; (b) Lee Boltin, BM. 274, Michel Zabe/DM. 275, (cl) Victor R. Boswell, Jr., MNA; (bl) Victor R. Boswell, Jr., Museo Preistorico et Etnografico Luigi Pigorini, Rome; (r) the Edward E. Ayer Collection, the Newberry Library.

South America: 278-279, Hans Jurgen Burkard/The Stock Market/BILDERBERG. 280, (t) Susan Griggs Agency, London; (bl) Dirk Bakker; (br) James L. Stanfield, NGP, Galeria Cano, Bogota, Colombia. 281, Victor Englebert. 282, William Albert Allard. 283, (l) Justin Kerr; (r) Lee Boltin, MMA; (br) Eduardo Gil/BLACK STAR. 284, (t) The Textile Museum, Washington, D.C.; (bl) Eduardo Gil/BLACK STAR; (br) Buckingham Fund, The Art Institute of Chicago. 284-285, William Albert Allard. 285, (l) Eduardo Gil/BLACK STAR; (r) Robert Frerck/Woodfin Camp & Assoc. 286, (t, both, cl, & bl) Martha Cooper; (cr) Bill Ballenberg. 287, Heinz Plenge. 288, (cl & b) Nathan Benn, MMA; 288, (t) & 288-289, Nathan Benn. 290-291, C. May/SUPERSTOCK. 291, (tl) Eduardo Gil/BLACK STAR; (r) Robert Harding Picture Library; (b) Wim Swaan, Archaeological Museum of the Central Bank, Quito, Ecuador. 292, Robert Harding Picture Library. 293, (t) Loren McIntyre, Museum & Institute of Archaeology, Univ. of San Antonio Abad, Cuzco, Peru; (b) Loren McIntyre; (r) John Bigelow Taylor, American Museum of Natural History, NY. 294-295, Peter Frey/The Image Bank. 295, (t) HF; (c) Eduardo Gil/BLACK STAR. 296-297, Georg Gerster, Zumikon/Zurich.

Acknowledgments

The Book Division is grateful to George E. Stuart, NGS Staff Archaeologist, for his expert advice at all stages of the book. We also thank the NGS Library, including its News Collection, the Image Collection, and Valerie F. Mattingley of the U.K. Office.

We also benefited from the assistance of the following: Robert D. Biggs, Oriental Institute, Univ. of Chicago; Annie Caubet, Louvre, Paris; Terry Childs, Nat'l Park Service, Washington, D.C.; Victor Englebert; Peter Hughes, Auckland Institute & Museum; Flemming Kaul, Nationalmuseet, Copenhagen; M.D. McLeod, Hunterian Museum, Univ. of Glasgow; Joseph F. Ochlak; Cemal Pulak, Institute of Nautical Archaeology, Texas A&M Univ.; Gesine Schulz-Berlekamp, Kunstgewerbemuseum, Berlin; Richard F. Townsend, The Art Institute of Chicago; Alan Walker, Johns Hopkins School of Medicine; Laurie Webster, Arizona State Museum, Univ. of Arizona; Gun Westholm, Gotlands Fornsal, Visby, Sweden; and Adam Woolfitt.

Index

Boldface indicates illustrations or broad treatment of a topic, including illustrations.

Note: Artifact measurements given in taglines refer to the height of the object unless otherwise stated.

A

Abbasids 109
Abell, Paul 23
Abeyadana temple, Burma: frieze 171
Aborigines, Australian 213, 213-215
Abraham 48, 98, 100, 102, 107
Abu Hureyra, Syria 34, 44
Abu Simbel, Egypt: temple 66
Acamapichtli 272
Achaemenid dynasty 58-61
Acropolis, Athens 84-85, 85
Adena culture 242
Afar Desert, Africa 20, 21
Africa 42, 126-143; early humans 18-25; Islam 109; metallurgy 150, 151; pottery 248, 250; Romans 94; trade 56-57; Viking raids 123
Afterlife, belief in: Europe 119, 250; Neandertals 27; reincarnation 154; South America 286, 290; *see also* Burial customs
Agamemnon 81
Agriculture 30, 40-45; Africa 142; Asia 164; Europe 111, 112; India 154; Middle East 34, 37, 38, 46, 148; North America 232-234, 242-244; Oceania 211, 223; slash-and-burn 220; South America 276, 280, 283, 284, 286, 293; Vikings 122-123
Ah Cacao: monument 263
Ahuitzotl 273, 274, 275
Ahura Mazda (deity) 60; relief 60
Ajanta, India 159; mural 159
Akan people 137; brass figure 137
Akhenaten 64
Akkadian language 50
Akkadians 46; cuneiform 71, 71
Akrotiri, Thera, Greece 78; frescoes 78-79
Aksum (kingdom) 132, 134-135
Alaca Hüyük, Turkey: bronze 50
Alaska 228, 229
Alemanni 120
Alexander the Great 52, 53, 59, 60, 64, 77, 86, 103, 147, 184, 196, 206; mosaic 86-87
Alexandria, Egypt 86, 95
Ali Kosh, Iran 34
Altai tribesmen 204-205
Altar, Israelite 100
Alva, Walter 288
Amazon Basin, South America 276
Ambrona, Spain 27
Amorites 46
Amphorae: Canaanite 17; Greek 83
Amu Dar'ya River, Asia 206
Amun (deity) 64, 66; temple, Jebel Barkal 130-131, 132
Amun-Re (deity) 64; Temple of, Karnak 66, 67
Amunhotep II: sarcophagus 73
Ananda temple, Pagan: gilded Buddha 170
Anasazi 2-3, 234, 235, 236-239; pottery 253; textiles 198
Anatolia (region) 34, 38, 38, 39,
44, 46, 50, 84
Anawrahta 170
Ancestor worship: China 179; Europe 112
Andean peoples 148, 276, 282-283, 286-297
Angkor, Cambodia 164, 166-169, 172; Angkor Thom 168-169, 169; Angkor Wat 166-167
Angles 120, 121
Anglo-Saxons 120
Animal domestication 34, 42, 44; Africa 142; Asia 200; Australia 213, 219; China 178; Europe 117, 150, 151; India 248; Mesoamerica 234, 255; Oceania 211
Animal sacrifice: Asia 181, 200, 202, 204, 219; Middle East 70; South America 199, 293
Antiochus I 34
Anuradhapura, Sri Lanka 162
Anyang, China 179
Apache Indians 234
Aphrodite (deity): pendant 206
Apollo, Temple of, Corinth 82
Aqueduct, Roman 96
Arch of Titus, Rome 91
Archaeology, 8, 10-17, 41, 139; aerial photography 129; computer modeling 169; conservation 169; dating techniques 14, 17, 142, 235, 251-252; excavation 10-12, 13, 15; looting risk 14, 17, 142, 202, 204, 295; metallurgy 145; pottery 250-252; remote-sensing 13, 14; restoration 13, 173, 175; underwater 16, 17, 251
Architecture: Aksum 134-135; Angkor 166-169; China 179; Greek 82, 83; Inca 294-297; India 158, 160, 161; Kush 132; Maori 223; Mesoamerica 260-263, 265, 267, 268, 270; Nan Madol 218-219; Neo-Babylonian 53; North America 224-225, 233, 234-235, 237, 238; Persian 61; Roman 90-91, 94-96, 132; South America 280, 281, 283, 290-291; Thailand 172, 173; Zimbabwe 142, 143; *see also* Temples
Arctic regions 226, 228-229; Vikings 151
Arctic Small Tool tradition 228, 228, 229
Ark of the Covenant 100, 102
Aryan tribes 154, 157, 160
Ashoka 154, 159, 162; capital 159
Ashurbanipal 54; relief 55
Asia 26, 44, 77, 109, 152-163, 205-208, 226, 229; Central Asia 200-209; East Asia 176-191; pottery 42, 248, 249-250, 251, 253; Southeast Asia 164-175; textiles 194-195, 197-198; writing 71-74
Aspelta: gold cylinder 132
Assyrians 46, 52, 54-55, 57-59, 98, 102, 130, 132, 202; cuneiform 71, 71; painting 70
Atahuallpa 146, 295
Athapaskans 226, 234
Athena (deity) 85
Athens, Greece 77, 82, 83, 84-85
Atlantis 137
Atlatl, Aztec gilded 275
Attic pottery: amphora 83; kylix 250
Aubrey, John 113
Augustus (Roman emperor) 77, 90, 95, 96

Australia 26, 211, 212-215
Australopithecines 20-22, 24
Austronesian 211
Avebury, England 113
Axayacatl 273
Axes: Minoan double-headed 79; Olmec 256; Syrian 151; Viking 122
Ayutthaya, Thailand 172-173
Aztec 255, 259-261, 269, 270-275; metallurgy 146, 148; pottery 13, 253; writing 74, 75

B

Baal (deity) 100; figurine 101
Babylonians 50, 52-54, 57, 58, 98, 102, 250; cuneiform 71, 71
Bacchus (deity): painting 93
Bactria 154, 206-207
Baffin Island, Canada 229
Baghdad, Iraq 124
Bahía culture: pottery 252
Balkan Peninsula 111
Balkh, Afghanistan 184
Ball game, ritual 233, 252, 266
Balts 124
Bangkok, Thailand 173
Banpo, China 178
bar-Kokhba, Simon 103
Basalt: Olmec sculpture 256
Basketmaking 193-194; North America 232, 232, 237
Bayon, temple, Angkor Thom 168-169, 169
Beaker People 149, 250, 250, 251
Beer making: figurine 43
Beidha, Jordan 34
Benin 129, 136-138; bronzes 138, 139, 150
Bering Sea 29, 226, 228, 229, 255
Berlin, Heinrich 263
Bezeklik, China 184-185
Bingham, Hiram 295
Bipedalism 20, 22
Bismarck Archipelago 216
Black Death 85, 208
Black Sea 124, 125, 202
Blood sacrifice: Mesoamerica 264
Bluefish Caves, Yukon Territory 29
Boats: Egypt 62-63; Minoans 78, 78-79; North America 228, 230; Phoenicians 56, 56; Polynesians 216; Vikings 122-124, rivet 151
Book of the Dead 73, 73
Boomerangs 213
Border Cave, South Africa 18-19
Borobudur (shrine), Java 152-153, 164, 174, 174
Botta, Paul 54
British Isles: Celts 118; Vikings 111, 123
Brittany, France: menhirs 112, 115; tomb 114
Brochtorff Circle, Malta 114
Bronze and bronzes 16, 17, 145, 148, 149-151; Africa 129, 136, 137, 138, 139; Asia 156, 160, 173, 179, 208; Europe 88, 118, 119, 120, 121; lost-wax casting 136, 138, 148-150; Middle East 50, 57, 101, 132
Buddha 154, 159; images 152, 158, 159, 159, 162, 170, 172, 173, 173, 186
Buddhism 154, 159, 162-164, 188, 190; monasteries 184-185, 186; stupas 152-153, 156, 158, 174, 174; temples 166-173, 175
Bulls: Çatal Hüyük 38, 39; Minoan pendant 79; Sumerian 48; Assyrian winged bull 55
Burgundians 120

Burial customs 199; Asia 179, 180-183, 188, 195, 208; Europe 27, 78, 88, 111, 112-114, 119, 122-125, 195, 250; Mesoamerica 262-265, 272; Middle East 49, 62-64, 100, 147, 194, 248; North America 198; Oceania 213, 216, 217; South America 193, 286-288, 290, 291; *see also* Burial mounds
Burial mounds: Asia 190, 191, 200, 202-207; Europe 112; North America 240-241; South America 276, 278-279
Burial structures: Europe 112-114
Burma 164, 170-171, 173
Byblos, Lebanon: golden calf 101
Byzantium (Istanbul), Turkey 96, 197

C

Cacaxtla, Mexico: murals 45, 266
Caesar, Julius 77, 94, 118, 120; statue 90; temple 94, 95
Cahokia, U.S. 244
Cajamarca, Peru 295
Calendar: Mesoamerica 255, 264, 270, 271; tapestry 197
Calima: gold mask 280
Cambodia 164, 166-169, 172
Canaanites 17, 56, 98, 100-101
Canute the Great 124
Canyon de Chelly, U.S. 236
Cape York Peninsula, Australia: rock art 213, 214
Cappadocia, Turkey: fresco 104; rock-cut dwellings 6
Carchemish, Turkey: gold figurine 51
Carnac, France: menhirs 112, 115
Carolingian Empire 124
Carter, Howard 65, 147
Carthage, Tunisia 56-57, 95
Casa Grande, U.S. 233, 234
Casas Grandes, Mexico 234, 235
Caso, Alfonso 256
Castor and Pollux, Temple of, Rome 91, 95
Çatal Hüyük, Turkey 34, 38-39; textiles 193, 194
The Catalan World Atlas of the Year 1375 141, 186
Caton-Thompson, Gertrude 142
Cattle: Africa 142
Cauac Sky 266
Cave paintings 28, 29, 186
Çayönü, Turkey 34; linen 193
Celts 111, 118-119, 120; metallurgy 150, 151
Central and North Asia 200-209
Ceramics *see* Pottery
Cerne Abbas giant, England 119
Cerro Chepen, Peru 288-289
chac mool 267
Chaco Canyon, U.S. 2-3, 239; pottery 237
Chaeronea, Greece 86
Chalcatzingo, Mexico 258
Chaldeans 46, 52
Chalukyas 160
Champollion, Jean François 71
Chan Chan, Peru 276, 290-291
Charlemagne 111
Charles V (Holy Roman Emperor) 274
Chavín culture 276, 282-283
Chavín de Huántar, Peru 276, 283
Chen-La (kingdom) 164, 167, 168
Cheops *see* Khufu
Chichen Itza, Mexico 266, 267, 269

Chichimec 269, 271
Chimor 276
Chimu Empire **290-291**, 293; gold gloves **146;** textiles **192-193**
China 164, 170, 172, 176, **178-187,** 190, 191, 205-208; agriculture 42, 44; Islam 109; jade **178,** 179, **179, 183;** pottery **178,** 248-250, **251,** 253; silk **194,** 195, 197, 198; writing 71-74
Cholas 160; bronze **160**
Chomsongdae observatory, Korea **189**
Chosun 188
Christianity 95, 96, 98, **104-105;** Ethiopia **134-135;** Germanic tribes 120; Spanish conquest 270, 280; Vikings 124, **146**
Cimbri 120
Cimmerians 202
City-states: Etruscan 88; Greek 77, 82, 84-86
Ciudad Perdida, Colombia 280, **281**
Clay tablets: Mesopotamia 48, 50, **52,** 69, **70, 71;** Mycenaean **72;** Syria **68-69**
Clovis points 30, **30**
Coatlicue 271; sculpture **271**
Coe, Michael D. 256
Coins **147;** Greek **84,** 85
Colima culture: pottery **253**
Colosseum, Rome **90-91,** 95
Concrete: use of 94
Confucianism 179, 188
Constantine the Great 96, 105
Constantinople (Istanbul), Turkey 96, 124
Cook, James 220, 223
Copan, Honduras 260, 265-266; effigy figures **246-247;** flint **264;** jade **264**
Copper **16,** 145, 148-150, 196, 248; Europe 116-117, **117;** Mesoamerica 269; North America **242;** South America **14,** 280, **288;** West Africa **137,** 141
Copts: textiles 194
Coricancha (deity) 295
Corinth, Greece 77, 83; temple **82**
Cortés, Hernán 274, 275
Cotton 194, 197, 198, **198**
Coyolxauhqui (deity) 271; stone disk **270,** 273, 274
Creation myths: Aborigines **214-215,** 216; Anasazi 238; Chimu 290; Dogon 151; Inca 293, 295; Mesoamerica 266; Olmec 259
Crete (island), Greece 77, 78
Cro-Magnon 29
Croesus 60, 147
Crucifixion: heel bone **105**
Cuello, Belize 262, 265
Cuneiform **70,** 71; Ebla **68-69;** Mesopotamia 48, 50, **52**
Cuzco, Peru 276, 293; fortress **294-295**
Cyclades (islands), Greece 82; figurine **82**
Cyprus: pottery **17**
Cyrus the Great 60, 102

Daggers: bronze inlaid **81;** gold **65**
Danube Basin: copper tool **148**
Darius I 60, 202; relief **60**
Darius II 87
Darius III 60
David 98, 100
de Soto, Hernando 244
Dead Sea scrolls 102, **102**
Decoys **232**

Delian League 84-85
Dendrochronology 14, 235
Denmark **120-123;** metallurgy **150-151**
Diaspora 103, 105
Diehl, Richard A. 256
Diomede Islands, Bering Strait **229**
Djénné, Mali: 141; mosque **140**
Dnieper River, Russia 124, 125
Dogon people 151
dogu 190, **190**
Dome of the Rock, Jerusalem **106**
Dong Son drums 150
Dorset culture 229; wood carving **228**
Douris 250
Dreamtime **214-215,** 216
Druids 118
Dublin, Ireland 124
Dunhuang, China 184; cave painting **186;** embroidery **194**

Eagles, Temple of the, Tenochtitlan: statue **274**
Early humans **18-25**
East Asia 44, 150, 151, **176-191;** *see also* China; Japan; Korea
Easter Island 211, 217, **220-221;** ancestral guardian **220**
Ebla, Syria: cuneiform **68-69,** 69
Ecbatana, Iran 60
Eccentric flints **264-265**
Egypt 11, 17, 44, 46, 50, **62-67,** 130, 132, 162, 245, 250; gold 146, 147; Hebrews 100, 101; hieroglyphs 69, 71, **73,** 157; pottery 249, **249,** 252; textiles 194, **194,** 196-198; tomb painting **42-43;** trade 56, 77
18 Rabbit 265, 266
El Lanzón **282,** 283
El Manatí, Mexico 259
El Mirador, Guatemala 265
El Paraíso, Peru 276
El Plomo, Chile: mummy **293**
Elamites 46, 58-59, 71, 148
Elgin, Thomas Bruce 11, 85
Epic of Gilgamesh 52
Epps, Meave 23
Eridu, Iraq: clay figurine **248**
Eskimos 226, 228, 229; *see also* Inuit
Essene sect 102
Etowah, U.S. 244
Ethiopia *see* Lalibela
Etruscans 77, **88-89,** 89, 90; alphabet 72; bronze work **88;** coin **147;** gold tablets **72;** inkwell **72;** trade 57
Euphrates River 42, 46, 48, 149
Europe 26, 44, **110-125;** bronze making 149; first civilization 78; Islam 109; Roman conquest 94; trade 88
Evans, Arthur 78, 79, 251
Evolution 20-24; diagram **20-21**
Exodus from Egypt 100, 101

Fash, William L. 266
Feathered Serpent (deity) 261
Fertile Crescent 42, 44, 46, 149
Fertility symbols **29,** 248; Aztec **253;** Çatal Hüyük **38, 39;** Celtic **119;** Malta **112,** 114
Fiji Islands 211
Finno-Ugrics 124
Fiorelli, Giuseppe 93
Fire 24, 25
Forum, Rome **90-91,** 95
Four Corners region, U.S. **224-225, 236-239**

Franks 111, 120, 124
Frescoes: Minoan **78-79;** Turkey **104**
Frisians 121
Frobenius, Leo 137
Funan (kingdom) 164, 166, 167

Games: Mesoamerica 233, 252, 266, 269; Viking gaming pieces **124**
Ganesha (deity): image **174**
Garlake, Peter 142
Garstang, John 37
Gaugamela, Iraq 60
Gaul 118, 120
Gavr'inis, France: tomb **114**
Genghis Khan 208, **208,** 209
Geoglyphs: Nazca **284-285**
Gila River, U.S. 233
Girsu, Iraq: clay tablet **70**
Giza, Egypt: pyramids **62-63**
Glass 250; blue glass ingots **17;** Phoenician **56,** 57; Viking gaming pieces **124**
Glyphs *see* Hieroglyphs
Gnezdovo Hoard, Smolensk, Russia 125
Gold and goldwork 125, 145-147; Africa 141-143; Assyrian **54,** 55; Bactrian **206, 207;** Canaan **101;** Egypt **64-65;** Greek **203;** Inca **293;** Korean **188;** Kushite **130, 132;** Macedonian **87;** Mesoamerica **275;** Middle East **101, 130, 132;** Minoan **79;** Moche **286, 288;** Mycenaean **81;** Persian rhyton **60;** Scythians **202-203;** South America 276, 280, **280,** 283, **283, 291,** 295; tablets **72;** Thrace **4-5**
Goths 120
Gotland, Sweden: carving **122;** runic stone **124**
Gozo (island), Malta 113
Grasshopper Pueblo, U.S. 234
Graaballe man 120, **121**
Great Basin, U.S. 232-234
Great Pyramid of Khufu 62, **62-63,** 63
Great Rift Valley, Africa 20-24
Great Wall, China 176, 182
Great Zimbabwe, Zimbabwe **142-143**
Greco-Persian wars 60
Greeks 11, **82-87,** 88, 103, 154; alphabet **72;** bronze 149; pottery **17, 250,** 252, 253; sculpture 94, 206, 207; textiles 197; trade 57, 82, 84, 202; *see also* Mycenaeans
Greenland 228, 229; Vikings 111, 124
Groslier, Bernard Philippe 167, 169
Gudea of Lagash 70; sculpture **71**
Gundestrup cauldron 118
Gupta dynasty 154, 159
Gurche, John: Iceman bust **116**
Gutians 46

Hacilar, Anatolia 34, 44
Hadrian 95, 103
Hadrian's Wall, England **95**
Hagar Qim, Malta: temple **112,** 113
Halafian pottery 250
Hallstatt Celts 118, 150, 151
Hammond, Norman 262
Hammurapi 52, 53
Han 164, 176; dynasty 181, **181-183;** empire 184, 188

Hanging Gardens of Babylon 52
haniwa **190,** 191
Hannibal 57
Haran, Anatolia 100
Harappa, Pakistan 156, 157
Harappan culture **156-157,** 252; copper tools **148;** seals **73, 157**
Harp, Sumerian **48**
Harrington, M. R. 232
Harvest Mountain Lord 74, 256
Hathor (deity) 130, **130**
Hattusha, Turkey 50; gateway **51**
Hawaiian Islands 211, 217
Hazor, Israel 100, **101**
Hebrews 98, 101-103
Helmets: Celts **118;** Mongolian **209;** Viking **122**
Hemudu, China 178
Herculaneum 77, **92,** 93
Herod the Great 104, **104**
Herodotus 202
Hesire (royal scribe) 73; carving **73**
Heyerdahl, Thor 220
Hieroglyphs 71, 72; Egypt 62, **67, 73,** 132; Hittite 50, **51;** Maya 251, **252,** 264, **265,** 266; Mesoamerica **74,** 255, 256
Hindu Kush 186
Hinduism 154, **156-157, 160-161,** 164, 166, 169, 175, 206; temple **174**
Hittites 46, **50-51,** 71, 150
Hogup Cave, U.S. 233
Hohokam people 226, 233, 234, 237; pottery **232, 253**
Holy Sepulcher, Church of the, Jerusalem: pilgrim crosses **107**
Homer 81, 83
Hominids **20-25**
Homo erectus **21,** 24, **25;** migration 26, 27
Homo habilis **20,** 22, 24
Homo sapiens 226; fossils 21; migration 26-27; tools 24
Hopewell culture 242-244; copper raven **148**
Horses: Asia 200; Egypt 64; silver and gold **147;** Tang ceramic **182;** terra-cotta 89
Horus (deity): eye of **65, 66;** figurine **249**
Hsiungnu 188, 200
Huaca de la Luna, Peru 286
Huaca del Sol, Peru 286
Huaca Prieta, Peru 276
Huari, Peru 276
Huayna Capac 295
Huemac 269
Huitzilopochtli (deity) 270, 271
Human sacrifice 107; Aztec 271-274; China 181; Europe 120, 121, mummies **121;** Inca 293, **293;** Maya 265, 266; North America 244; Phoenicians 57; Scythians 202; South America 193, 252
Humboldt Sink 232
Hungary: pottery **44**
Huns 120, 200, 206
Hunter-gatherers 26, 30, 41, 148, 248; Aborigines 213; Japan 190; Mesoamerica 255; North America 198, 226, 228, 232-233, 241
Hurrians 46
Hyksos 64, 100

Ibiza (island), Spain 57
Ice Age 29, 30, 111; cave paintings **28, 29**
Iceland: Vikings 111, 123, 124
Iceman 111, **116-117,** 145
Ife culture 136-137, 138;

bronze heads **136**
Igbo-Ukwu, Nigeria 129, 136, **136**
Iguegha 138
Ijebu (kingdom) 136-137
Inca 199, 76, 286, **292-297**; metal-lurgy 146, 148; quipu 75
India 77, **154-161**, 164, 166, 186, 206, 207; Islam 109; pottery **42, 248**; textiles 197-198
Inscriptions, Temple of the, Palenque 264
Inuit 229, **229**; *see also* Eskimos
Ipiutak peoples 229; burial mask **228**
Ireland 112, 113, 123, 124
Iron 145, 148, 150-151, **151**; Africa 132; Asia **209**; Europe 118, 120, **122**; Mesoamerica 258
Irwin, Geoffrey 217
Ishtar (deity): figurine **52**
Isis (deity): figurine **249**; hieroglyph **73**
Islam 98, 107-109, 160, 197; Africa 134, 135, 141; China 186
Isokelekel 219
Israel 98, 102; pottery **249**; textiles 193, 194
Issos, battle of 87
Itzcoatl 273, 275
Ivory carvings: North America **228, 229**; Phoenician panel **57**; salt cellar **138**
Ivory trade 134, 138
Ixtilxochitl, Fernando de Alva 270, 275
Ixtlilton (deity): mask **273**

Jade: China **178, 179, 183**; Korea **188**; Maori **223**; Mesoamerica 256, **259, 264**
Jaina, Mexico: pottery **252**
Jainism 161
Japan 176, 188, **190-191**, 251; pottery **248**; silk **195**, 198
Jarmo, Iraq 34
Java, Indonesia 164, 167, **174-175**
Jayavarman II 168
Jayavarman VII 169
Jebel Barkal, Sudan **126-127, 130-131, 133**
Jenne-jeno, Mali 129, **140-141**; terra-cotta **251**
Jericho 34, **36-37**, 44, 100; cup **100**
Jerusalem 98, 100, 102-103, 105, **106-107**
Jesus Christ 98, 104-105, 107; fresco **104**; mosaic **105**
Jingdi: tomb guardians 181, **181**
Johanson, Donald C. 20, 21
Jomon 190; pottery 248, **248**
Joshua 101
Judaea 103
Judaeans 90
Judah 102
Judaism 98, 102-103, 105, 107
Justinian I 120
Jutes 120, 121
Jutland: wool 198

Kaaba, Mecca 109, **109**
Kabul, Afghanistan 207
Kalibangan, India: copper tools **148**
Kamares, Crete: pottery **249**
Kaminaljuyu, Guatemala 260
Kamoya, Kamoya 23
Karnak, Egypt 64; temple 66, **67**
Kashgar, China 186
Kassapa I 163
Kassites 46; boundary stone **52**
Kayenta, U.S.: wood carvings **238**

Kenyon, Kathleen 37
Ketu (kingdom) 136-137
Khafre: pyramid **62-63**
Khajuraho, India: temples **161**
Khanbaliq, China 209
Khmer 164, **166-169**, 172, 173
Khorat Plateau, Thailand 148, 150
Khufu: pyramid **62-63**
Khwarazm (region), Afghanistan 208
Kimeu, Kamoya 23
Kivas **224-225**, 234, 237, **238**
Knossos, Crete 251; palace 78, **79**
kofun **190**, 191
Kogi 280
Koldewey, Robert 53
Konarak, India: temple **160**
Kongo, Kingdom of 138
Koobi Fora, Kenya 22, **23**
Koran 109
Korea 176, **188-189**, 190, 191
Kostenki, Russia: mammoth-bone shelters **10-11**
Kostromskaya, Russia 202
Kourion, Cyprus 77
Krater, Greek **85**
Kublai Khan 164, 170, 208, **208**, 209
Kurgans 200, 202, 203, **204**, 205
Kush, Kingdom of 129-134, 151; computer model **13**; pot **250**
Kushan 154, 200, **206-207**

La Hougue Bie, Jersey 114
La Mojarra stela **74**, 256
La Tène culture 118
La Venta, Mexico 256, 258; statuettes **259**
Laetoli, Tanzania 21; fossil footprints 21, **22**
Laguna de los Cerros, Mexico **258-259**
Lake Mungo, Australia **212**, 213
Lake Texcoco, Mexico 272-275
Lalibela, Ethiopia **134-135**
L'Anse aux Meadows, New-foundland 124
Laozi 179
Lapita culture 211; pottery **217**
Lascaux Cave, France **28**, 29
Latins 90
Law codes: Mongolian 208; Hammurapi 52, **53**; Hittite 50
Layard, Austen Henry 54
Leakey, Louis 22
Leakey, Mary 21, 22
Leakey, Richard **23**, 24
Leptis Magna, Libya: amphitheater **94-95**
Levant (region) 44
Limerick, Ireland 124
Lindholm, Denmark: graveyard **122-123**
Lindisfarne, England: monastery 123
Linear B 69, **72**, 81,
Linen 193, **194**, 194, 196, 198
Lintong, China: tomb guardians **180**, 181
Liu Yan: jade burial suit **183**
Llamas 293; silver figurine **293**
Longshan culture 178
Looms 194, 195, 197-199
Lord of Sipán: tomb 286, **287**, 288
Lord of the Dead: disk **261**
Lost-wax casting 136, 138, 148-150
Lothal, India 157
Loud, Llewellyn L. 232
Lovelock Cave, U.S. 232
"Lucy" (australopithecine) 20, 21; model **22**
Lusterware bowl, Iraq **109**
Luxor, Egypt: temple 64

Lydia 147; coinage **84**, 85

Macaw Chac 264
Maccabaeus, Judas 103
Macedonians 86
Machu Picchu, Peru 292, 295, **296-297**
Mackey, Carol J. 193
Maggi, Giuseppe 93
Maize cultivation 44; Mesoamerica 255; North America 233, 234, 237, 244; South America 276, 280, 286
Makah **230-231**
Malaysia 164, 170
Malinalco, Mexico 275
Malta (island): temples **112, 113**
Mansa Musa 141
Maori **222-223**
Marquesas Islands 211
Mars (deity) 95
Marduk (deity) 52
Marshall, Sir John 157
Masada (fortress), Israel **102-103**
Masks: Greek 85; Ipiutak **228**; Mesoamerica 258, 259, **273**; Mycenaean **81**; North America **244**; South America 280, 288
Mathematics: Babylon 52; Maya 262
Matos Moctezuma, Eduardo 271, 272, 273
Matthiae, Paolo 69
Mauch, Karl 142
Maya 148, 251, 255, 256, **262-267**; glyphs **74, 75**; mural **45**; pottery **246-247**, 252
McIntosh, Roderick 140-141
McIntosh, Susan 140-141
Meadowcroft site, U.S.: painting **30**
Mecca, Saudi Arabia 98, 109, **109**
Medes 46, 59-60
Medina, Saudi Arabia 109
Mediterranean Sea and region 56-57, **77-97**
Megalithic monuments: Europe 111, **112-115**
Megiddo, Israel 100; altar **100**
Mehrgarh, Pakistan 44
Mellaart, James 38
Melrose, Scotland 77
Melanesia 211, **216-217**
Menkaure: pyramid **62-63**
Meroë, Sudan 130, 132, 134, 151
Merv, Turkmenistan 184
Mesa Verde, U.S. **224-225**, 237, 238
Mesoamerica 42, 44, 226, 233, 235, 244, **254-275**, 276; pottery **1, 246-247, 252, 253, 261, 262, 265, 269**; writing 71, 74, **74, 75**
Mesopotamia 12, 14, 42, **46-49**, 50, **52-55**, 62, 57-59, 62, **70**, 98, 100, 102, 130, 132, 157, 196, 198, 202, 250; metallurgy **146, 148, 150**; pottery 249, 250; textiles 196, 198; writing 69-72
Metallurgy **144-151**; Africa 137, 138, 141, 143; China 178; Europe 111; Korea 188, **188**; Mesoamerica 269; New Guinea 211; South America 276; Sumer 48, 49; Thule 228; *see also* Bronze and bronzes; Copper; Gold and goldwork; Iron; Silver; Tin; Tumbaga
Mexica 270, 271, 272; *see also* Aztec
Mexico City *see* Tenochtitlan
Mica cutouts, Hopewell **242**
Michoacan 269, 273
Micronesians 211, **216-219**
Middle East **8-9**, 44, **46-67**, 98,

100-109, 145; early settlements **32-39**; metallurgy 148, 149; pottery 248, 249, **249**, 250; writing 69, 71
Migrations, human 26-27, 29-30, 255; North America 226; Oceania **210-223**
Mimbres people: pottery 234, **234**
Mingdi 182
Minoans 77, **78, 79**, 81, 82, 251; pottery **249**
Minos 78
Minotaur 78, 79
Mississippian culture 226, 244, **244-245**
Mixtec 74, 273; codex **75**
Mnajdra, Malta: temple 113, **113**
moai 220, **220, 221**
Moche **14, 15**, 276, **286-289**, 290; pottery **45, 252**
Mogollon 234, **234-235**, 237
Mohenjo Daro, Pakistan **156-157**, 157, 197
Mon (kingdom) 164, 170
Monasteries, Buddhist **184-185**, 186
Mongols 164, 172, 176, 186, 200, **208-209**
Monks Mound, U.S. 244
Monotheism 98, 100, 101, 107
Monte Albán, Mexico 255
Monte Verde, Chile 29, 30
Mosaics: Italy **105**; Mesoamerica **269, 272, 273**; Pompeii 72, **86-87**; Sumerian panel **42-43**
Moseley, Michael E. 193
Moses 100, 102
Mosques: Iraq **108**; Mali **140**; Mecca **109**
Motecuhzoma Ilhuicamina 273
Motecuzoma Xocoyotzin 274, 275
Mouhot, Henri 169
Mound builders 226, **240-245**
Moundville, U.S. 244, **244-245**
Muhammad (prophet) 98, 107, 109; miniature **109**
Muhammad of Khwarazm 208
Mummies 199; Egypt 197; Europe 120, **121**; Inca **293**
Murals: Aksum 135; Anasazi **238**; India 159; Maya **45, 266**
Mureybit, Syria 34
Muslims 109, **109**, 154; *see also* Mosques
Mycenaeans 56, 72, 77, 78, 80-82; bronze making 149, 150; clay tablet **72**; pottery **17**, **249**
Myron 85

Nabataean tomb, Petra, Jordan **8-9**
Nakbe, Guatemala 265
Nan Madol, Pohnpei **218-219**
Napata, Sudan 129, 130
Naqa, Sudan: kiosk **132**
Nara, Japan: temple guardian **191**
Naram-Sin of Akkad: bronze **150**
Narmer 62
Navigation: Micronesians 216-217, chart **216**
Nazca 276, **284-285**, 286, 290
Neandertals 27
Nebuchadrezzar II 52, 53; throne room **53**
Nemrud Dagh, Turkey: statues **32-33**
Neo-Babylonian Empire 52-54
Nero 105
New Guinea 211
New Zealand 211, 217, **222-223**
Newgrange, Ireland 112
Nezahualcoyotl 275

Niger River 140, 141
Nigeria 129, 136; sculpture **136, 137**
Nile, Africa 62, 130
Nimrud, Iraq 54
Nineveh, Iraq 54, 197; bronze **150**
Nintoku tomb **190**
Nippur, Iraq **12**
Nok culture 136; iron 151; terra-cotta head **136**
Nomads 34, 54; Asia 176, 197, 200-209; India 154; Middle East 98, 100; North America 228, 233; *see also* Hunter-gatherers
Normandy, Duchy of 124
North America **226-245**; earliest known settlement 29; pottery **253**; Vikings 111
North Asia 188, 189
Norton peoples 228
Norway 123, 124; silk **197**
Nubia (region) 64, 130, 146
Nullarbor Plain, Australia 213

Oaxaca, Mexico 273; hieroglyphs 74
Obsidian 34, 37, **38**; dating 17; Mesoamerica 265, 269, **273**; North America 242, **243**
Oceania **210-223**
Odoacer 96
Oguola 138
Ohio River Valley, U.S. **240-243**
Oldowan toolmakers 22
Olduvai Gorge, Tanzania 22
Olmec 255, **256-259**; colossal head **259**; glyphs **74**
Olokun (deity) 137
Oracle bones 73, **73**, 179
Orkney Islands, Scotland 112
Oseberg, Norway: ship burial 124, 125, carving **125**
Osiris (deity) 66
Oyo (kingdom) 136-137
Ozette **230-231**

Pacal the Great 265; bust **264**
Pachacuti 293
Pacific Ocean 176, 211
Pactolus River, Lydia 147
Pagan, Burma 164, **170-171**
Pagodas: Burma **170-171**
Paintings: earliest known 38; frescoes **78-79**, **104**; murals **45**, **135**, **159**, **238**, **266**; *see also* Cave paintings; Rock art; Tombs: paintings
Pakistan 154, **156-157**
Palas 160
Palenque, Mexico 264, 266
Paleo-Arctic cultures 228
Palestine 64, 103; pottery **17**
Pallavas 160
Pamirs, Asia 184, 186
Papago Indians 234
Paracas, Peru 276; wool **198-199**
Parthenon, Athens **84**, 85
Parthians 154
Pasargadae, Iran 60
Patagonia: rock art **31**
Paul, Saint 105
Pazyryk, Russia: carpet **196**, 197; kurgan **204**, 205
Peloponnese, Greece 81
Pericles 85, 111
Persepolis: stairway **58-59**
Persians 46, 52, 53, 57, **58-61**, 84, 102-103, 184, 196-198, 202
Peter the Great 202
Peter, Saint 105

Petra, Jordan 8, **8-9**
Petrie, William M. Flinders 250, 251
Philistines 100; sarcophagus lid **100**
Phillip II of Macedon 86; gold wreath **87**
Phoenicians **56-57**, 196, 198; alphabet **72**; pendant **56**
Pima Indians 234
Pipes: North America **243, 245**
Pitcairn Island 220
Piye 132
Pizarro, Francisco 146, 295
Plaques: Benin **139**; Chimu **291**; Greek **82**
Platinum 148
Pleistocene epoch 226, 240, 241
Pohnpeians **218-219**
Polo, Marco 208; map illustration **186**
Polonnaruva, Sri Lanka 162; reclining Buddha **162**
Polynesians 211, 217, 220, 222; sea god 216, **216**
Pompeii 77, 93, **93**; mosaics **72, 86-87**
Pompey 103
Popul Vuh 252, 266
Porcelain 186, **188, 251**
Portuguese 138, 142
Poseidon: temple 83
Potassium-argon dating 17
Pottery 145, 149, 197, **246-253**; Africa 141; Bronze Age **17**; China 178, **178, 182, 184**; Europe **44**; Greek **83**; Harappan 157; Japan 190, **190**; Korea 188, **188, 189**; Lapita ware 211, **217**; Mesoamerica **1, 74, 252, 253, 261, 262**, 265, **269**; North America 228, **233-235, 237**, 240, **244**, 245; South America **45**, 276, **283-285**, 286, 291; Thai **173**; toys **42, 157**; *see also* Terra-cotta
Prambanan, Java **174**, 175
Preuss, Konrad 278
Ptolemies (Egyptian dynasty) 64
Pueblo Bonito, Chaco Canyon **2-3**, 237, **239**
Pueblos **2-3, 224-225**, 226, 233, **234-236**, 237, 238
Puuc (region) 266
Pyramids: Egypt **62-63**, 162; Kush **126-127**; Mesoamerica **260, 263**, 265; Moche tomb **287**, 288; South America 283, 284, 290
Pyrgi, Italy: gold tablets **72**
Pyu (kingdom) 164, 170

Qin Shi Huangdi 181, 182; terra-cotta army **180**
Qorqor, Ethiopia: mural **135**
Quechua (language) 293
Quetzalcoatl: mask **273**
Quipus **75**, 293
Quirigua, Guatemala 265, 266
Qumran: caves 102, **102**

Radiocarbon dating 14, 17, 113, 116, 117, 262
Raiatea, Society Islands **216-217**
Rama I 173
Ram Kamheng 172
Ramses II: statue **66**
Ramses III 64
Randall-MacIver, David 142
Rano Raraku (volcano), Easter Island 220
Rapa Nui *see* Easter Island

Rapu, Sergio 220
Rawlinson, Henry C. 69
Re (deity) 64, 66
Red River, Vietnam 150
Red Sea 134
Reisner, George 130
Relief sculpture: Assyria **54-56**; Hittite **50**; Persian **60**; Phoenician **56**; Roman **97**; South American **291**; Sumerian **43**
Reshef (deity) 101
Retoka, Vanuatu: mass burial **216**, 217
Rhodes, Cecil 142
Rhodesia *see* Zimbabwe
Rice cultivation 41, 44; China 178; Japan 190, 191; Southeast Asia 164, 168
Roads: Persian 60; Roman **96**; South American 280, 286, 293
Rock art: Aborigines **213-215**; Maori 222; North America **230, 235**; South America **31**
Romans 57, 64, 77, 86, 88, **90-97**, 98, 103, 111, 118, 120, 121, 134, 147, 148, 206; alphabet 72, **72**; Christianity 104, 105, 107; legions **97**; textile fragment **194**
Rosetta Stone 71
Roy Mata: mass burial **216**, 217
Rua (mythical hero) 222
Rudenko, Sergei 197
Runic stone, Gotland, Sweden **124**
Rus (Vikings) 124, 125
Russia 176, 184, 186, 188; Vikings 111, 124, 125, graves **125**
Ruz, Alberto 264

Sabi River Valley, Africa 142
Sabines 90
Sacrifice *see* Animal sacrifice; Blood sacrifice; Human sacrifice
Sacsahuaman (fortress), Cuzco, Peru **294-295**
Sahagún, Bernardino de 270
Sahul 211
Sailendra dynasty 164
St. George, Ethiopia **134-135**
St. Mary, Ethiopia: mural **135**
Salamis, Greece 60; battle of 84
Salt River, U.S. 234
Samarkand, Uzbekistan 184, 186
Samarra, Iraq: mosque **108**
Samoa Islands 211, 217
Samurai: armor **195**
San Agustín, Colombia 276, **278-279**
San Lorenzo, Mexico 256, 258; colossal head **259**
Sanchi, India: stupa **158**
Sanjaya dynasty 175
Sargon of Akkad 46, 150
Sargon II 55
Sarianidi, Viktor Ivanovich 207
Sarmatians 200, 202
Satricum: terra-cotta ornament **89**
Saudeleur dynasty 218-219
Saul 98, 100
Saxons 120, 121, 124
Scandinavia 111, 120; *see also* Vikings
Schliemann, Heinrich 81, 150
Scotland 77; carved stone ball **114**; Vikings 123
Sculpture: Africa **143**; Egypt **66**; Greek 85, 87, copy **85**; Hittite **50, 51**; Ice Age **29**; India **157, 159-161**; Java **174, 175**; Khmer **169**; Kushite **130, 131**; Mesoamerica **256-259, 261, 264-265, 267-274**; Minoan **78**;

Nigeria **136, 137**; Scotland **114**; South America **278-279**, 283, **283**; Sumer 49, **49**; Thai **172, 173**; Viking **122, 124**; *see also* Relief sculpture
Scythians 154, 200, **202-203**, 206, 207
Seals: Akkadian **71**; Harappan **73, 157**
Segovia, Spain: aqueduct **96**
Seleucid Empire 103
Semitic people 134; alphabet 71, **72**
Sennacherib 197
Septimius Severus 95
Serpent Mound, U.S. **240-241**
Shang dynasty 150, 178, 179
Shanidar, Iraq 148
Shapur 197
Shell art: North America **233, 245**; Oceania **216**
Shield, Aztec feathered **275**
Shield Jaguar: image on lintel **265**
Shiite sect 109
Shinto 191
Ships *see* Boats
Shiva (deity) 160, 164, 175; bronze **160**
Shona culture 142
Sialk, Iran 148
Siberia 188, 206, 207, 226, 228; tomb looting 202, 204
Siddhartha Gautama *see* Buddha
Sierra Nevada de Santa Marta, Colombia 276, 280
Sigiriya, Sri Lanka: cliff painting **163**; fortress **162-163**
Silk **194-197**, 198
Silk Road 182, 184, 186, 195, 206
Silla (kingdom) 188; observatory **189**
Silver 146-148; Celts **118**; Inca 293, 295; Moche 288; Thrace **4-5**; Vikings **125, 146**
Simon, Helmut and Erika 116, 117
Sinhalese 162
Sipán, Peru **15**, **286-288**; sketch **14**
Skulls: australopithecine 21, 22, **23**; inlaid **273**; painted **37**
Slavery: Africa 138; Assyrians 54; Easter Islanders 220; Etruscans 88; Hebrews 100; Hittites 50; Indus Valley 156; Kushites 132; Makah 231; Romans 90; Scythians 202
Slavs 124
Snaketown, U.S. 233; incense burner **232**
Society Islands **216-217**
Solís, Felipe 275
Solokha, Russia: gold comb **203**
Solomon 57, 98, 100-103, 107
Solomon Islands 216
Sondok 189
South America 42, 44, 220, **276-297**; looms 195
Southeast Asia 42, 44, **164-175**, 211; looms 195; metallurgy 148-150; pottery 250
Spain 27, 57, **96**; conquests 146, 148, 255, 266, 270, 276, 278, 280, 288, 295; silk **196**
Sparta, Greece 77; gold cup **81**
Spartans 85, 86
Spindler, Konrad 116
Spiro, U.S. 244
Sri Lanka **162-163**, 170
Srivijaya empire 164
Standard of Ur **42-43, 48-49**
Stratigraphy **12**, 13, 14
Stelae: Aksum **134**; Babylonian **52**; Mesoamerica **74**, 256, 258, 265; South America **278-279**

Stephens, John Lloyd 8
Stirling, Matthew W. 256
Stirrups, iron **209**
Stonehenge, England 113, **114**
Stuart, David S. 75, 266
Stuart, George E. 8, 244
Stupas 159; India **158**; Java **152-153**; Pakistan **156**
Sudan: pyramids **126-127**
Sueves 120
Sukhothai, Thailand 172-173
Sumatra 164
Sumerians **12**, 14, 46, **48-49**, 52, 54, 62, 157; copper cudgel **148**; gold **146**; writing 69, 71
Sun Stone, Aztec **271**
"sun-chariot" **150-151**
Sunni sect 109
Suryavarman II 167
Susa, Iran 60; relief **60**
Sutton Hoo, England 120-121; drinking horns **120**
Sweden 124-125; silk **197**
Sweet potatoes: New Zealand 223
Syria 46, 48, 50, 64, 197; ax **151**; Roman road **96**

Tada, Nigeria: copper figure **137**
Taharqa 130
Tairona culture 276, **280-281**
Taklimakan Desert, China 184, 186
Tal-i-Iblis, Iran 148
The Tale of Genji (Murasaki) 198
Talmud 102
Tang dynasty 188; porcelain **251**; pottery **182, 184**
Tangaroa (deity) 216, 222; figurine **216**
Tarascans 273
Tarquinia, Italy: tomb painting **88-89**
Tasmania (island), Australia 211
Tayasal, Guatemala 266
Tell Brak, Syria 34
Tell el-Amarna, Egypt 64
Tell Halaf, Iraq 250
Temples: Buddhist **152-153, 156, 158**, 159, **166-173, 175, 191**; Egypt **66, 67**; Etruscan ornaments **89**; Greek 83; Hindu **160-161, 174**; Jebel Barkal **120-131**; Jerusalem 57, 100, 102, 103, **106-107**; Malta **112, 113**; Mesoamerica **253, 260, 263**, 264-266, **267, 268, 270**, 271-275; Oceania 211; Roman **91**, 94, 95; South America **282**, 284, 293, 295; Ur **49**
Tenochtitlan, Mexico 259, **270-271, 274-275**; map **275**; pottery **253**; writing 75
Teotihuacan, Mexico 259, **260-261**, 264-266, 269
Tepanec 272, 273, 275
Terebinth resin 17
Terra-cotta: Africa **141, 136**, 137, **251**; Chinese tomb figures **180-181**; Etruscan **89**; Greek **87**; Harappan **157**
Teutons 120
Texcoco, Mexico 272-275
Textiles 145, **192-199**; Pazyryk **205**; South America 276, 283, 284, 291
Tezcatlipoca (deity) 273, **273**
Thai 164, 169, **172-173**
Thanjavur, India: temple 160
Thebes, Egypt 44, 64, 66
Thebes, Greece 86
Thor (deity): hammer **146**
Thracians: metallurgy **147, 149**

Thule culture **228**, 229
Tiahuanaco, Bolivia 276
Tian Shan (mountains), China-Kyrgyzstan **186-187**
Tiber River, Italy 90
Tibetan Plateau 176
Tiglath-pileser III 54
Tigris River 42, 46, 48
Tikal, Guatemala 260, **262-263**, 265
Tillya Tepe, Afghanistan **206-207**
Timbuktu, Mali 141
Tin 17, 150
Titus: triumphal arch, Rome **91**
Tizoc 273
Tlacopan, Mexico 273
Tlaloc (deity) 266, 271, 273
Tlaloc, Mount, Mexico 275
Toldense people: rock art **31**
Tollund man 120, **121**
Tolstaya Mogila, Ukraine: gold pectoral **202-203**
Toltec 255, 266, **268-269**, 272, 273
Tombs: Chinese figures **180, 181, 251**; looting 14, 142, 202, 204, 286, 288, 295; paintings: Egypt **42-43**, 44, 66, Etruscan **88-89**
Tools: Aborigines 213; Acheulian 24, **24**; agriculture 44, **44**; Anatolia 193; Arctic regions **228, 229**; Clovis points **30**; copper **117, 148**, 149; Cro-Magnon 29; earliest 22; fire 24, 25; food utensils **38**; *Homo sapiens* 24; iron 150; Japan 190; Maori 222-223; Mousterian 27; North America 232, **232**, 233, 234, 241; Oceania **218**; Oldowan 22, **24**; South America 278, 283; Upper Paleolithic **24**; Zhoukoudian 26
Topa Inca 293
Torah 102
Torralba, Spain 27
Townsend, Richard F. 275
Toys: Harappan **42, 157**; Mali 129
Trade 69, 70, 196, 249; Aborigines 213; Africa 134, 138, 140-143; Asia 164, 166, 167, 170, 202, 251; Benin 150; Bronze Age 17; China 182, 184, 186; Copper Age 117; Etruscans 88; Germanic tribes 121; India 156, 157, 164, 166, 170; Kush 130, 132; Kushan 206; Maori 222-223, 234, 258, 265; Middle East 34, 37, 38, 149; Minoans 78; Mycenaeans 81; North America 232, 237, 241, 242, 243, 244; Phoenicians 56-57; South America 283, 284, 286; Vikings 123, 124, 125
Trajan 53, 94, 95
Trojan War 81, 83
Troy, Turkey 149, 150
Tula, Mexico 266, **268**, 269, 270, 273
tumbaga 280, **280**
"Turkana Boy" 24
Turquoise 237; inlaid scraper **237**; mask 273; mosaics 269, **272**; studded shoe buckle **207**
Tuscany, Italy 77, 88
Tutankhamun 64, 147; burial goods **64-65**
Tuxtla Statuette **257**

Ubaid, Iraq: frieze **43**; sculpture **248**
Uhle, Max 286
Ukraine 200, 202
Ulu Burun, Turkey: shipwreck

16, 17
Umayyads 109
UNESCO 173
Ur, Iraq **42-43**, 48-49, 100; gold 146, **146**; harp **48**; pottery 249; textiles 198; ziggurat **49**
Urnfielders 111
Ushabtis **130**
Uyghurs 208

Valley of the Kings, Egypt 64
Valley of the Nobles, Egypt 66
Vandals 120
Varna, Bulgaria: gold 145, **146**
Venus (deity) 95
Venus figurines *see* Fertility symbols
Veracruz, Mexico: pottery **1**; stela 74
Verghina, Greece: Macedonian tomb 87, **87**
Vespasian (Roman emperor) 90
Vesuvius, Mount, Italy 93, **93**
Vietnam 164
Vikings 111, **122-125**, 228, 229; iron rivets **151**; silk **197**; silver **146**
Viracocha (deity) 295
Vishnu (deity) 160, 164
Visigoths 96, 121; bronze fibula **120**
Vogelsang-Eastwood, Gillian 194
Volga River, Russia 124

Waikato: memorial post **223**
Wairau Bar, New Zealand 222
Walker, Alan 24
Warfare: Assyrians 52, 54, 55; bronze weapons 148, **149**; Celts 118, 119, helmet **118**; copper weapons 149; Easter Island 220; Hittites 50; Inca 293, **295**; Kushan belt **207**; Maori war club **223**; Mesoamerica 266, 269, 271-273, **275**; Mongols **208-209**; Mycenaeans 81, **81**; North America 243, 245; Scythians 202; South America 284, 286, 288; Viking battle gear **122**
Warriors, Temple of the, Chichen Itza **267**
Wat Lokaya Sutha, Thailand **173**
Wat Mahathat, Thailand **172**
Wat Yai Chai Mongkol, Thailand **173**
Waterford, Ireland 124
West Africa **136-141**

West Kennet, England 112
Western Wall, Temple Mount, Jerusalem **106**
Whale-tooth pendant, Maori **223**
Whaling: North America 228, **229**, 230
White Huns 154
Wood, Bryant 37
Wood carvings: Japan **191**; Makah **231**; Maori **222-223**; North America **228, 237, 238, 244**; Pazyryk **205**; South America **291, 295**; Viking **124**
Woodcut: Tenochtitlan map **275**
Wool **192-193**, 194, 196, **198-199**
Woolley, Sir Leonard 48, 49, 146, 198
"Wrestler" **256**
Writing **69-75**; Harappan 157, **157**; Kushites 132; Mesopotamia 46; Minoan 78; Mongols 208; Mycenaean 81; Phoenicians 57; Sumer 48; Syria 48; Vikings 124
Wudi 184, 188

Xerxes: tomb **61**
Xia dynasty 178, 179
Xi'an, China 178, 179, 184; tomb figures 181, **181**
Xianyang, China 181
Xoc: image **265**

Yadin, Yigael 100-101
Yamato 191
Yangshao culture 178, 253
Yangtze River Valley, China 176
Yaxchilan, Mexico: glyphs **75, 265**
Yayoi culture 191
Yellow River Valley, China 176, 178
Yoruba people 136-137
Yuan dynasty 176, 208; pottery **182**
Yueh-chi 200

Zagros Mountains, Iran 42, 148
Zagwe dynasty 134, 135
Zakros, Crete 79
Zapotec 255
Zhang Chien 184
Zhou dynasty 178-179, 181; dou (vessel) **73**; iron 151
Zhoukoudian Caves, China 26
Ziggurat: Ur **49**
Zimbabwe 142, 143

Library of Congress ⊡ data

Wonders of the ancient world : National Geographic atlas of archaeology / prepared by the Book Division, National Geographic Society, Washington, D. C.
  p. cm.
  Includes index.
  ISBN 0-87044-982-6 ISBN 0-87044-983-4 (deluxe)
  1. Civilization, Ancient. 2. Antiquities. 3. Antiquities—Pictorial works. 4. Archaeology. I. National Geographic Society (U.S.). Book Division.
  CB311.W63 1994
  930'.022'3—dc20   94-16650
                       ⊡

Composition for this book by the National Geographic Society Book Division with the assistance of the Typographic section of National Geographic Production Services, Pre-Press Division. Set in Stone Serif. Printed and bound by R. R. Donnelley & Sons, Willard, Ohio. Color separations by Graphic Art Service, Inc., Nashville, Tenn.; Lanman Progressive Co., Washington, D.C.; Lincoln Graphics, Inc., Cherry Hill, N.J.; and Phototype Color Graphics, Pennsauken, N.J. Dust jacket printed by Miken Systems, Inc., Cheektowaga, N.Y. Map relief by National Geographic Society Cartographic Division; map production by Maryland Cartographics, Inc., Columbia, Md.